# Democracy and Complexity

A certain prince of the present day, whom I shall refrain from naming, preaches nothing but peace and faith, and to both one and the other he is entirely opposed; and both, if he had put them into practice, would have cost him many times over either his reputation or his state.

Machiavelli, *Il Principe*

# DEMOCRACY AND COMPLEXITY

## A Realist Approach

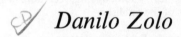 *Danilo Zolo*

Translated from the Italian
by David McKie

The Pennsylvania State University Press
University Park, Pennsylvania

First published in 1992 in the United States and Canada by
The Pennsylvania State University Press, Barbara Building, Suite C,
University Park, PA 16802

**Library of Congress Cataloging-in-Publication Data**

Zolo, Danilo,
    Democracy and complexity: a realistic approach/Danilo Zolo:
translated by David McKie.
        p.  cm.
    Includes bibliographical references and indexes.
    ISBN 0–271–00891–1 (cloth: acid-free paper).—ISBN
0–271–00892–X (paper: acid-free paper)
    1. Democracy.  2. Political sociology.  I. Title.
JC423.Z6713  1992                                            92–10234
321.8—dc20                                                      CIP

Typeset in 10 on 12pt Times
by Butler & Tanner Ltd, Frome, Somerset
Printed in Great Britain
by T J Press (Padstow) Ltd, Padstow, Cornwall

It is the policy of The Pennsylvania State University Press to use acid-free
paper for the first printing of all clothbound books. Publications on
uncoated stock satisfy the minimum requirements of American National
Standard for Information Sciences—Permanence of Paper for Printed
Library Materials, ANSI Z39.48–1984.

# Contents

# Preface

Following the collapse of communism, Western democracy appears to have become the world's only viable political system. Democracy itself, however, is at present undergoing unparalleled evolutionary stresses in modern post-industrial societies. So strong have these stresses become that the explanatory power – perhaps even the ability to convey any meaning at all – of the very notion of 'representative democracy' is now seriously called into question. In the same way, other large sections of the vocabulary of European political theory appear to have been emptied of their content. Terms such as 'sovereignty of the people', 'common good', 'consensus', 'control', 'participation', 'pluralism', 'party competition', 'public opinion', have long been detached from the values they originally bore. Indeed, it is hard to avoid the impression that even the acknowledged classics of political thought have now ceased to be able to provide us with any real help.

Nor is the situation any less problematical in the area of political research. The epistemological paradigms postulated by the various theories of democracy – including the economic theory, the empirical theory, and the ethico-political theories of contractualistic or utilitarian origin – have all succumbed to the prevailing uncertainty over the foundations of scientific knowledge and the situation of crisis in the social sciences. This uncertainty has followed the demise of empiricist philosophies of science and is still characteristic of the movement which, for want of a better name, it has been convenient to call 'post-empiricism'.

For all these reasons the need for a thoroughgoing reconstruction of democratic theory will form the principal concern of this book. By democratic theory I shall mean liberal-democratic theory *tout court*, in the sense in which it has become established in the political culture of Europe, without intending to draw any precise distinction between liberalism and democracy. I hope that the argument of this book will serve to justify the loss of this philosophically significant distinction, as well as certain other historiographical simplifications which will be made necessary by my approach.

For many, of course, the ideal of democracy remains an important symbol. In certain political contexts, especially, but not only, in the Third World, the word 'democracy' still represents a revolutionary challenge to power on the part of political and military groups. This has dramatically become the case in the countries of 'actually existing socialism', where the political and institutional legacy of Marxism-Leninism has manifestly failed to withstand the test of experience. After the democratic revolution of 1989 and the decline of the Soviet Union, the communist system stands widely revealed in its true light as unbearably regressive rather than a transcendence of the formalism of representative democracy. At the same time, however, it is not hard to predict that the Eastern European countries which are now so fulsome in their praise of democratic liberties and of free-market economics will, after the removal of the Iron Curtain and the anticipated arrest of their economic decline, all too rapidly find themselves faced with exactly the same problems as those that typically afflict Western democracies.

In fact the notion of representative democracy, especially at a time when its traditional conservative and progressive alternatives are breaking down, no longer appears capable of successfully describing the political systems of post-industrial countries and of adequately distinguishing the democratic from the non-democratic. This is especially true of the notion of democracy which has developed out of what I propose to call the 'neo-classical' doctrine. I have in mind the theories of democratic pluralism which extend from Schumpeter to, amongst others, Lipset, Dahl, Plamenatz, Aron and Sartori. To my mind, these theories are nowadays no less rudimentary or unrealistic than the classical doctrine of democracy whose lack of complexity and realism they originally set out to oppose. Fifty years after *Capitalism, Socialism and Democracy*, it is necessary to realize that Schumpeter's brand of realism has been displaced, not to say wholly superseded, by the realism contained in a reality of infinitely greater complexity. Once again, therefore, we are faced with the need to evolve another theory of democracy of still greater complexity and realism than those previously transmitted to us by the Western tradition, both classical and 'neo-classical'.

Far more than the classical doctrine, it is the neo-classical theories of democracy that provide political theodicies of the 'prince of the present day'. By designating such a 'prince' democratic, and by seeing pluralistic democracy as 'one of the most extraordinary of all human artifacts',[1] they

---

[1] R. A. Dahl, *Democracy and Its Critics*, New Haven (Conn.) and London: Yale University Press, 1989, p. 223.

simply justify the principality of today, in all its forms, as the best of all possible principalities. However, it is not my purpose to attempt here any fruitless (and inevitably moralistic) resurrection of the ethico-political prescription of classical democracy in the old European tradition. A sufficient number of such attempts have appeared on both sides of the Atlantic in the last twenty years, of which John Rawls has provided the most prominent example. To my mind they add up to little more in substance than a harking back to the puritan individualism of European proto-capitalism, whose political ideals, it has been said, extended no further than the intellectual horizon of the eighteenth-century ironmonger.

For myself, I remain unconvinced that the underlying assumption behind the notion of representative democracy – i.e. the sovereignty, rationality, and moral autonomy of the individual – remains in any sense valid as an assumption rather than as an extremely difficult goal in the context of what have now become the truly effective factors in the political systems of modern, complex societies. Consequently, I intend to argue for the elaboration of a 'post-representative' theory of the political system capable of matching the levels of complexity now reached by industrial societies in the midst of the 'infomation revolution': a theory which would take account of the 'evolutionary risks' which democracy encounters in those societies.

In doing this, I consciously ally myself with the tradition of European political realism which leads from Machiavelli to Hobbes, Marx, the Italian elitists, Weber and Schumpeter. Naturally I hope to remain aware of the difficulties inherent in such a proposition, but I shall aim not to lose sight of the essential lesson to be drawn from this tradition: that the salient characteristic of all political decision-making is its lack of impartiality, and the randomness of its morality. In contrast with the moralism which at present holds sway in political philosophy in the English-speaking world, one of my basic assumptions will be that the primary function of the political system is that of reducing fear, through a selective regulation of social risks.

At the same time, however, it is important to state that I ally myself with classical notions of the resistance to power and the struggle against its insolence, abuses and privileges. For this apparent contradiction, the lessons of recent times will perhaps form my best apology.

# Acknowledgements

My first thanks are due to Richard Bellamy and John B. Thompson for the encouragement they gave me to develop a number of ideas which I had begun to advance in a previous collection of essays. That those ideas should finally have emerged as a book to be published in English is owed to the kind suggestion of Anthony Giddens, David Held and John B. Thompson, who also offered some valuable advice about its structure. To Anthony Giddens I owe in addition the opportunity to stay in Cambridge during the autumn of 1988 as Visiting Scholar of the University's Social and Political Sciences Committee. Through the kindness also of Jeremy Butterfield, Fellow of Jesus College, my stay in Cambridge at that time enabled me to lay the ground for the book in near ideal conditions.

In June 1989 I spent a brief, but closely packed, time at Bielefeld, where the ample resources of the University Library, and especially of its sociology section, greatly assisted my further research. The success of the visit was largely made possible by the expert bibliographical help I received from Elena Esposito.

A book which saw its beginnings in one Cambridge reached an equally happy conclusion in another. As a result of a much appreciated invitation from its chairman, Guido Goldman, I was able to spend the winter of 1989–90 at Harvard, as Visiting Scholar at the Center for European Studies.

My book naturally owes a great deal to the English-speaking environment in which it was both conceived and, in large part, written. But I should not wish, for all that, to pass over the large debts I have incurred in discussing its ideas with numerous Italian friends. In thanking Luca Baccelli, Franca Bonichi, Antonio Cassese, Furio Cerutti, Pietro Costa, Raimondo Cubeddu, Luigi Ferrajoli, Giovan Francesco Lanzara, Giovanni Mari, Virgilio Mura, Andrea Orsi Battaglini, Emilio Santoro and Francesco Vertova, I am able to acknowledge just a few of those debts.

The greatest, however, as always, is to Norberto Bobbio, whose views are so constantly in my mind that it is as if I have discussed every page of the book with him, even those he has never seen.

Finally, on the literary side, it is a pleasure to express my thanks to David McKie, Fellow of Robinson College, Cambridge, who once again has been kind enough to lend a text of mine the elegant precision of his English.

Danilo Zolo
*Florence and Cambridge*

# 1 Some General Assumptions

## Complexity

In *Democracy and Its Critics* Robert Dahl has argued that any proper discussion of the problems of democracy must begin by addressing itself to the half-hidden assumptions lying behind democratic theory. These assumptions, he reminds us, are present in all conceptions of democracy, but are ones which proponents of democracy tend to dismiss as a sort of unexplored and unrecognized 'shadow theory'.[1] The result is that this grey area in fact receives greater illumination at the hands of critics of democracy. This is an opinion not usually voiced in American political science and one with which I find myself largely in agreement. It is important, therefore, that I should first lay bare the assumptions behind my work and attempt to argue their case. In doing this, I shall aim to reduce the extent of my own 'grey area', although it would naturally be foolish to hope to eliminate it entirely.

The general premiss behind my thought is the hypothesis that it is the idea of complexity – along with the closely related notion of social complexity – which opens the way to a realistic analysis of the condition and fate of democracy in post-industrial societies.[2] The idea of complexity, at least in the sense in which I propose to use it, involves a very broad range of philosophical assumptions which cannot be taken for granted. In addition I shall make reference to a 'reflexive epistemology' and, albeit critically, to system theory.

The idea of complexity is plagued with controversy. A decade ago Herbert Simon was able to identify no less than seven distinct meanings then given to the term.[3] It is true that in certain disciplines a number of rigorous definitions have been reached: for instance in dynamic topology, information theory, artificial-intelligence research, and, above all, in computer science, where the notion of computational complexity has well established itself.[4] Such formalized definitions are useful, in these as in other contexts, for mathematical calculation. They fail, however, to admit of any significant application in the social sciences. Their practical utilization requires a large number of supplementary assumptions or *ceteris paribus* clauses which can only annul the logical rigour of their point of departure and hence their utility.

Once we abandon narrow subject confines and enter into the domain of the social sciences (or the related area of political and journalistic language), we find ourselves confronted with a pathological situation. For here the notion of complexity, despite all the value it has acquired in specialized contexts, has only an awkward and, usually, trivial meaning, as in the reply so often given by European politicians to tricky questions, namely that 'the problem is more complex than that'. Often the word 'complex' appears to stand for little more than the psychological unease of someone who finds himself in the position of having recently made the discovery that the world in which he lives is no longer that of his parents and grandparents.

In fact, even in its more sophisticated uses, the concept of complexity remains vague and ambiguous, to an extent which goes beyond the vagueness and ambiguity of terms normally employed in the social (and natural) sciences. It has to be admitted that philosophers of complexity have hardly distinguished themselves in their attempts to bring their subject up to the standards required for rigorous scientific debate. The examples of Edgar Morin and Niklas Luhmann[5] come to mind, not to mention the proponents of *autopoiesis*, and 'second-order cybernetics'.[6]

My first task, therefore, is to set out in specific terms the idea of complexity which I intend to use, and, in doing this, to offer some defence of it. For epistemological reasons which I hope will become clear by the end of this chapter, I shall make no attempt to give it a formal definition which aspires to some grade of verifiability (or falsifiability) within a properly axiomatized theory. Instead, I shall restrict myself to suggesting a possible line of interpretation. And this I shall put forward, after the event, not for its methodological rigour, but for its ability to select and arrange in coherent fashion certain problems which I consider important. In this way, I hope to set out the premises, naturally entirely stipulative, of a clear and accessible argument, matching what I am in a position to offer with what I hope will be the reasonable requirements of my readers.

In my theoretical lexicon the term 'complexity' does not describe objective properties of natural or social phenomena. Nor does it denote complex objects as contrasted with simple objects. Rather, it refers to the cognitive situation in which agents, whether they are individuals or social groups, find themselves. The relations which agents construct and project on their environment in their attempts at self-orientation – i.e. at arrangement, prediction, planning, manipulation – will be more or less complex according to circumstances. In the same way their actual connection with the environment will be more or less complex.

These premises allow the conditions of complexity to be expressed under the following four headings:

1   The wider the scope of possible choices and the higher the number of variables which agents have to take account of in their attempts to resolve problems of knowledge, adaptation and organization, the more complex their environmental situation becomes. For example, life in a metropolitan environment offers more complexity than life in a rural environment in proportion to the greater variety of experience it provides. The complexity is further increased, the more the inhabitants become aware of the possibility they have of being exposed to pollutive substances. In Western countries, political life has become more complex with the introduction into elections of opinion polls. These extend the range of available information and influence the choice of voters by anticipating the result of the ballot.

2   An environment grows in complexity, the more interdependent the variables become. Variations in the value of one variable inevitably act on other variables (and so too they on it), making the task of cognition (and operation) necessarily more difficult. A larger amount of information is then needed to arrange and control the environment. Once a certain threshold of complexity is crossed, the very quality changes of the calculations needed to predict the effects of the recursive relations which interconnect the environmental factors. Even analysis of individual phenomena becomes less certain, given that their basic condition – and developments from that condition – can scarcely be separated from the nexus of non-linear connections.

3   A third element of complexity is formed by the instability or turbulence of the environment and by the tendency of its variables to change along swift or unpredictable trajectories.[7] This facet of complexity is of a dynamic nature, and is all the more important the more it is connected to processes which lead either from order to disorder (revolution, chaotic evolution, catastrophic bifurcation, etc.) or, and still more significantly, to the birth of order from disorder.[8]

4   The fourth condition of complexity, which itself embraces the first three, is the state of cognitive circularity reached by agents who become aware of the high level of the complexity of their own environment. These agents realize that the difficulty they encounter in their attempts to explain and predict environmental phenomena according to linear (i.e. monocausal, monofunctional, or simple-law) schemes, itself conditions their overall

relationship with the environment. The difficulty in fact arises from what is actually their own cognitive activity in constructing and altering their environment through their attempt to grasp it intellectually. (This situation seems to receive confirmation from the prevalent interpretations of the uncertainty principle.) Consequently, the agents take account of the fact that they are not in a position to define their environment in objective terms, i.e. by neutralizing the distortions introduced by their own cognitive activity and, circularly, that they are not in a position to define themselves without reference to the complexity and turbulence of the environment which, over time, condition and modity their own cognitive activities. The situation they find themselves in, therefore, is one of epistemological complexity. From this there arises, as we shall see, the need for a 'reflexive epistemology', based on recognition of the cognitive intertwining of agent (or system) and environment in conditions of heightened complexity.

## Social complexity

By 'social complexity' I have in mind a specific configuration of social relations in modern post-industrial societies as it is perceived by the social agents themselves. This configuration may be seen – as it is, for example, by Niklas Luhmann[9] – as the outcome of a very general evolutive tendency. The underlying hypothesis behind his and others' views is that social groups tend over time to modify their organizational structure according to a logic of increasing differentiation. This hypothesis is now generally considered to be well established, having been advanced by many of the founders of modern sociology, such as Spencer, Simmel, Durkheim, Weber and Parsons, who form the tradition to which Luhmann himself subscribes.[10]

Luhmann's argument is that social evolution has historically taken the form first of a phase of segmentary differentiation, second as differentiation through stratification, and finally, in modern times, as functional differentiation, arising from an increase in the quantity and variety of the functional subsystems of each social system.[11] The subsystems (economic, political, scientific, etc.) develop more specific roles than were present in the system from which they were originally differentiated, creating to this end separate organizational structures and shaping themselves to working criteria – 'functional codes' – which open the way towards autonomous specialization.

I should say at the outset that, in contrast to Luhmann,[12] the establishment of an evolutionary basis for a theory of social complexity holds little of value for me. I doubt even whether such a basis could ever be affirmed, especially if the attempt to do so is made by means of a rough combination, on the most general of theoretical planes, of System Theory and the 'Darwinistic approach'.[13] More significant, from my point of view, is the analysis of the actual level of complexity of contemporary political systems, the ramifications of this development and the issue of whether this level will increase or diminish in the immediate future.

My use of the term 'social complexity' should therefore be seen in the light of this more toned-down assessment. The following four propositions will help to make clear what it is:

1   In post-industrial societies, typified by a high level of division of labour and functional differentiation, social complexity manifests itself as the variety and semantic discontinuity of the languages, understandings, techniques and values which are practised within each subsystem and its further differentiations. Every subsystem tends to seek specialization and to work on the basis of distinct and autonomous functional codes. The meaning of an event experienced within one social environment – a religious experience, for example – cannot be conveyed in the terms relevant to the experience of a different environment – a sports club, for instance, or an office, or a nuclear research laboratory. The different experiences are not at root commensurable. The variables of social behaviour increase in correlation, and there is a consequent growth in the difficulty of its understanding and prediction.

2   Alongside the tendency to autonomy of the functional codes, there exist phenomena of growing interdependence between the various subsystems. These phenomena are a condition of their coordination within the wider social orbit. Study of the different forms taken by this interdependence reveals diffuse and polycentric activity, with a characteristic tendency towards the breaking down of hierarchical structures. Political campaigns, for example, are nowadays conditioned by the requirements of the medium of television, but this medium is subordinate to legislation governing political use of the media, and both of these agents, the politicians and the television company, have to submit to the exigencies of the advertising market. This process is in turn conditioned not only by general economic legislation, but also by the increasingly fierce competition between television and more traditional forms of publicity. Herbert Simon and Raymond Boudon have demonstrated how, in the fields of economics, business studies and sociology, an increase in phenomena of interdependence is accompanied by an increased difficulty of prediction and social intervention. Since they are forced to make their predictions and projections in the absence of full information and sufficient knowledge of the lines of interaction, the economist, politician and social engineer have to accommodate themselves to a significant body of 'perverse effects': that

is, of results they had not predicted and which are hardly welcome to them.[14] More generally, any growth in phenomena of functional inter-dependence is matched by a significant increase in negative external factors.[15]

3   Differentiation of experience favours social mobility. In place of a society weighted with the ballast of universal and unchanging principles, there is a pluralism of social spaces regulated by contingent and flexible criteria. Removal of the constraints of tradition, stratification, and loca-lization leads to a marked acceleration of social change. Moral 'polytheism' and widespread agnosticism over the 'final questions' take the place of institutionalized collective beliefs brought into being by political coercion.

4   As seen by individual agents (or systems), increased levels of differe-ntiation lead to a greater 'depersonalization' and 'abstractness' of social relations. Variety of experience increases, but the experiences are more directly moulded by functional needs or expectations. The individuals, who give or receive specialized services within ever more differentiated roles, become interchangeable elements within those roles. The multiplicity of possible actions and the increase in the range of services produce a kind of 'selective overload' in a context of increasing insecurity and instability.[16] The wider the spectrum of possible choices extends, the more pressing and hazardous becomes the need for each agent to choose between options and to 'reduce the complexity'.[17]

## Epistemological complexity

My treatment of the problem of complexity (including social complexity) is quite clearly only one of the many which are possible. It cannot claim, in absolute terms, to be preferable to any other. My outlook is unavoidably context dependent and cannot avoid a certain evaluative bias. But one feature essential to my treatment is the attempt to deal with the complexity of political and social relations in post-industrial societies on the basis of a further, no less complex, cognitive approach: that is, on the basis of a reflexive epistemology.

The meaning I attach to reflexive epistemology may be conveyed most directly by reference to the metaphor first used forty years ago by Otto Neurath to describe the position of the philosopher of science in the post-Einsteinian period.[18] It has more recently been given even greater celebrity by Quine, who took it as a symbol of his own critique of dogmatic empiricism.[19] Philosophers, according to Neurath, are like sailors who are prevented by storm from returning to port and so are forced to repair their disintegrating ship in mid-ocean, supporting themselves, while they carry out the repair, on the very structures threatened with collapse by the waves.

The reflexive nature of this metaphor well conveys the idea of 'epistemological complexity' which I have referred to as one of the summary conditions of complexity. The metaphor alludes to a cognitive situation in which any possibility of certainty or, following Popper, of 'approximation' to the truth, is excluded because agents themselves are included in the environment which they attempt to make the object of their own cognition. The agents may take critical – i.e. reflexive – account of the situation of circularity in which they find themselves, but they cannot remove themselves from their own historical and social perspective, or free themselves from the biases of the scientific community, culture or civilization to which they belong and which influence their own perception of themselves. They cannot know themselves objectively, but they cannot even know objectively their environmental either, since they themselves alter the environment by projecting upon it their own biases when they interact with it in making it the object of their cognition.

Agents may well attempt to deal with the problem of circularity by including themselves among the objects which they study. But they will never succeed in forming the perfect circle of cognitive self-transparency by neutralizing, so to speak, all the anthropological, semantic, and sociological preconditions of their own intellectual biographies. They can only try to reduce, but never succeed in suppressing, the element of epistemological complexity. And in this respect, as post-empiricist philosophers, historians and sociologists of science such as Thomas Kuhn, Ludwik Fleck, and the Edinburgh School have persuasively argued, the epistemological situation of social groups, and even of scientific communities, is no different from that of individual agents.[20]

Moreover, if agents wish to avoid condemning themselves to total cognitive and communicative paralysis, they have to avoid calling into question the whole conceptual apparatus set in place for them by the environment. At least in part, they have to accept, acritically and non-reflexively, the linguistic and theoretical presuppositions handed down to them by the 'folklore' of the tradition to which they belong.[21] They are not therefore in a position to occupy some neutral ground, a Cartesian *tabula rasa*, which they can take as a 'methodological starting-point' for an objective foundation of knowledge. Nor is it possible for individuals, as Edmund Husserl and Edith Stein suggested,[22] to attain at least some inner certainty, a basic insight at the end of a psychological journey made within the phenomenological context of the 'world of life' (*Lebenswelt*). If the situation of circularity is truly one which may not be overcome, all possibility of the justification for, or of an objective foundation of, knowledge must fail, whether it be of an empirical, Galilean nature or of an intuitive, consciential kind.

From this 'reflexive' standpoint, philosophies of science based on realistic or idealistic stances can only appear, for symmetrically opposite reasons, wholly inadequate. And this is no less the case with more sophisticated recent versions such as 'internal realism' and 'radical constructivism' respectively. Such philosophies ignore the situation of circularity from which no cognitive construct is free, and, in so doing, set out to establish linear, causal and 'directional' relations between agent and environment. They conjure up ingenuously – that is, through their inability to grasp the complexity of the cognitive position – relations of objective mirroring of the environment or, conversely, of subjective 'production' of it.

Thus there are good reasons for seeing neo-positivism in particular as being the most thoroughgoing attempt in our time at the scientistic and logicistic denial of 'epistemological complexity'. The so-called North American empiricist 'received view' comes most to mind, advanced by such writers as Rudolf Carnap, Carl G. Hempel, Ernest Nagel, R. B. Braithwaite, Alan Kaplan, and exercising a deep influence on contemporary social sciences.[23] Amongst other things it has, as we shall see, contributed significantly to the establishment of political science and to the development, within it, of 'revisionist' theories of procedural democracy. But the fault of this version of empiricism is that not only does it rest on an ingenuously realistic epistemology, but it has also presupposed the universality and constancy of scientific language, conceiving it as an organic system of perfectly rigorous statements, free (or freeable) from all ambiguity, metaphorical vagueness, and evaluative content, and therefore capable of being logically formalized and subjected to control.

As to the construction of theories, this conception of empiricism demands that scientific explanation and prediction be based deductively on universal laws, valid for every possible time and every possible space. It binds the scholar, whether on the arts or the science side, to the discovery of causal connections between phenomena, according to the nomological and deductive model of scientific explanation advanced by Popper and formalized by Hempel.[24]

The basic failure of such philosophies of science to take into account the problem of 'epistemological complexity' cannot be subject to doubt. Following the ideal of maximum epistemic parsimony and a conception of the truth as the correspondence of linguistic statements to reality, they set out to make knowledge of the environment coincide with its reduction to highly simplified, linear and 'directional' explanatory principles. From this viewpoint, even the universe itself comes to be seen as a fixed and objective structure rather than as an environment interacting with its observer and changing as the observer changes.

As opposed to dogmatic empiricism, a 'reflexive' epistemological position argues that the point of departure and the point of arrival in every cognitive process consists, circularly, in the propositions of linguistic communication and not in the data or facts of a supposed environmental objectivity, which both precedes, and is external to, language. For it is on the symbolic plane that agents (both individual and collective) develop the selective structures which enable them to represent the environment, to adapt themselves to it or to form arrangements of it. As an instrument for reducing the complexity of the environment, language may not therefore be superseded. For it is not possible, while still using linguistic instruments, to separate language from some hypothetical extra-linguistic dimension of the environment.

'Reflexive' epistemology is bound to deny the possibility of a nomological and deductive explanation in either the natural or the political and social sciences. The reasons for this are entirely straightforward. First, any general law can only really be held valid within a particular defined area and, even within this area, only with exceptions and anomalies. Second, any empirical phenomenon can always be interpreted in the light of a plurality of different theories which are even, in many cases, mutually exclusive. This is as true in, say, sociology as it is in physics.

From this point of view, the distinction between the science of nature and the science of man rapidly diminishes. The science of nature also operates circularly. There are no absolute terms for it to be based on, because no theory can be confirmed or falsified empirically, except within the context of linguistic forms, theoretical assumptions and practices which have themselves led to the formation of that theory and in the light of which only that theory makes sense. An epistemological enquiry into the general meaning of scientific knowledge can only start from the self-interpretation of its own particular symbolic universe – it may be called 'paradigm', 'disciplinary matrix', 'thought-style', or *Denkkollektiv* – which it is bound to accept as a *tabula inscripta*. Such has been the lesson of European conventionalism, from Duhem to Poincaré, Rey, Le Roy, Neurath and Fleck.[25]

If theoretical propositions are not rigorously 'avaluative', but are instead conditioned by the systems of belief (biases, vested interests, ideologies, etc.) of the communities which develop them, then it might well be possible to conclude that there is no difference in principle between the language of theory and the language of prescription, between scientific knowledge and moral imperatives. Recognition of 'epistemological complexity' could then be a premiss for an overall acceptance of the reasons behind 'ethical cognitivism', at least in its weaker forms.

My own argument, as will emerge later on, is entirely opposed to this conclusion. The fact that an evaluative element is always present in the language of theory provides, to my mind, a further and decisive reason for rejecting the viewpoint of moral cognitivism and of the related ethico-political philosophies, such as, for example, the 'theory of justice' advanced by John Rawls. It is only on the basis of an implicit realistic metaphysics, which sees knowledge as intuition of the truth or as the discovery of the laws of Nature, that it is possible to claim to derive a deontology from an underlying ontology, extracting imperatives from assertions, and pre-scriptive propositions from observational propositions. The ethical principles based on natural law which the Roman Catholic church preaches in the area of sexuality – in practice without great success – provide a typical example of this stance.

## Increasing complexity

It would be impossible to conclude a chapter setting out my theoretical assumptions without alluding to two hypotheses which inform a number of my arguments on the crisis of European political theory and, more particularly, on the need for a reconstruction of democratic theory.

The first hypothesis is that the development of scientific research and the increase in knowledge which it has brought about both inside and outside the scientific subsystem does not, as one would naturally expect, reduce, but instead increases, the complexity of the environment in modern societies. This hypothesis is closely linked with a premiss which has been rightly insisted upon in the history and philosophy of science by, amongst others, Thomas Kuhn and Mary Hesse.[26] The central point of this premiss is that growth in scientific knowledge does not come about in accordance with rational criteria, in the sense of a logical coherence and organic evolution of theories, but instead is segmentary and discontinuous.

It is well recognized that there exist within areas of empirical research (not least physics) various theoretical models which allow reliable predictions to be made within their respective domains, but fail to apply even to adjoining areas. Indeed, not only is there no discernible tendency of these theories to converge towards a common centre, but grave difficulties are encountered in any attempt to reduce their multiplicity by removing the elements of incompatibility. The best example of this situation is the extent to which theoretical physicists have so far found it impossible to gather both quantum physics and general relativity within a single unified theory.[27]

The transition from one general theory to another – from Ptolemaic physics to Galilean, for example, or, again, from Galilean physics to relativity – is a kind of revolutionary leap from one scientific paradigm to another. Adherence to the new paradigm, as Thomas Kuhn has argued, has more of the quality of a conversion than of rational persuasion. From this standpoint, even the idea of the 'convergence' of scientific developments towards cumulative results capable of integration within a unitary synthesis lacks foundation.[28] In fact quite the opposite seems to be the case. All the main categories, for instance, of classical physics – space, time, matter, energy, causality – have undergone far-reaching alterations in contemporary developments of the subject, but without this process of alteration corresponding to any kind of internal logic. Instead, it looks very much as if the entire body of inherited knowledge in the subject is finding increasing difficulty in orientating scientific research within its newly widened horizons on both the cosmic and the subatomic level and that this difficulty is therefore leading to continual changes of paradigm.

Growth in scientific knowledge enlarges the range of possible experience for *homo sapiens* and reduces our ignorance. But our certainties do not thereby increase. On the contrary, the more theory advances, drawing new technological advances in its train, the more new horizons open up, raising unforeseen questions which stimulate ever more hazardous attempts at explanation, less underwritten by the preceding stages of knowledge. The uncertainty and complexity of the environment increase in proportion.

Mary Hesse has argued that, while the idea of convergence and logical transition of scientific theories has to be rejected, it is necessary to recognize all the same that scientific progress admits of a 'pragmatic criterion': the progress is instrumental in terms of the increasing ability it affords for both the prediction and the control of the environment.[29] I do not expect that there can be any doubts on the first of these two points, if by prediction we mean that science is able to provide rules of a hypothetical kind for the weighing of risks connected with practical decisions taken in conditions of uncertainty. This is the same as saying that science is essentially the begetter or provider of technical progress. But the point must still be stressed, as it is by Raymond Aron,[30] that notable irregularities and discontinuities are present not only in scientific development, but also in purely technical development. In both areas, European history has witnessed long phases both of stagnation and of unexpected acceleration. It is probably worth stressing in addition that increased ability for technical prediction takes place within ever more specialized areas governed by criteria of local and 'bounded' rationality.

As for the second point, 'control of the environment', I believe that Mary Hesse's formulation could be usefully improved by the specification that it is a matter of purely potential progress. The reason for this is that, paradoxical though it may seem, progress goes hand in hand with a dramatic increase in the quantity and variety of risks brought about by technical scientific development – witness the recent proposition of the notion of a 'risk society' (*Risikogesellschaft*) as an interpretative category of post-industrial societies.[31] In an environment of increased technology there is a progressive reduction of what Gehlen called the 'invariant reservoir' of 'cultural real estate'.[32] Individuals are required to maintain constant vigilance, to remain in a kind of chronic state of alarm, and to improvise fundamental decisions at any given time.

The development of technical applications of science in fact demands a growing complexity of strategies to control the environment in the light of the new factors of risk brought about circularly by the development itself. One need think only of the unlooked-for and unwelcome discoveries of the last two decades: the limits to economic progress, the potential exhaustion of traditional energy resources, the tight ecological rules for human survival in conditions of rapid and unbalanced demographic expansion, the dangers of nuclear power, the continually increasing gap between varying conditions of life for human beings on different parts of the planet – an inequality which seems poised in coming decades to bring about large migratory pressures and the accompanying threat of violent conflict over the apportionment of citizenship, together with new forms of xenophobia and of racial discrimination.[33]

The second hypothesis may be formulated as follows: the development of advanced technologies, especially of electronic and information technology, is not simply a factor in the growth of social complexity, but is also a powerful accelerator of that growth. This acceleration is created to a large degree by the fact that advanced technical innovation – e.g. in biotechnology, genetic engineering, artificial intelligence, new materials and new sources of energy – possesses to a hitherto unknown degree a particular aptitude for reflexive application to the biological, anthropological and cognitive characteristics of *homo sapiens*. A central role in this large-scale feed-back has been played by the so-called 'information revolution' with its multiple developments of a robotic, telematic or multimedial nature.[34]

The reduction in working hours and the saving of resources and physical energy brought about by the automation of productive processes and by customer-operated techniques in the service sector (banks, shops, etc.)

have transferred a large amount of human energy from work time to leisure time. Simultaneously average life expectancy has been prolonged, with a resulting increase in the range of possible experience for each individual. Thus the need becomes all the more pressing for individuals to respond to growing social complexity by making a meaningful selection from the multitude of possible roles and differentiated functions open to them.

Telematic developments are bringing into existence a world-wide network capable of being filled at virtually the speed of light with millions of units of information which are potentially at the fingertips of any possessor of a personal computer. Individuals are being exposed to a mass of information and stimuli which tax their attention and selection abilities outside the traditional centres for exchange and digestion of knowledge, such as the family, school, church, trade union, etc. Delicate problems of interaction come into being between these telematic sources and the great majority of their users, who are not possessed of selective mechanisms sufficient to cope with the mass and variety of information they are provided with. The risk of a slight, fortuitous, or even chaotic, reduction of complexity threatens the normal processes by which individual identities are shaped, and new forms of socialization appreciably interfere with the forms traditionally taken by collective identities. Overall, the acceleration of the pace of life brought about by new technologies – an acceleration which has given rise to Paul Virilio's term 'dromocracy' (i.e. domination by speed in the transmission of objects and symbols) – appears to be the cause of a growing sensory privation in human beings.[35]

Mass communication has undoubtedly, over the course of time, produced politically important cognitive effects – I shall deal with these in depth in a subsequent chapter – but it has also come to play a surrogate role for experience itself. The medium of television, in particular, creates as a symbolical substitute for direct experience what the 'slavery of the concrete' would otherwise make impossible. Direct experience is then marginalized by this symbolical realization of the possible, and the need for personal activity is reduced. In time, even sensory perception is influenced by it, to the extent that it is symbolic interaction with the media which provides the primary 'frames' of direct experience, and not vice versa.[36]

The mass media have the effect, therefore, of excluding as 'non-real' anything extraneous to their own image of reality. They produce a sort of dematerialization of life and a 'spectacular' stylization of social relations. This effect brings about a general increase in the symbolical abstraction, contingency, and plasticity of the social environment, so that it can to an ever-decreasing degree be thought of and experienced as an objective, static and unidimensional 'reality'. Instead, it appears as the highly change-able result of the interaction between selective representations of a 'reality' over which individuals no longer feel they have control.[37] They have in fact lost any possibility of relating it to something which is not an experience 'mediated' to them by the means of mass communication.

## Notes

1  R. A. Dahl, *Democracy and Its Critics*, pp. 3–5.
2  I shall use the phrase 'post-industrial societies', although it is in a number of respects open to criticism, to refer very simply to contemporary industrial societies as they have been affected by the 'information revolution' in its three fundamental developments: telematics, which deals with electronic filing and transmitting of data; robotics, which deals with the automatization of indus-trial processes and social services; and mass-media communication, which principally concerns communication via television.
3  Cf. H. Simon, 'How Complex are Complex Systems?', in *Proceedings of the 1976 Biennial Meeting of the Philosophy of Science Association*, ed. F. Suppe and P. H. Asquith, East Lansing (Mich.): Philosophy of Science Association, 1976, vol. 2, pp. 501–22.
4  Cf. H. W. Gottinger, *Coping with Complexity*, Dordrecht and Boston (Mass.) D. Reidel, 1983, particularly pp. ix-xv; see R. L. Flood, *Dealing with Complexity*, New York: Plenum Press, 1988; C. Calude, *Theories of Com-putational Complexity*, Amsterdam and New York: North Holland, 1988; see also C. Cherniak, *Minimal Rationality*, Cambridge (Mass.): The MIT Press, 1986.
5  See e.g. E. Morin, *La Méthode*, I. *La Nature de la Nature*, Paris: Éditions du Seuil, 1977; N. Luhmann, *Soziologische Aufklärung*, I, Opladen: Westdeu-tscher Verlag, 1970.
6  The (highly controversial) theory of *autopoiesis* has been advanced by two Chilean biologists, H. R. Maturana and F. J. Varela. They maintain that life is characterized in every living system by the recursive and self-referential organization of its own constitutive elements, i.e. that 'the very organization of processes is generated by the interaction between their products'; see H. R. Maturana and F. J. Varela, *Autopoiesis and Cognition: The Realization of the Living*, Dordrecht and Boston (Mass): D. Reidel, 1980; M. Zeleny (ed.), *Autopoiesis. A Theory of Living Organization*, New York and Oxford: North Holland, 1981. On 'second-order cybernetics' see H. von Foerster, *Observing Systems*, Seaside (Calif.): Intersystems Publications, 1984.
7  Cf. J. Casti, *Connectivity, Complexity and Catastrophe in Large-scale Systems*, New York: John Wiley and Sons, 1979, pp. 102–5.
8  Phenomena of the first type have been studied under the theory of 'attractors' and have been formalized by, amongst others, René Thom and Christopher Zeeman; see R. Thom, *Stabilité structurelle et morphogénèse*, Paris: Inter-

éditions, 1972, Eng. trans. Reading (Mass.): W. A. Benjamin, 1975; C. Zeeman, *Catastrophe Theory*, Reading (Mass.): Benjamin, 1977. Those of the second have generated the idea of complexity as self-organization. This idea has been shared by the studies of Henri Atlan on 'order through noise', of Ilya Prigogine on dissipative structures, of Eric Jantsch on the self-organization of the universe, and of Friedrich von Hayek on the processes of spontaneous morphogenesis of social groups; see H. Atlan, *Entre le cristal et la fumée. Essai sur l'organisation du vivant*, Paris: Seuil, 1979; I. Prigogine and I. Stengers, *La Nouvelle Alliance: Métamorphose de la science*, Paris: Gallimard, 1979, Eng. trans. Boulder (Col.) and London: Shambhala, 1984; E. Jantsch, *The Self-Organizing Universe*, Oxford: Pergamon Press, 1980; F. A. von Hayek, *Kinds of Order in Society*, Studies in Social Theory no. 5, Menlo Park (Calif.): Institute for Humane Studies, 1975; F. A. Hayek, 'The Theory of Complex Phenomena', in M. Bunge (ed.), *The Critical Approach to Science and Philosophy*, New York: Free Press, 1964.

9 Cf. N. Luhmann, *The Differentiation of Society*, New York: Columbia University Press, 1981, pp. 229–70.

10 See N. Luhmann (ed.), *Soziale Differenzierung*, Opladen: Westdeutscher Verlag, 1985.

11 Cf. N. Luhmann, *The Differentiation of Society*, pp. 232–8.

12 Ibid., pp. 229–54.

13 Ibid., p. 252. One objection is provided by the study of biological evolution itself, where the 'Darwinistic approach' is far from being taken as unassailable truth. It is entirely in keeping with the adaptive and directional nature of evolution that it should not be immune to doubt, especially given the general crisis of the conception of progressive enlightenment to which Darwin himself adhered. Another objection is the poor credibility in itself of the notion of functional differentiation as the core of a theory of social evolution. See N. Eldredge and S. J. Gould, 'Punctuated Equilibria: The Tempo and Mode of Evolution Reconsidered', *Paleobiology*, 3 (1977), 2. 115–51; and cf. H. Tyrell, 'Anfragen an die Theorie der gesellschaftlichen Differenzierung', *Zeitschrift für Soziologie*, 7 (1978), 2. 175–93.

14 See H. E. Simon, 'Bounded Rationality', in C. B. McGuire and R. Radner (eds), *Decision and Organization*, Amsterdam: North Holland, 1971; R. Boudon, *Effets perverses et ordre social*, Paris: Presses Universitaires de France, 1977, Eng. trans. New York: St Martin's Press, 1982.

15 Cf. R. Benjamin, *The Limits of Politics. Collective Goods and Political Change in Postindustrial Societies*, Chicago and London: The University of Chicago Press, 1980, pp. vii–xi.

16 Cf. A. Gehlen, *Der Mensch. Seine Natur und Seine Stellung in der Welt*, Wiesbaden: Akademische Verlagsgesellschaft Athenaion, 1978, Eng. trans. New York: Columbia University Press, 1988, pp. 49–64. On the increasing demand for symbolic reassurance which individuals and groups convey to the political system within complex societies see T. R. La Porte (ed.), *Organized Social Complexity: Challenge to Politics and Polity*, Princeton (NJ): Princeton University Press, 1975.

17    Cf. A. Gehlen, *Die Seele im technischen Zeitalter*, Reinbek bei Hamburg: Rowohlt, 1957, Eng. trans. New York: Columbia University Press, 1980, p. 75; J. Habermas and N. Luhmann, *Theorie der Gesellschaft oder Sozialtechnologie*, Frankfurt a.M.: Suhrkamp Verlag, 1971, pp. 156–62. As a final explanation of terms I should make clear that by 'system' I mean a social unity which presents a sufficient degree of organization to stabilize itself within its environment. By 'environment' I mean the framework of exogenous conditions of stability or of growth of the system. The debt this outline bears to system research and to established theories of complexity, such as those of Ludwig von Bertalanffy, Herbert Simon, Ross Ashby, Ilya Prigogine and Niklas Luhmann will be clear. See L. von Bertalanffy, *General System Theory*, New York: Braziller, 1968; H. A. Simon, 'The Architecture of Complexity', in H. A. Simon, *The Sciences of the Artificial*, Cambridge (Mass.): The MIT Press, 1981; W. R. Ashby, 'Principles of the Self-Organizing System', in W. Buckley (ed.), *Modern System Research for the Behavioral Scientist*, pp. 108–18; I. Prigogine and I. Stengers, *La Nouvelle Alliance: Métamorphose de la science*; N. Luhmann, *The Differentiation of Society*.

18    Cf. O. Neurath, *Foundations of the Social Sciences*, Chicago: University of Chicago Press, 1944, p. 47; and see O. Neurath, *Gesammelte philosophische und methodologische Schriften*, Vienna: Hölder-Pichler-Tempsky Verlag, 1981; cf. also my *Reflexive Epistemology. The Philosophical Legacy of Otto Neurath*, Dordrecht, Boston (Mass.) and London: Kluwer Academic Publishers, 1989, pp. xv–xviii, 22–3, 36, 48.

19    See W. V. O. Quine, 'Two Dogmas of Empiricism', in W. V. O. Quine, *From a Logical Point of View*, Cambridge (Mass.): Harvard University Press, 1980. On Neurath's metaphor see also H. Blumenberg, *Schiffbruch mit Zuschauer. Paradigma einer Daseinsmetapher*, Frankfurt a.M.: Suhrkamp Verlag, 1979; P. Lorenzen, *Methodisches Denken*, Frankfurt a.M.: Suhrkamp Verlag, 1968, Eng. trans. Amherst (Mass.): University of Massachusetts Press, 1987; C. Cherniak, *Minimal Rationality*; and see also my *Reflexive Epistemology*.

20    See T. Kuhn, *The Structure of Scientific Revolutions*, Chicago: University of Chicago Press, 1970; L. Fleck, *Entstehung und Entwicklung einer wissenschaftlichen Tatsache*, Frankfurt a.M.: Suhrkamp Verlag, 1980, Eng. trans. Chicago: University of Chicago Press, 1979; B. Barnes, *Interests and the Growth of Knowledge*, London and Boston (Mass.): Routledge and Kegan Paul, 1977.

21    I use the term to convey the very broad meaning proposed for it by Neurath, i.e. the ensemble of social habits and moral and religious beliefs which are transmitted from one generation to the next within some specific historical tradition; cf. my *Reflexive Epistemology*, pp. 146, 152, 175.

22    See E. Stein, *Werke*, Louvain: Nauwelaerts, 1950–87, Eng. trans. Washington (DC): ICS Publications, 1986.

23    See F. Suppe, *The Structure of Scientific Theories*, Urbana (Ill.): University of Illinois Press, 1977.

24 See K. Popper, *The Logic of Scientific Discovery*, London: Hutchinson, 1968; C. G. Hempel, *Aspects of Scientific Explanation*, New York: The Free Press, 1965.

25 Cf. again on this subject my *Reflexive Epistemology*, particularly pp. xiii–xviii, 169–70.

26 See R. Kuhn, *The Structure of Scientific Revolutions*; M. Hesse, *Revolutions and Reconstructions in the Philosophy of Science*, Brighton (Sussex): The Harvester Press, 1980.

27 See e.g. S. W. Hawking, *A Brief History of Time. From the Big Bang to Black Holes*, Toronto and New York: Bantam Books, 1988. This attempt at broad scientific dissemination is optimistically committed to the hope that the unification of physics is still an open question. This may go some way to accounting for the book's wide international acclaim.

28 See N. Rescher, *The Limits of Science*, Berkeley (Calif.): University of California Press, 1984.

29 Cf. M. Hesse, *Revolutions and Reconstructions in the Philosophy of Science*, pp. vii–xiv.

30 See R. Aron, *Dix-huit leçons sur la société industrielle*, Paris: Gallimard, 1962, Eng. trans. London: Weidenfeld and Nicolson, 1967. In order to reach Rome from Paris, Caesar took nearly the same time as Napoleon. By and large a Roman of the upper class enjoyed the same resources as a member of the French bourgeoisie at the time of Louis XIV. Afterwards the differences suddenly became enormous.

31 See U. Beck, *Risikogesellschaft. Auf dem Weg in eine andere Moderne*, Frankfurt a.M.: Suhrkamp Verlag, 1986; U. Beck, *Gegengifte. Die organisierte Unverantwortlichkeit*, Frankfurt a.M.: Suhrkamp Verlag, 1988; see also M. Douglas, *Risk Acceptability According to the Social Sciences*, London: Routledge and Kegan Paul, 1986; J. Keane, 'Democracy and the Decline of the Left', unpublished paper, London: Centre for the Study of Democracy, 1989, pp. 10–1.

32 Cf. A. Gehlen, *Die Seele im technischen Zeitalter*, Eng. trans., pp. 67–8 and *passim*; see also F. Rapp, *Analytical Philosophy of Technology*, Dordrecht, Boston (Mass.) and London: D. Reidel, 1981.

33 On this subject see the important collection, V. Reynolds, V. Falger and I. Wine (eds), *The Sociobiology of Ethnocentrism. Evolutionary Dimensions of Xenophobia, Discrimination, Racism and Nationalism*, London: Croom Helm, 1987.

34 See D. Lyon, *The Information Society: Issues and Illusions*, Cambridge: Polity Press, 1988; W. P. Dizard, Jr., *The Coming Information Age*, New York and London: Longman, 1985.

35 See P. Virilio, *Vitesse et politique*, Paris: Galilée, 1976.

36 See D. L. Altheide, *Media Power*, Beverly Hills (Calif.): Sage Publications, 1985; P. Elliot, 'Intellectuals, the Information Society and the Disappearance of the Public Sphere', in R. Collins et al. (eds), *Media, Culture and Society. A Critical Reader*, London: Sage Publications, 1986; J. Curran, A. Smith and P. Wingate (eds), *Impact and Influences. Essay on Media Power in the Twentieth*

*Century*, London: Methuen, 1987; see also A. Door, *Television and Children*, Beverly Hills (Calif.): Sage Publications, 1986.

37   Gianni Vattimo perceptively identifies the fundamental characteristics of 'post-modernity' as the crumbling of the principle of reality and the fragmentation of the cognitive horizon brought about by the growth of the mass media. But he also believes that there may be a new chance for human emancipation as a result of the increasing social complexity which develops out of the emerging plurality of fluid social subsystems. Unfortunately this kind of philosophical optimism seems contradicted, at least to date, by analytical evidence provided by communication research. Cf. G. Vattimo, *La società trasparente*, Milan: Garzanti, 1989, pp. 8–20, and cf. ch. 5 below.

# 2 Complexity and Political Theory

## Economic theories of politics

Now that the 'grey area' of my theoretical assumptions, however impossible to remove, has at least been more clearly defined, I move on to the
proposition of more explicit theses. My purpose in this chapter will be
to argue that there is a substantial incompatibility between a reflexive
epistemology and the theoretical paradigms which lie behind some of the
most influential conceptions of democracy current today in the West. I
shall then argue that a reflexive epistemology provides several important
premises for a realistic conception of democracy based on a non-meta-
physical version of political realism.

Acceptance of the notion of 'epistemological complexity' inevitably
calls into question the epistemological basis of a number of branches of
contemporary social science which have come into existence since the
last war under the influence of American neo-empiricism. Above all, the
paradigm of 'political science' suggests itself, a discipline which from its
very origin has embraced the ideals of the 'behaviourist revolution', one
of the most dogmatic expressions of neo-empiricism.[1] Other related areas
also come to mind, such the 'public choice' school and, more generally,
the application of rational action theories to politics, which surface most
typically in the economic theories of democracy and of the political system.

Separate consideration should also be devoted to the political applications of game theory. Here the pioneering work of Thomas Schelling
led to some enthusiastic hopes in the 1970s that a 'formal theory of politics'
would emerge from the collaboration of mathematicians and political
scientists.[2] In practice, however, at least so far as can be judged at present,
the influence of game theory on political and democratic theory has

extended little further than the modest use by some political scientists of basic notions of strategic decision-making in situations involving the interdependence of decisions. As for the mathematicians, little has been achieved on their side beyond the formulation of some highly abstract theorems. By their very nature these can only be devoid of the 'requisite variety' needed for them to be in any sense applicable to the complexity of political games, still less for them to be assumed as premises for any political decision.

The one factor which does, however, bind these disciplinary areas together from the epistemological point of view (leaving aside specific theoretical aspects which it would not be relevant to examine here) is their 'strong' conception of the scientific status of political research. According to this thesis, conjunction of these areas results in the strengthening of the language used in political research, the employment of mathematical models and, in some cases, the construction of axiomatized theorems which have a claim to empirical verification. In other words, what these disciplines attempt to do is to apply to the political and social sciences explanatory and predictive models derived from the natural sciences (physics especially) via the mediation of mathematical economics.

The most significant element which the economic theories of politics have introduced into the analysis of democratic systems is the assumption, which they draw from neo-classical economics, of the rationality of the social agent. This has assured them widespread academic success, not least in English- and German-speaking countries.[3] The equation between *homo politicus* and *homo oeconomicus* has appeared in three notable classical works: Antony Downs's *An Economic Theory of Democracy*, Mancur Olson's *The Logic of Collective Action* and James M. Buchanan and Gordon Tullock's *The Calculus of Consent*.[4] In all of these studies, political agents are taken to be 'rational self-interested beings' who are concerned to maximize their utility function. They are assumed to operate therefore by utilizing the minimum of resources (which are by definition scarce) necessary to obtain the maximum possible result in terms of profit, prestige and power. In particular they strive to acquire the maximum political information necessary for them to calculate what is the most advantageous investment in their political market. Their gathering of information, including their actual participation in the electoral processes, are taken to represent pure costs.

The theory does not end at this point, however. In the work both of authors such as Downs, Riker and Fiorina and of the Virginia School of Public Choice,[5] the assumption of individual rationality which was so central to the methodology of the neo-classical economists is extended to include collective political agents. Political parties, governments and administrative bureaucracies also respond, according to this view, to the postulation of 'egotistical interest'. Their 'rational behaviour' is directly modelled on the logic of the entrepreneur operating in conditions of free competition. Thus the maximization of political support they aim for in terms of electoral votes (or, in the case of the bureaucracies, physical and financial expansion) corresponds to the entrepreneur's maximization of profit. Political parties present their manifestos to the electoral body with the sole aim of maximizing their own 'political return', i.e. the profit, prestige and power of their own members.[6] Electoral support is not sought with the aim of realizing political programmes which have been consciously devised with a supposed 'public interest' in mind.

The least that can be said against these attempts is that they operate on the basis of assumptions which drastically reduce in number and import-ance the motives, expectations and aims with which political agents actu-ally operate within a liberal-democratic regime. But they fail also to grasp certain other fundamental aspects of political activity, and, as I shall attempt to show, they ignore the particular functional logic of modern political systems. Leaving aside the force of conservative ideology by which the work of the Virginia School in particular is dominated, the utilitarian realism of the economic theories of democracy goes wholly astray when, to put it most simply, it confuses the 'egotistical' reasons behind political action with the 'egotistical' reasons behind economic behaviour.

In practice the subsystem of politics in advanced industrial societies is nowadays clearly differentiated from other primary subsystems and their functional codes. Quite apart from the insuperable technical difficulties noted in the specialist literature, this is the main reason why any attempt at interpreting the behaviour of *homo politicus* by borrowing categories and explanatory models from the functional code of economics can only be seen as simplistic and outdated. This was a concept entirely grasped, even though he was in point of fact the first to propose the use of mercantile metaphors in political theory, by Joseph Schumpeter, whose example the 'mathematical democrats' wrongly, to my mind, persist in holding up for themselves.[7] Unlike Downs, Schumpeter was careful not to adopt the orthodox assumptions of neo-classical economics and, at the very least, rejected the hypothesis of the unlimited rationality and perfect information of the 'political consumer'. Nor did he make the unrealistic supposition that electors' choices were impervious to the manipulative effects of pol-itical propaganda.[8]

To my epistemological view, the reason behind the cognitive sterility of the economic theories of politics is their devotion to the principle of explanatory parsimony, which is very radically opposed to the require-ments of what I have called a 'reflexive epistemology'. Such an epistemology, as we have already seen, excludes the general possibility that complex social phenomena – which is what the phenomena of politics typically are – can be reduced to simple principles or to general laws. In fact the empirical propositions which these theories claim to enunciate in the case of phenomena such as electoral behaviour, competition between parties, the working of the systems of representation, the mechanics of public spending, etc., restrict themselves for the most part to the inference of simple truisms or the confirmation of propositions belonging to other, methodologically far less ambitious, theories.[9] Emblematic confirmation is to be found here for the rule which states that an inverse relation exists between the level of complexity in social phenomena and the hermeneutic capacity (not to mention the explanatory and, in a strict sense, predictive capacity) allowed by drastically simplified models of methodological individualism and rational calculation.

Downs, for example, openly acknowledges the triteness of his conclusions concerning the theses contained in Walter Lippmann's celebrated trilogy on the relations between public opinion and democratic government. But, in accordance with his highly personal view of the aims both of logic and of empirical research, he goes on to claim that he has 'proved logically' what in Lippmann and others was simply the product of empirical observation.[10] Downs's book is also an excellent quarry for conclusions which are either obvious or of minimal political importance. The following are some of the astounding 'empirical' inferences with which he ends his classic work: that diminution of the costs of voting leads to an increase in electoral participation; that in certain circumstances rational political agents will vote ('strategically') for a different party from the one they actually wish to see in power; that when a change in electoral laws alters the distribution of political preferences, new parties are likely to come into being;[11] and, lastly, the bizarre idea that democratic rulers, notwithstanding their 'egotistical' propensities, obey the inner logic of the political market and transfer the profit of the richer, less numerous social classes to the benefit of the larger and poorer classes.[12] All of these inferences, however, are expressed through propositions which could never in practice be subjected to empirical verification or falsification.

The same criticism can also be made, to my mind, of the 'voting paradox', an idea which has prompted a vast amount of academic writing, from Tullock to Riker, Ordeshook, Mueller and Brams.[13] The paradox arises, as is well known, from the supposed 'rationality' of democratic citizens' abstention or deliberate attempt to avoid informing themselves politically. Given the minute possibility that their individual votes will have any effect at all on the overall result of the election, voters have scarcely any practical interest either in taking the trouble to cast their votes or, if they do, in making sure in advance that they are sufficiently apprised of the possible gains and losses which hang on it. In practice, however, the obsession which this type of approach has with the wholly marginal element of electoral costs means that it offers no significant contribution, as I see it, to the understanding of the problem either of electoral abstentionism or, on the other hand, of why people do choose to vote in democratic elections.[14] In order to reach any understanding at all, the whole notion of economic rationality in political behaviour has to be discarded. In its place, rational theorists need to examine the political motives which lead one section of the citizen body to participate in the ritual of election, the other not to, some to express their vote after a careful attempt at gaining information, and others to do so with no relevant information at all. Others still, such as revolutionaries or terrorists operating within democratic regimes, opt for dangerous or violent forms of political intervention. These forms, despite Tullock's idea that such figures conform to the model of the entrepreneur in that they pursue some advantage they believe to be gainable for themselves from revolution or terrorist outrage, lie wholly outside any system of rational 'economic' expectations.

## The tragedy of political science

The development of an empirical theory of democracy has been the central aim of American and European political science for at least the last three decades. Following the canons of the behaviourist revolution[15] of the 1950s, political scientists have understood the term to mean the development of a purely 'procedural' and 'non-normative' model of the democratic method.[16] In direct opposition to the philosophical conceptions of democracy, which were seen as being incapable of distinguishing scientific ascertainment of the facts from their evaluation and normative projection, the empirical theory was to be concerned with the simple description of observable phenomena[17] and, at most, with the inductive generalization of them.[18] By avoiding any idealization or philosophical justification of democracy, political science would thus demonstrate 'what democracies really are in the real world'.[19] A rigorous demonstration of the necessary and sufficient conditions of democracy would lead to the explanation and prediction of democratic phenomena and behaviour patterns on the basis of an empirical ascertainment of their general causes.[20]

Today, at the beginning of the 1990s, not only has this ambitious programme receded, but it is now not even clear what meaning is actually conveyed by 'political science'. Its epistemological status is decidedly uncertain, given that the last decade has left it torn by internal divisions which threaten not only the theoretical identity of the discipline, but also the rationale itself behind its standing as an autonomous subject, once proudly arrayed against political philosophy and related areas such as political sociology.

In some respects blame is due to a kind of corporate inertia which, especially in continental Europe, imprisons political science in the fetters of a by now greatly outmoded loyalty to its original starting-point as a branch of neo-empiricism. In this respect the theoretical position of Giovanni Sartori, one of the most convinced proponents of the empirical theory of democracy, is quite typical. He is still putting forward the idea, without a trace of irony, that political science is the sole discipline capable of forming a 'verifiable political knowledge' because it alone respects 'the methodological canons of empirical science'. These 'canons' he still identifies without qualification as logical rigour in definitions, empirical verifiability of theories and the cumulativity of discoveries.[21] It is possibly for this reason that, in reissuing a book on democracy which had some success thirty years ago, Sartori feels able to claim that his own empirical theory of democracy contains an implicit refutation of all that has been thought or written in the meantime on political philosophy and democratic theory. Accordingly no mention at all of this new work appears in the book.[22]

Other writers, however, are to be found, especially in the English-speaking world, who are aware of how contrary this type of loyalty runs to the more important gains made by contemporary epistemology, and how such blindness threatens to close the discipline off from the wider framework of political thought, nowadays distinguished by a lively revival of political philosophy.[23] There is also an implicit realization that the reductive assumptions and thematic restrictions imposed on the discipline by neo-empiricism are in ever more marked contrast with the social condition of the developed countries, now characterized by increasing complexity and variability and by a growing unpredictability of political phenomena.

It is worth recalling at this point that political science set out forty years ago with two distinct objectives: first – its acknowledged aim – of attaining certain and objective knowledge of political facts, inasmuch as its own approach was based, unlike idealism and Marxist historicism, on the empirical analysis of social phenomena; and second – an unacknowledged aim, but one deeply rooted in the subjective motivations of its practitioners – of demonstrating the optimality of (American) democratic institutions, as forming the realization of liberty, pluralism and equality of opportunity.[24] Adherence to this programme implied, according to the belief of the founding fathers of the discipline,[25] the following assumptions, attached to each of which was a goal which had to be met in order for the results of the research to be considered scientific:

*Explanation and prediction on the basis of general laws*   In both the behaviour of political agents and the functioning of political systems there were regular recurrences to be observed. The basic job of the political scientist was to identify these recurrences and to express them in the form of general laws of a causal or statistical nature which would permit the explanation or prediction of political phenomena.

*Empirical verifiability and objectivity*   The validity of nomological generalizations in political science could be ascertained at root by means of empirical verification which took the behaviour of political agents as its reference point.

*Quantification and measurement*   The political scientist had to adopt the techniques of quantification and precise measurement which were already employed in the 'exact sciences' and which produced results also in such social sciences as economics and psychology.

*Systematicity and cumulativity*   The research carried out by political scientists would have to be performed 'systematically'; that is, there would be constant interaction between a logically structured and consistent language of theory and empirical research governed by a rigorous inductive method. The progressive accumulation of empirical data would permit the gradual development of theories and thus the formation would be achieved of a nucleus of general principles shared by the whole community of political scientists.

*Avaluativity*   The explanation and empirical prediction of political phenomena should be kept strictly separate from evaluations or prescriptions of an ethical or ideological kind. The political scientist was therefore under an intellectual obligation to abstain from any kind of ethical or ideological evaluation in the course of his studies.

It will be obvious that the elements of this methodological list, which was intended to express the core of a 'scientific' attitude, implied a series of very general epistemological options derived from the standard empiricist view. Central to such options was the decision to take political questions as belonging to the sphere of the empirical sciences on the grounds that no difference in complexity exists between the 'behaviour' of natural objects and the individual and collective behaviour of human beings.

As things stand, however, according to the judgement of certain influential political scientists themselves – such as Ed Lindblom, Gabriel A. Almond, David Easton[26] and most recently David M. Ricci, author of an especially critical study of the history of the discipline, *The Tragedy of Political Science*[27] – not a single one of these requirements has been met by political science. The discipline, as Ricci sees it, has been prevented from producing an effective form of 'political knowledge' by the self-imposed obligation to reach an unreachable scientific knowledge. This obligation drives the political scientist away from the very political issues, including in particular the crisis of democratic institutions, which are crucial to the society in which he lives. These issues cannot be properly handled by one whose profession commits him to political neutrality. Political science runs the risk therefore of a tragic self-negation by virtue of being a 'politically disinterested' science.[28]

Gabriel Almond, for his part, has ironically suggested that the attempt by political scientists to reach full scientific status has led them to create a sort of 'cargo cult', fashioning cardboard imitations of the tools and products of the hard sciences in the hope that their incantations will make them real. In place of such 'flirtation with mistaken metaphors'[29] he advises the use of 'weak' heuristic theories which make no claim to legitimacy on the basis of their explanatory and predictive power, but instead confine themselves to the interpretation and understanding of politics as a process of adaptation and attainment of goals within bounded decisional frameworks.[30]

David Easton is still more radical. In his thorough review of the history of political science in the United States, he has linked the outcome of the discipline (including its assertion of the ideological neutrality of the political scientist) to its adherence to the myth of the 'end of ideologies', a myth which, in his view, has served in practice to conceal the domination of the democratic-conservative ideology. He attributes the failure of behaviouristic political science to such factors as an underestimation of the very real transformations which have occurred in American society, an inability to make social prediction, scant regard for the historical dimension, reliance on a dogmatic conception of the 'scientific method' drawn from neo-positivism and a touching faith in the evaluative neutrality of science. In Easton's view, American political science, following the crisis of behaviourism, now lacks any common aim or standpoint, and is devoid of cognitive tautness and imagination, having reached a particularly crucial point of uncertainty over its own theoretical identity.[31]

These different criticisms from within the discipline share a common theme which it is difficult not to find persuasive. The fact is that political science has entirely failed to produce any law of a causal or statistical nature capable of leading to explanations, still less to general political predictions, either inside or outside the democratic political systems. Nor has it provided any logical or mathematical model capable of being applied to the political system. No nucleus of political theorems has emerged, nor any unanimously agreed general principles which can provide the basis for an empirical theory of democracy. Even the more modest attempt to produce a unified language of political science – a particular aim of Giovanni Sartori – has so far borne little fruit, to judge from Sartori's own continued complaints of the Babel-like confusion which reigns within the discipline quite apart from within the minds of ordinary people.[32]

The problem remains that the generalizations of political science and of any possible empirical theory of democracy will never be susceptible to empirical verification or falsification. In politics, more than anywhere, there exists no 'observation language' that can be separated from the language of theories. In addition, the theories themselves are always indissolubly linked with ideologies, general philosophies and historically and socially conditioned *Weltanschauungen*. All of this explains why political scientists find it impossible not only to unify their language, but also to honour the obligation to avoid all judgements of value, a poisoned chalice, if ever there was one, from which they still find themselves forced to drink.

The reason for all these difficulties can be quite simply expressed: not a single one of the requirements of political science can be met in the face of actual political phenomena and the need to develop something other than purely trivial political theories. As soon as one passes from elementary levels of classification of data to the development of political theories sufficiently complex to be applied to the complexity of the environment, it becomes inevitable that political scientists will be forced to violate and contradict their own methodological requirements.

Once such crucial questions are raised as what mechanisms lie behind 'invisible power'[33] how political obligation can be justified in the context of a plurality of values and moral beliefs, how the crisis of the representative function of political parties is to be resolved, how post-industrial societies can be governed, what the political effects of a long period of exposure to the mass media are, then it becomes clear that these are problems so complex that they cannot be posed, even in linguistic terms, without some violation of the canons of neo-empiricism.

Nor, as I see it, is it any accident that political science has been so slow in addressing such problems as these, given the commitment it has to a kind of ever-present implicit defence of Western political institutions as they are. It seems unavoidable that a science which has sacrificed any discussion of the values of politics on the altar of methodological rigour and has become involved exclusively with the facts should have abandoned all claim to be able to state, let alone advance or solve, the problems of politics, inasmuch as these problems can hardly not involve some decision on the aims, limits or meaning of politics.[34] It is equally inevitable that this attitude should lead political scientists to an uncritical acceptance of such general categories of the Western political 'encyclopedia' as, above all, democracy, public opinion, consensus and pluralism, which they then take as unproblematical points of departure for their 'neutral' research into the 'real' functioning of democratic institutions.

The conclusion may safely be drawn, therefore, that the various attempts to introduce rigorous scientific models into the study of political phenomena have failed to produce any worthwhile results. The symbolic complexity of political phenomena, whose agents are themselves producers and interpreters of symbolic systems, ensures that simple political explanations of a linear, causal or statistical type can attain no level of real significance. In order to attach political significance to instances of human behaviour, and so to understand and interpret them, it is above all necessary to take account of the agents' political motivations; that is, of their symbolic references and ideologies, and also of the declared, latent or pretended aims of their actions or political choices.[35]

As Otto Neurath first pointed out in the context of conventionalism, complexity of individual motivation is an element which, in sociology or the study of politics, can only lead to 'scientific suicide' for the claim to operate with the observation methods and quantitative measurement of natural science. The high level of evolutive indeterminacy in human groups and the diversity of their linguistic, cultural and organizational forms leads to surprising and virtually unpredictable forms of political change. Even non-trivial political behaviour on the part of individual agents within any group emerges as statistically improbable as a result of the factors of dispersion and instability with which individual choices are shot through.[36]

The more advanced a society is, the more it will manifest these phenomena, especially if my opening hypothesis is accepted: that advanced societies are typified by characteristics such as the deepening of the semantic discontinuity between social experiences, the increase of interdependence between different functions and the growing contingency and symbolic abstractness of the environment.

## A Kantian version of Menenius Agrippa's apologue

A reflexive epistemology, while it excludes the possibility of a science of politics (and democracy), and rejects any form of explanatory parsimony, does at the same time reassert the need for truly theoretical or philosophical political research. Given the complexity of political phenomena, and given that their complexity tends to increase along with social differentiation, the value of an analysis which claims to restrict itself to 'empirically observable' phenomena can only decline. Growing differentiation and specialization of political life mean that attempts to borrow explanatory models from other subsystems can only become less plausible. Instead the need is for even greater focus to be applied to the newer and more specific functions which the political subsystem is continuously acquiring in complex societies. In itself, this will necessitate a comprehensive theoretical investigation into the goals, values and meaning of politics. And then, at a further level of reflexivity, this investigation will need to be extended to cover its own goals, values and meaning. In particular, it will need to question the significance and heuristic value of certain of its own fundamental categories, such as the notions of politics, political obligation and democracy.[37]

For these reasons, the reawakening of interest in political philosophy in the West is greatly to be welcomed.[38] All the more so because this revival coincides with the crises in neo-empiricism and orthodox Marxism, two systems which, for all their differences, had in common a basic denial of the legitimacy of any philosophy of politics. For neo-empiricism, any approach to political and social problems which was not pure factual description, free from any philosophical or ideological presuppositions, was irrelevant. Orthodox Marxist theory envisaged the withering away of philosophy along with the State, and consequently allowed of no political philosophy which did not coincide with the theoretical and practical activity required by the revolutionary process. It was a process which, after the destruction of the economic, political and ideological power of the bourgeoisie, was to lead to the establishment of a communist society 'without law and without the State'.[39]

With the decline of these two dogmatic positions, new areas for political philosophy open up. But, less fortunately, this has also coincided with a return, not solely in the English-speaking world, to the grand fashion of the ethico-political tradition which Niklas Luhmann has ironically termed 'vetero-European'. Within German culture the *Rehabilitierung der praktischen Philosophie* has attempted in recent years to reinstate the philosophical tradition of Aristotle in opposition to ethical relativism, formalism and scientism, which are decried as typically modern manifestations.[40] There has also been the nostalgic appeal to the republican tradition of Aristotelian civic virtues which is found in otherwise important works by John Pocock, Alasdair MacIntyre and the 'communitarians'.[41] Above all, there has been the reassertion of liberal-democratic thought along natural-law and contractualist lines which has appeared in the work of such writers as, amongst many others, Ronald Dworkin, Robert Nozick,

Bruce Ackerman and, most especially, John Rawls. Later in this section I shall deal directly with Rawls's theses as providing an exemplary expression of contemporary political moralism.[42]

The abandonment of positivist and Marxist prejudices can only, to my mind, be a step in the right direction. But the danger lies in the possibility of their being replaced by a rehabilitation of the ethical approach to politics, which both neo-empiricism and Marxism set out to combat. As I have already indicated, a reflexive epistemology can only view the thesis of ethical cognitivism, on which the tradition of political moralism in Europe has been based, as an outright 'deontological fallacy'. The various doctrines of the 'knowability' of moral precepts in fact base their prescriptive force on a postulated ontology. For the existence of a natural order is the objective basis on which the prescriptive claim of universal morals rests. Whether the postulated ontology is claimed to be demonstrable, as is the case in Aristotelianism and Thomism, or whether, as for Kant, the ontology is supposed to rest on intuition, universal moral systems still demand a gnostic position, over and beyond a profound metaphysical optimism. Moral values are knowable, and so have force, only in so far as the world objectively 'exists' and its order is rigorously arguable. A system of deontological ethics cannot admit to being based on the contingency of subjective preferences, particular traditions or mystical beliefs.

Quite differently, a reflexive epistemology aims to refute the contradistinction between a cognitive dimension, which has regard for the 'facts', and an ethico-evaluative dimension, which includes both subjective preferences and moral prescriptions. In one respect, as we have seen, it in fact argues that the language of theory, even at the highest scientific levels, cannot avoid including elements of evaluation. And in another, it proposes a clear-cut distinction between the axiological dimension of evaluations and the deontological dimension of prescriptions. The first are made up of judgements which involve no claim to prescriptive generalization. The preferences they express are purely subjective, know their own nature and intend to stay as they are, even if, quite clearly, the question of the indirectly prescriptive worth which evaluations can assume within certain power frameworks remains open, as has been made clear by Michel Foucault.[43] Prescriptions, on the other hand, assert the imperative, and often universal, character of a determined value, or system of values, and so advance a 'categorical' expectation of generalized compliance.[44]

It is clear, therefore, that in this context the polarity 'facts/values' of positivist origin should give place to the distinction between the language of theory (or of science) and the language of prescription. The first necessarily includes judgements of value, but excludes prescriptions. The second not only expresses evaluations, but also asserts the prescriptive force of a determined value or system of values, from which can be drawn the claim to universality, rationality and so obligatoriness on all. It should also appear equally clear that recognition of the unavoidably evaluative nature of the language of theory rules out both the objectivity of scientific knowledge and the possibility of basing a system of prescriptive ethics on them. Once it is recognized that knowledge, even in its more rigorous forms, is never *wertfrei*, then it follows that to take it as the basis of a moral deontology means arbitrarily raising to the status of a general rule of behaviour what is in fact the result of subjective evaluations, conventions and methodological decisions: *stat pro ratione voluntas*. It is a case in fact of a 'deontological fallacy' which attributes prescriptive value to particular evaluations and decisions rather than of a 'naturalist fallacy' along the lines of Hume's classic argument, which forbids the logical step from 'being' to 'ought to be'.[45]

Thus ethical doctrines cannot lay claim to any ontological foundation or specific rationality: they are systems of beliefs, established in society to varying degrees, which make up a part of the totality of habits, practical rules and symbolic codes on which groups and individuals choose to base their social life. They form an integral part of the 'folklore' transmitted from one generation to the next by cultural traditions. Their general function, just like that of any other social structure, is to reduce environmental complexity by preselecting decisional options and thus allowing individuals to make speedier and more coherent choices. Their specific function is to provide standardized reasons for preferring certain modes of behaviour and excluding others on the basis of a particular code which defines every possible human action as morally permitted, or illicit, or required by duty.

An ethical system has no other claim to be followed apart from the decision taken by individual agents, in varying degrees of freedom and consciousness, to make their behaviour conform to certain general rules. Put in slightly different terms, ethical – as well as legal and political – systems lack any basic rule which makes them intrinsically obligatory. This is true not only of morals derived from mythical or religious cosmologies, but also, and perhaps with even greater force, of modern systems of formalistic ethics, justified on the basis of an intuition of moral conscience. Otto Neurath made the observation that ethics arose in antiquity, along with penal law, as a theory of sin, and thus as a doctrine of divine prohibitions. A categorical imperative was therefore for him nothing other than a theological residue – divine law divorced from its agent and constructed as a law in itself, a logically arbitrary construct, as if one were to speak of 'a neighbour in himself, without neighbours'.[46]

So too Kantian ethics, in just the same way as any other universal morality, are ethics without foundation: they can invoke no 'reason', either theoretical or practical, why they should be objeyed. Even the staunchest modern defender of the imperative character of morality is powerless to do any more, in justifying its authority, than appeal to the 'intuitive' nature of categorical prescriptions. In Kant the moral quality of the human being is taken as a postulate of practical reason, on the same level as the existence of God and the immortality of the soul. It is a postulate which Kant himself recognized as not being susceptible to argument on the level of 'pure reason', but one which makes appeal rather to the 'primacy' of practical reason. Refusing the inner evidence of the categorical imperative is therefore not allowed to a rational being.

It is surprising, in view of the powerful proof offered by modern anthropology of the historical relativity of ethical and religious beliefs, that the founder of the most notable ethico-political system of our time, John Rawls,[47] has had nothing to add to – let alone raise in objection against – this type of dogmatic justification of morality. As it is, the entire edifice of Rawls's neo-contractualism rests, precisely as in Kant, on the inbuilt intuition that 'human beings are moral by nature' or on the 'natural sense of justice' existing in each and every one of us.[48] Far from attempting to supersede the intuitional basis of Kantian ethics, Rawls is dominated by precisely the opposite concern: to show the exact coincidence of his own position with that of Kant.[49] Convinced that the ethics of Kant are superior to the ethics of Bentham, he concludes that contractualism is superior to utilitarianism, and makes not the slightest attempt to offer new answers to the realistic and historicist criticisms of contractualism which have been made in the course of at least two centuries by, for instance, Hume, Hegel, Marx, Weber or Schumpeter.

The upshot of all this is that there is nothing to distinguish Rawls's neo-contractualism from classical contractualism. Criticisms of the latter therefore still hold force against the former. The only element, if any, of novelty in Rawls concerns his ultimate basis in the formal and procedural nature of justification. In place of the argumentative fiction of a natural state and of an original contract, he puts the argumentative fiction of the 'original position' and the 'veil of ignorance', which he himself says must be understood as 'a procedural interpretation of Kant's conception of autonomy and the categorical imperative'.[50] This veil of ignorance, as is now well known, requires the original contractors to agree on the rules which will govern their life plans without their knowing, or being able rationally to predict, what course their life will take. The device clearly corresponds to the Kantian requirement to neutralize empirical individuals to the extent of making them anaemic noumenic hypostases, i.e. free and equal agents, capable of making decisions impersonally and *sub specie aeternitatis.* It is difficult, however, to envisage a scheme of 'rational' decision which could be further removed from the actual 'rationality' of political decisions taken in modern societies. For within this context, rational decision-making means the attempt to reduce the risks of disappointment of our own expectations, i.e. the attempt to lessen, on the basis of the most accurate information possible, the conditions of uncertainty present in our decisions.

The rhetorical device of the original position and the veil of ignorance means in effect that moral decision-making in politics is possible only on condition that individuals ignore their personal identity and, along with it, their own situation of inequality and dependence. It is this that makes possible the assumption of the universal negotiability of social conflicts, because even the 'the least-favoured elements' – as in the apologue of Menenius Agrippa[51] – give legitimacy to the political institutions, feeling themselves to be limbs of the same body and disposing themselves spiritually for social co-operation within a fair and democratic regime.[52]

In reality, the members of social groups – or at least the majority of them – justify their own political structures, but they do this by starting from the historical and sociological conditions of the distribution of resources, advantages and status within their own group. This justification, especially in differentiated societies, has little in common with the categories of universal ethics: it is a particularistic, contingent and highly variable justification. Rather than agreeing once and for all on general and immutable ethical principles – and the distributive criteria connected with them[53] – organized groups and individuals are constantly involved in a nexus of mutually interactive circuits which give expression to the potential for conflict and need for security felt by each group, and which give realization to the ever-precarious equilibrium between the different systems of expectations which different social agents carry within them.

Far from applying criteria of distributive justice, the allocation of resources by modern political systems – especially in democratic regimes and Welfare State societies – follows the logic of 'opportunistic attribution'. The expectations of the groups which coalesce and represent primary interests of the social body are satisfied or discouraged as part of the working of political balances which take account of the organizational capacities, potential for conflict and functional significance of the different social agents and take no account at all, on the other hand, of their being more or less favoured by the natural or social 'lottery'.[54] Even within the most democratic regimes, social conflict is regulated through the authoritarian imposition of distributive criteria which have little to do with any ethical foundation of laws and political duties. Even trade-union demands, and the 'intuitive' criteria of social justice which in some sense they express, tend to model themselves on this segmented and heterogeneous social phenomenology rather than setting out to resist it in the name of a universal moral code.

Nor are objections from the standpoint of social complexity less relevant. Rawls's *A Theory of Justice* is a confident endorsement of representative institutions at just the time when one of the most serious problems emerging in advanced industrial societies is the crisis of representation. It is a justification of the well-ordered, co-operative society, informed by clear, simple, universal and universally shared principles,[55] at a time when the central problem in post-industrial societies is in fact the decline in standards of rationality in political action, and the contingency and plurality of values and social affiliations. It is a work of social theory which starts from the epistemological premiss of methodological individualism at the very time when the sociology of complex societies is giving its greatest attention to the homologizing mechanisms of the large organizational structures which tend to shape individuals' motives and plans.

For a prescriptive scheme of ethics to be applied, an overall transparency would be needed of political, economic and military institutions, in addition both to exhaustive information being available about the presuppositions behind political decisions and to the predictability of their effects. It would mean that the circuitry of political communication would have to promote the establishment of a competent, active and substantially homogeneous public opinion, capable of directing itself discursively in the choice of common values.[56] Such conditions, however, can exist only in an idealized or moralistically abstract vision of the functioning of democratic institutions. The attention which Rawls, like all moralists, gives almost exclusively to the problem of distribution presupposes furthermore that the essential goods – which he calls 'social primary goods' – should be those which are 'distributable'. In complex societies, however, it seems, on the contrary, that those goods become primary which are the object of 'diffused interests'. Increasingly important are elements such as the environment, energy, peace, demographic balance, information, scientific knowledge, protection against technological dangers, all of them goods for which no system of apportionment or measurement can easily be envisaged.[57]

Passing over other details that need not be questioned here,[58] it may be said that Rawls's assessment of the problems boils down to the meta-question of the 'political function' of a neo-contractualistic theory of justice. In this respect, the Marxist conception of ideology or Pareto's notion of *derivazioni*, despite their abstractness, seem to me to retain some relevance.[59] If the moralistic hypothesis on which neo-contractualism is based is wholly superfluous from the explanatory or interpretative standpoint – it is not moral consensus which holds men together in a political community but, if anything, as Hume argued, fear, the need for security and necessity[60] – then the neo-contractualist doctrine is not for this reason politically unimportant. By providing, albeit in highly generic terms, a list in two columns of reasons and conditions under which the exercise of democratic power should be considered rationally justified and obligatory – from the standpoint of the prince and from the standpoint of the people – it can claim to introduce democratic political obligation as a moral obligation into the consciousness of the citizens.

Like any other mythological, religious or moral legitimation of a given political order, the neo-contractualistic doctrine should be considered an element internal to the political system: it is an attempt, of however dubious efficacy, to achieve the symbolic absorption of disappointment and the neutralization of dissent through an emotional reinforcement of the democratic political code.[61] In Rawls's case the appeasing middle ground of his assumptions sets out to justify in moral terms everything that is politically 'average' or 'mixed' – e.g. the balance between freedom and equality, industrial peace, the mixed economy, reconciliation of social conflict. In sum: a Kantian version of the apologue of Menenius Agrippa.

## Politics as selective regulation of social risks

The argument I shall advance in this final section of the chapter is that an important contribution towards a realistic conception of politics can be provided by a theory of social complexity inspired by system research. The theory can provide an alternative both to the moralistic conceptions of politics and to the false realism of the economic or empirical theories. In the next chapter I shall attempt to show how, starting from this conception, a realistic view can be developed of the problem of democracy.

The core of political realism is most usually held to reside in Thrasymachus' argument in Plato's *Republic*. Even the thought of Machiavelli and the elitists is taken to be reducible in essence to its central message: that politics is ruled not by principles of justice, but by the interest of the strongest. Indeed, justice itself is in any given case identical with the advantage of whoever holds power in the state, be it a 'prince' or an oligarchy. Thus politics would seem to be reducible to questions of pure force, threat, betrayal or deception.

But when put in this way, the argument of Thrasymachus expresses only partially, and in a reductive fashion, what seems to me to be the true theoretical core of political realism, which is not the simplistic idea of a zero-sum opposition of the interests of rulers and ruled. Instead, its true character – which makes it still relevant to modern societies – should be seen in the conflict between the universalist nature of the idea of justice and the particularism of the interests at play in the political arena. Politics, as classical realism has traditionally maintained, from the Epicurean school to Machiavelli, Guicciardini and the reason of state theorists, is the domain of 'prudence' and not of justice. Justice imposes the duty to respect all citizens and see to the good of all, ensuring that all receive what is owed to them according to the principle of the natural equality of man. Prudence, on the contrary, recommends to political individuals a clever and resourceful use of power as a means of preserving, and  quite possibly increasing, their own interests, and thus the power, possessions and prestige of their own group or of their own political corner.[62]

In this conception we see the root of the classical distinction between the pessimistic view of human nature, which conceives politics as unalterably incompatible with ethics, and the optimistic view, which argues for the universalist nature of politics and the compatibility of politics with values, and sees the function of politics as being the harmonization of interests towards the common good. It is this optimistic position which lies behind Aristotelianism, Thomism, the natural-law basis of Protestantism and the so-called 'social doctrine' of the Roman Catholic Church – a tradition which brands Machiavelli's political realism as treacherous and nihilistic and his *Prince* as the 'work of the devil'.[63]

The 'vetero-European' tradition, whether in Plato or Cicero, the eighteenth-century Protestant preachers or the Jesuits, Frederick II of Prussia or the Roman pontiffs, has an implicit tendency to view the arguments of political realism as an expression of irrationality or emotionalism, an individualistic denial of the moral unity of the human race or, simply, as the exaltation of a 'power wish' inimical to social solidarity and democratic values. More wisely – e.g. in Apel and Rawls – the arguments of realism are passed over as unimportant for the ethico-political debate. But even Habermas, following Hannah Arendt, argues for an implicit ethical dimension in political communication: i.e. that exponents of political arguments place themselves automatically in the transcendental dimension of practical reason.[64] It would seem to follow therefore that the theses of political realism, insofar as they deny the rational and moral dimension of political communication, relegate themselves to the class of self-defeating arguments. Only political silence – the denial of politics through apathy or terrorism – would be consistent with a repudiation of the transcendental dimension of ethics.

For my own part, I do not believe that the arguments of political realism are self-defeating. They can, on the contrary, prove helpful in grasping the specific logic of political activity and in distinguishing it from the logic of other functional codes, especially the moral one. In this, as I see it, lies their especial relevance for societies enmeshed in processes of increasing differentiation and social complexity. But it is none the less necessary to free the realistic position from its traditional pessimistic view of man. It is essentially a metaphysical option which derives from Augustine and which is clearly present also in Machiavelli. For Machiavelli, at least in the *Prince*,[65] politics is the domain in which man's potential for evil, cunning, duplicity, aggressiveness and lust for power reveals itself most dramatically. The Prince must be ever mindful that men are 'ungrateful, fickle, feigners and dissemblers, avoiders of danger, eager for gain'.[66] In contrast to the optimistic outlook of classical moralists and humanists, such as Seneca and Giovanni Pontano, 'effective' politics was taken to show that egoism is an ineradicable component of the human spirit. The autonomy of politics was therefore the autonomy of worldly aims as contrasted with the spiritual aims of Christian ethics and humanistic culture.

This pessimism constitutes, to my mind, one of the limitations of classical realism – the residual universalist conception of ethics which continues to judge politics in moral terms, while at the same time realizing its autonomy or arguing for it. It reveals, amongst other things, the crudeness of the conservative realism preached by the Virginia School of Public Choice, given especially the recent reformulation by Gordon Tullock of the 'self-interest axiom' in terms of Tullock's Law which states that 'individuals are altruistic 5% of the time.'[67]

Political realism does not, I think, require a pessimistic view of man in order to be philosophically justified. I reject the view that there are decisive arguments, deducible from some hypothetical 'human nature' or extract-able from historical experience, which can either legitimate the adoption of a pessimistic view, with Augustine, or engender, on the other hand, an optimistic view, such as that of Rousseau or Kant. History is full of examples of generosity and self-sacrifice taken to the limits of heroism, just as it is full, as our own century has amply demonstrated, of examples of cruelty of every sort. There is no need even to make a profession of moral nihilism, because there is no reason to maintain that repudiation of universalist ethics necessitates the denial of all forms of moral experience. Indeed, according to the view of Epicurus in antiquity, it is precisely when one moves beyond the dimension of the political ethos that the moral experience of friendship and deep communion does become possible.

Within modern societies, to give my own view, political realism finds its foundation in the very process of functional differentiation and the attend-ant increase in complexity. In complex societies, morals and politics receive expression within clearly differentiated spheres of experience and submit to 'codes' which cannot be superimposed one upon another without risk to their functioning and general meaning. In such societies there exists, in other words, a growing semantic discontinuity between the domain of morality and the domain of politics.

The only view of humanity this realistic foundation of politics requires is the thesis of the historical, and not 'natural' or 'ontological', nature of the human faculties, along with the recognition of the high 'plasticity' of human beings. By plasticity I have in mind, in common with Arnold Gehlen, the variety and indeterminacy of the impulses, and hence behavioural attitudes, of *homo sapiens*, our lack of instinctual specialization and our 'world-openness'.[68] This make-up enables us to reduce the complexity of the environment through very free symbolic and manipulative activities, which are not bound deterministically to refer to any immediate situation, and hence are capable of extending themselves to cover a very wide range of possibilities, from attitudes of an adaptive, ritual, risk-free nature, oriented towards stabilization, to ones of a playful and explorative nature, oriented towards risk and innovation. Here, as we shall see, may lie the biological origin of the conflict between the search for security and the need for freedom which manifests itself in the political life of *homo sapiens*. Our lack of instinctual specialization may be the ultimate reason both for our especial sense of fear and for our especial courage in free and risk-filled exploration.

In this context, my 'realistic' thesis, suggested by the systemic approach, is that the criteria of political decision-making are essentially incompatible with the criteria of a system of public ethics. More precisely, it can be stated thus: political decision-making is typified by an ineradicable lack of impartiality and universality, and one of the most prominent aspects of political power is precisely its lack of moral foundation. This does not mean to exclude its 'functionality' or to argue that it can or should be replaced by functional equivalents which are in some sense preferable, as being more moral – as has been the hope of a large number of spiritualistic philosophies, and as the Marxist theory of the withering away of the state implicitly suggested.

What, then, are the functions of political power in differentiated and complex societies? What do people expect from the political system? On what criteria are our political decisions based? What, in other terms, is the specific functionality of the political code?

My attempt to provide an answer to these questions is that in modern societies the specific function of the political system is that of *regulating selectively the distribution of social risks, and so of reducing fear, through the competitive allocation of 'security values'*. Seen thus, the two most specific criteria of the political code are the principle of internal/external differentiation and the asymmetric relation of power/subordination.

In general terms, this means that political action essentially includes functions and behaviour patterns of an adaptive type which tend towards the collective alleviation of insecurity and which are based on a logic of the avoidance of risk. Central to this scheme is the question of the relations between politics and fear – a classic topic from Thomas Hobbes to Guglielmo Ferrero[69] and Franz Neumann[70] – and especially important are some recent contributions in anthropology and human ethology made by, e.g., Konrad Lorenz,[71] Irenäus Eibl-Eibesfeldt,[72] and, above all, Arnold Gehlen.

For Gehlen the reason for fear being one of man's basic impulses is our 'organic primitivism'. Our lack of instinctual specialization makes us freer than any other biological being, but also peculiarly ill adapted to survival, and thus places us in a condition of perpetual insecurity. It is precisely this fragility of life, due to our excessive exposure to the environment, which seems to have stimulated in *homo sapiens* the singular ability to reduce environmental complexity not through processes of adaptive specialization or by trusting ourselves exclusively to habitual repetitions of collective behaviour, but through the production of selective structures of a symbolic nature. This is the principle which Gehlen has termed 'relief' (*Entlastung*).[73]

Fear, in this view of humanity, is the reaction of the individual (or social group) when faced with the uncontrollable variety of possibilities present in a complex environment.[74] Individuals strive to inject elements of order and stability into the chaotic flux of environmental phenomena, but they notice that within the range of possibilities there also exists the possibility of their own dissolution. Their stability is not guaranteed by any law or general tendency: on the contrary, it is threatened by the tendency of the environment towards maximum entropy. They therefore interpret their own sense of selective stress as 'contingency' and 'risk': that is, as unpredictability, disorder and the possibility of failure.[75] They respond to the situation of risk by bringing into play 'homoeostatic' mechanisms which hold them in balance with the environment and 'reassure' them by removing or making the sources of their fear less visible.

In this context, then, the political system, just like language and thought itself in other ways,[76] can be interpreted as a homoeostatic mechanism for the lessening of fear. The political system works as a prescriptive structure of preselection of possibilities. It selects from the totality of possible events a much more restricted range of alternatives, reinforcing their probability and making them the object of social expectation. On the basis of decisions binding on all (in particular cases through direct action or coercive measures) the structure of political power forbids, imposes, promotes or authorizes certain social behaviour, penalizing contrary behaviour with consequences unwelcome to the individuals responsible for it.

In this way, certain events become socially more probable, while others, considered less probable, are thrown into more distant relief or are wholly removed from consideration. The political system thus achieves two ends. First, it produces 'trust' by allowing social agents to operate on the basis of stable expectations of behaviour conforming to collective rules.[77] This, amongst other things, achieves a notable saving of time, energy and trouble which would otherwise have to be spent on the continuous search for reassurance and the securing of guarantees of a concrete rather than a predominantly symbolic nature. Second, the political system succeeds in excluding from collective expectations that part of the risks and frustrations of social life which could not fall on its members without serious social upset (such as panic, violence, collapse of confidence, lawlessness, etc.), while it leaves to the 'liberty' of individuals the job of neutralizing instance by instance those risks and disappointments which are fundamentally less important.[78] Modern political systems, for example, tend to reduce significantly the chances citizens have (or perhaps rather, think they have) of being murdered, while they leave it to individuals to absorb the disappointments arising from the break-up of friendships, love, loss of job, etc.

In this light, the 'selective regulation of risks' (i.e. the definition of which risks should be politically covered and absorbed by the power structure) is the fundamental variable of a political system. In quantitative terms, this variable may be depicted as a typological continuum which goes from the 'minimal' State to the interventionist, paternalistic or totalitarian State.[79] From a more complex qualitative point of view of the same variable, a state can be described as clerical or lay, as liberal or 'social' (or socialist), as constitutional or despotic. So it is clear that a greater demand for protection, that is, for reduction in political complexity, corresponds to a wider collective perception of the risks and potential for conflict present in the environment, and vice versa. It is also equally clear that different social groups, possessed of different interests and therefore threatened by different dangers, will devote themselves in political terms to gaining, in competition with other groups, different configurations of the quantitative and qualitative distribution of the 'security values'. This will, correlatively, bring about the establishment of different configurations not only of socially accepted risks, but also of politically allowed 'liberties'. For widespread political protection will normally imply not only a reduction of risks, but also a restriction of liberties, and vice versa. Also, as matter of principle, groups which have wider resources at their disposal will tend to be interested in higher levels of political protection for those resources, while less privileged groups will call for the protective intervention of the political system to guarantee not the ownership of, but the possibility of access to, those resources and will feel less exposed than the other groups to the danger of social change. The more acute the collective perception of the scarcity of the commodity 'security', the more conflictual will be the competition between the groups, because higher levels of 'social fear' will tend to lead to higher levels of aggressiveness.[80]

The most basic political mechanism which brings about security, through a reduction of the complexity of the environment, is the definition of an internal/external boundary. Once a 'political space' is marked off, factors of risk are projected beyond the boundaries of a group, while factors of security are organized within it. In this way, the social group encompasses individuals and behaviour patterns which are compatible with its own stability, and encourages, through what Schattschneider has called the 'mobilization of bias'[81] the collective definition of 'extraneous' individuals and 'deviant' behaviour patterns which it considers inimical to its own survival.

In order to achieve its own stabilization, the political group not only needs to equip itself with decision structures aimed at the compulsory enforcement of both positive and negative selection of risks, but it must also set in order the wider range of pre-selective filters which Bachrach and Baratz have, perhaps not entirely properly, called 'nondecisions'.[82] In practice it is a matter of selective mechanisms which precede the ritualized process of political decision and form a kind of invisible and uncontrollable 'face' of power – a structure of 'bias' which predetermines the distribution of social risks and security through the tacit definition of what can be subjected to political decision. Thus the political code asserts its criterion for exclusion/inclusion less in the choice between alternatives prepared for the making of a political decision than at the prior stage of allowing the decision itself, exerting at that time its informal and invisible influence on the definition of the political agenda and of its priorities. In this way, the selective distribution of risks acts not so much on interests and behaviour patterns as on the cognitive processes of the formation of wishes and political preferences.[83] Central, therefore, and to an ever increasing extent, are the means of mass communication, both in respect of political communication in a strict sense and, more particularly, as we shall see, in respect of the political long-term effects of exposure to the media.

All complex political formations, whether they be international organizations, political parties, social movements or clandestine societies, conform without exception to this dialectic of 'inclusion-exclusion'. Without fail a particularistic logic operates, making a group the more cohesive – and thus more aggressive towards the outside and repressive towards the inside – the more it perceives the risks present in the environment. By a functional paradox, these very demands of self-identification will cause a political group to 'produce' its own enemies, internal or external.[84] The demand for security, just like the offer of protection, always contains a designation of agents or groups *against* whom the political service of the 'reduction of fear' is requested or offered. Of necessity, therefore, it cannot avoid having an excluding and discriminating value. This logic seems bound to grow ever stronger in societies of advanced technological development, given the tendency that exists in them for the level of environmental dangers, and consequent social alarm, to increase.

Political particularism is clearly incompatible with universal ethical principles such as the duty to tell no lies or not to commit murder, still less with the teleological respect for the dignity of each person. Secrecy, for example, and therefore pretence and falsehood, are normal functional practices in relations between the inside and outside of political groups. Power does not exist without *arcana*, because transparency and complete openness renders it vulnerable to other, antagonistic, powers. There are no states that are able to dispense with the apparatus of police and secret service, and no police or secret service that can do without spies and infiltrators into the world of crime, i.e. without professionals in the use of falsehood, deception and, not infrequently, violence. Nor are there any states that do not fail to define not only their territorial limits towards the outside, but also their internal frontiers in the shape of custodial exclusion from the legitimized political space. This exclusion may even extend to the death penalty.

The relation between power and subordination – the second functional criterion of the political code – is closely tied to the process whereby the political system is concentrated in specific institutions of authority, in order to fulfil its regulatory function. This institutional concentration of power, together with the distinction of roles and functions between governors and governed, appears to typify all social groups capable of stabilizing and reproducing themselves, as research in anthropology has indicated.[85] The concentration is particularly marked in Western societies which have attained a high degree of industrial and technological development, where the functions of political power are strongly differentiated (which does not mean centralized or hierarchical). From this point of view, both the communist theory of the withering away of the state and classical and contemporary ideas (such as those of Max Stirner and Robert Nozick) of individualistic anarchy lose much credibility.[86] Though they start from different motives, both types of theory are equally flawed by an idealized project for the simplification of social relations for which, in differentiated societies, all indications appear to be lacking. It would amount to the surmounting of the asymmetrical and heteronomous nature of the power relationship.

The 'concentrated' political system has the ability to produce binding decisions, backed up in the last resort by the use of force. It places itself at the centre of a network for allocating factors of social security made up of asymmetrical relations between individuals who hold power and individuals who are subordinate to that power. Holders of power are able – in proportion to the extent to which they hold it – both to guarantee their own security and to regulate the expectations of security of subordinate individuals, as a result of their ability in any given case to determine the distribution of risks and social guarantees.

*Ceteris paribus*, it is possible to say that more power means less social insecurity, and that more subordination means less security. But the existence and relative efficiency of institutions of authority represent for all members of any given group a symbolic factor of the reduction of fear. For the political system functions as a 'social structure', i.e. as a collective mechanism for the reduction of complexity and the production of security and trust. As Thomas Hobbes first saw, the unlimited complexity and unpredictability of risks which are present in the social environment equates to a maximum level of fear.

The political system thus performs a function of symbolic protection far beyond its specific role as an apparatus of the selective regulation of social risks. There can be no doubt that the physical protection of life, the legal guarantee of property and contracts, military defence, the national insurance provided by the modern Welfare State, the limitation itself of the State's powers of intervention in the private lives of individuals according to the tradition of *habeas corpus*, are all specific mechanisms for the 'reduction of fear'. But it is most of all on the symbolic level that the institutions of authority, with all their show, ritual, prescriptions, and even codes of manners and etiquette, satisfy a latent need for social protection and spread a gratifying sensation of order and security – an irrational or 'residual' need, to use the vocabulary of Paretian political sociology.[87] Even the leadership of a charismatic head of a state[88] such as that provided in the 1980s by Ronald Reagan in the United States or, in Britain, by Margaret Thatcher, in France by François Mitterrand and in Italy by Bettino Craxi – has its roots in this world of symbolic interactions, in which both rational and irrational elements are profoundly interwoven, rather than in the expectations of concrete utilitarian advantages which the 'assumption of rationality' of the economic theory of politics rather crudely supposes.

Writers such as Downs, Buchanan and Tullock seem to miss entirely the point that modern forms of political participation, such as the rituals of representation, chiefly fulfil a function of symbolic reassurance. The stylization and legal formalization of conflictual behaviour – especially as seen in the procedures for electoral competition – offer to the protagonists in the rite and to the public which assists in it opportunities for symbolic gratification. The thrust for collective action engendered by political militancy results in confirmation of the identity of the militants – an effect which 'free riders' cannot expect to obtain – as well as in strengthening the bonds of their social belonging.[89] Individuals who are ordinarily dispersed in private life and generally unpossessed of political power of any kind are gratified by the chance to participate in a public ritual in which people collectively decide their common destiny or at least collectively pretend to decide it. The institutional fiction of their 'sovereignty' and, at the same time, of their belonging to a community of free and equal deciders stimulates for one and all the sense of solidarity and political responsibility and gratifies them in the exercise of their role. This is the key, as I see it, for interpreting *a contrario* the phenomenon of political abstentionism in democratic societies: i.e. in terms of a lack of any expectations of political protection. Absence of expectations can be generated as much by a superabundance as by a total lack of 'security' in the social condition of those who absent themselves from the ritual of representation. The calculation of electoral costs does not seem at all significant, except in very special (and in any case wholly marginal) circumstances.

It need hardly be emphasized that even in the relationship between power and subordination universal ethical criteria do not, and cannot, operate. Instead we find all the particularisms and collective egoisms which are connected with the struggle for power, competition between corporations, leadership relations, patronage and political bartering. Individual and group interests compete for power within a context of the structural 'scarcity of power'; that is, of the resource whose possession allows the allocation of every other politically distributable resource.

This should not of course be taken to mean that political categories coincide with Carl Schmitt's 'friend–enemy' scheme.[90] Schmitt's doctrine is nothing other than a totalitarian and – to use the word in the sense suggested by Julien Freund – 'polemical'[91] version of the particularistic and agonistic conception of politics which characterizes the realistic approach. The functionality of politics does not rest on the view of conflict as a binary friend-enemy polarization. On the contrary, politics in a modern sense only begins at the point at which this polarization is overcome, and power, as Hobbes again well appreciated, dons the robe of the Sovereign State, i.e. the Leviathan which removes war between citizens by monopolizing the 'legitimate' use of force. Politics, unlike civil war, is therefore not a zero-sum game which expresses itself in a struggle without rules, having no possibility of mediation or of compromise, and finding no solution except in the total defeat, i.e. violent suppression, of the enemy.

The functional rationality of politics consists rather in its capacity to engender 'mixed games', to use a term familiar in game theory. Mixed games are not zero-sum games (i.e. ones which carry total risk). Instead, they are in part co-operative and in part conflictual, and at all times contain elements of coordination and consensual acceptance of the rules of the game, without this in any sense meaning that it is a matter of 'free' games or of games played by equal opposing forces. Although victory over the adversary is the objective of each player – so excluding any altruistic or universalist attitude – such a victory does not entail total loss for any of the players, because this is a risk considered by all to be excessive.

Under these circumstances, it is not at all necessary to proclaim, with Kant, Apel or Rawls, that 'agreements must be kept' (*pacta sunt servanda*), i.e. that citizens have a moral duty of fidelity to an original social pact or, more generally, that political obligation has an ethical basis. It is sufficient to recognize that, so to speak, 'agreements *have been* kept' (*pacta sunt servata*). The quality of life of one and all would be endangered if, once a certain threshold of social tension had been crossed, competition according to rules gave way to open conflict right up to the limit of armed struggle and implicit renunciation of the protective function of the Leviathan. For weaker or less expert players, the violation of pacts could be politically extremely dangerous.

Three examples may be given. First, a partially co-operative, i.e. political, game may be seen in the sort of conflict which regularly takes place between workers' trade unions and employers' confederations in advanced societies. Second, denial of the expediency of standing by agreements – and so the denial of the functionality of politics – was exemplified by the refusal of the Red Brigade to recognize the Italian State's legitimate monopoly of the use of force, and their consequent acceptance of the risk of total struggle – precisely in Schmitt's sense – which resulted in the return of society as a whole to a condition of unregulated fear. Finally, for an example of a wholly co-operative, and therefore no longer political, game we need look no further than the way in which political parties compete in 'self-referential' democracies; that is, as I shall argue in chapter 4, in almost all the cases of what Robert Dahl has termed 'pluralistic democracy'.

## Notes

1   See D. Easton, 'The Current Meaning of "Behavioralism" ', in G. C. Charles-

worth (ed.), *The Limits of Behavioralism in Political Science*, Philadelphia: American Academy of Political and Social Sciences, 1962.

2  See T. Schelling, *The Strategy of Conflict*, New York: Oxford University Press, 1963; for examples of the enthusiasm aroused by Schelling's research see W. H. Riker and P. C. Ordeshook, *An Introduction to Positive Political Theory*, Englewood Cliffs (NJ): Prentice Hall, 1973; M. P. Fiorina, 'Formal Models in Political Science', *American Journal of Political Science*, 19 (1975), 2. 133–59; P. C. Ordeshook, *Game Theory and Political Science*, New York: New York University Press, 1978; K. Deutsch provided a much more prudent evaluation in 'Game Theory and Politics: Some Problems of Application', *Canadian Journal of Economics and Political Science*, 20 (1954), 1. 76–83.

3  Cf. the relevant bibliography in D. K. Whynes and R. A. Bowles, *The Economic Theory of the State*, Oxford: Martin Robertson, 1981, pp. 225–34; for German bibliography see, e.g., P. Herder-Dorneich and M. Groser, *Ökonomische Theorie des politischen Wettbewerbs*, Göttingen: Vandenhoeck and Ruprecht, 1977; F. Schneider, *Politisch-ökonomische Modelle*, Königstein/Ts: Hain, 1978; F. Meyer-Krahmer, *Politische Entscheidungsprozesse und ökonomische Theorie der Politik*, Frankfurt a.M. and New York: Campus Verlag, 1979; C. Hillinger and M. J. Holler, *Ökonomische Theorie der Politik*, Munich: Wolfgang Dummer and Co., 1979.

4  See A. Downs, *An Economic Theory of Democracy*, New York: Harper and Row, 1957; M. Olson, *The Logic of Collective Action*, Cambridge (Mass.): Harvard University Press, 1965; J. M. Buchanan and G. Tullock, *The Calculus of Consent. Logical Foundations of Constitutional Democracy*, Ann Arbor (Mich.): University of Michigan Press, 1962; on the subject as a whole, see J. R. Pennock, *Democratic Political Theory*, Princeton: Princeton University Press, 1979.

5  Which includes among its major exponents J. M. Buchanan, G. Tullock and R. Tollison; cf. C. K. Rowley, *Democracy and Public Choice*, New York: Basil Blackwell, 1987, pp. 1–19.

6  Cf. A. Downs, *An Economic Theory of Democracy*, pp. 21–35; J. M. Buchanan et al., *The Economics of Politics*, Lansing (Mich.): The Institute of Economic Affairs, 1978, pp. 3–20; see A. Breton and R. Wintrobe, *The Logic of Bureaucratic Conduct*, Cambridge: Cambridge University Press, 1982.

7  Cf. A. Downs, *An Economic Theory of Democracy*, pp. 29, 284; J. M. Buchanan et al., *The Economics of Politics*, p. 11. I shall return to this point at pp. 66 ff.

8  For a criticism of Downs's model and a precise individuation of the aspects which differentiate it from Schumpeter's cf. D. Miller, 'The Competitive Model of Democracy', in G. Duncan (ed.), *Democratic Theory and Practice*, Cambridge: Cambridge University Press, 1985, pp. 141–6.

9  For an equally severe criticism, even if based on very different premisses, see J. Plamenatz, 'Some American Images of Democracy', in R. M. Hutchins and M. J. Adler (eds), *The Great Ideas of Today*, New York: Praeger, 1968; C. B. Macpherson, *Democratic Theory. Essays in Retrieval*, Oxford: Clarendon

Press, 1973, pp. 185–94; cf. in addition: J. F. J. Toye, 'Economic Theories of Politics and Public Finance', *British Journal of Political Science*, 6 (1976), 4. 433–47; S. I. Benn, 'The Problematic Rationality of Political Participation', in P. Laslett and J. Fishkin (eds), *Philosophy, Politics and Society*, Oxford: Basil Blackwell, 1979, pp. 291–312; W. N. Nelson, *On Justifying Democracy*, London: Routledge and Kegan Paul, 1980, pp. 72–93; A. Pizzorno, 'Sulla razionalità della scelta democratica', *Stato e mercato*, 3 (1983), 7. 3–46. B. Barry's analysis in *Sociologists, Economists and Democracy*, Chicago and London: Chicago University Press, 1978, lacks focus.

10  A. Downs, *An Economic Theory of Democracy*, p. 14.

11  Ibid., pp. 295–300.

12  Ibid., p. 198.

13  Cf. G. Tullock, *Towards a Mathematics of Politics*, Ann Arbor (Mich.): University of Michigan Press, 1967, pp. 110–14; see also C. Ordeshook, *An Introduction to Positive Political Theory*; D. C. Mueller, 'Voting Paradox', in C. K. Rowley, *Democracy and Public Choice*, pp. 78–99; S. J. Brams, *Paradoxes in Politics*, New York: The Free Press, 1976, pp. 53–66.

14  For a discussion of the (economic or political) reasons for electoral abstentionism in the United States see R. Teixera, *Why Americans Don't Vote: Turnout Decline in the United States 1960–1984*, Westport (Colo.), Greenwood Press, 1987; F. F. Piven and R. A. Cloward, *Why Americans Don't Vote*, New York: Pantheon Books, 1988.

15  Cf. G. Sartori, *The Theory of Democracy Revisited*, Chatham (NJ): Chatham House Publishers, 1987, vol. 1, p. x.

16  The first attempt at defining democracy as a 'method' or as a mere *modus procedendi* is owed, as is well known, to Joseph Schumpeter (cf. *Capitalism, Socialism and Democracy*, London: Allen and Unwin, 1987, pp. 242–3, 269–70). I shall return to this subject in the final section of ch. 3.

17  Cf. C. F. Cnudde and D. E. Neubauer (eds), *Empirical Democratic Theory*, Chicago: Markham Publishing Company, 1969, p. 2; for a criticism see W. J. Stankiewicz, *Approaches to Democracy*, London: Edward Arnold, 1980, pp. 157–9.

18  Cf. G. Sartori, *The Theory of Democracy Revisited*, vol. 1, pp. 16–7.

19  Ibid., p. xii.

20  Cf. C. F. Cnudde and D. E. Neubauer (eds), *Empirical Democratic Theory*, pp. 3–5.

21  Cf. G. Sartori, 'La scienza politica', *Mondoperaio*, 38 (1985), 11. 118.

22  Cf. G. Sartori, *The Theory of Democracy Revisited*, vol. 1, pp. ix–xiii. Today, however, Sartori maintains in a contradictory and very confused way that democracy is characterized by a tension between 'facts' and 'values' and that a theory of democracy should therefore result from the interplay between the descriptions of facts and their evaluation (ibid., pp. 5–6); cf. also my review of Sartori's book in *Ethics*, 99 (1989), 2. 431–3.

23  See D. Miller and L. Siedentop, 'Introduction', in D. Miller and L. Siedentop (eds), *The Nature of Political Theory*, Oxford: Clarendon Press, 1983.

24   Cf. R. A. Dahl, *A Preface to Democratic Theory*, Chicago: The University of Chicago Press, 1956, pp. 149–51.

25   See D. Lerner and H. D. Lasswell (eds), *The Policy Sciences: Recent Developments in Scope and Method*, Stanford (Calif.): Stanford University Press, 1951; D. B. Truman, 'The Implications of Political Behavior Research', *Items* 5 (1951), 4; R. A. Dahl, 'The Behavioral Approach in Political Science: Epitaph for a Monument to a Successful Protest', *American Political Science Review*, 55 (1961), 4; D. Easton, 'The Current Meaning of "Behavioralism"'; H. Eulau, *The Behavioral Persuasion in Politics*, New York: Random House, 1963; G. A. Almond, 'Political Theory and Political Science', *American Political Science Review*, 40 (1966), 4; K. Deutsch, 'Recent Trends in Research Methods', in J. Charlesworth (ed.), *A Design for Political Science: Scope, Objectives, and Methods*, Philadelphia: The American Academy of Political and Social Sciences, 1966. On the epistemological debate within American political science see J. F. Falter, *Der 'Positivismusstreit' in der amerikanischen Politikwissenschaft*, Opladen: Westdeutscher Verlag, 1962.

26   Cf. C. E. Lindblom, 'The Science of "Muddling Through"', *Public Administration Review*, 19 (1959), 2. 79–88; G. A. Almond and S. J. Genco, 'Clouds, Clocks, and the Study of Politics', *World Politics*, 29 (1977), 4. 489–522; D. Easton, 'Political Science in the United States. Past and Present', *International Political Science Review*, 6 (1985), 1. 133–52.

27   See D. M. Ricci, *The Tragedy of Political Science*, New Haven (Conn.): Yale University Press, 1984.

28   Ibid., pp. 20–5, 291–318.

29.   G. A. Almond and S. J. Genco, 'Clouds, Clocks, and the Study of Politics', p. 522.

30   Ibid., pp. 504, 518.

31   D. Easton, 'Political Science in the United States. Past and Present', pp. 139–43, 148–51.

32   See G. Sartori, 'The Tower of Babel', in G. Sartori, F. W. Riggs and H. Teune, *Tower of Babel*, Pittsburgh (Pa.): International Study Association, 1975.

33   Cf. N. Bobbio, *Il futuro della democrazia*, Turin: Einaudi, 1984, Eng. trans. Cambridge: Polity Press, 1987, pp. 79–97.

34   The criticism of political science by the 'traditional' political philosophers who first reacted against its hegemony by charging it with having caused a 'decline' in political theory still retains some interest. See, e.g., L. Strauss, 'What is Political Philosophy?', in L. Strauss, *What is Political Philosophy and Other Studies*, Glencoe (Ill.): The Free Press, 1959; P. H. Partridge, 'Politics, Philosophy, Ideology', *Political Studies*, 9 (1961), 3. 217–35; I. Berlin, 'Does Political Theory Still Exist?', in P. Laslett and W. G. Runciman (eds), *Philosophy, Politics and Society*, Oxford: Blackwell, 1962; J. Plamenatz, 'The Use of Political Theory', in A. Quinton (ed.), *Political Philosophy*, Oxford: Oxford University Press, 1967.

35   Cf. N. Bobbio, 'Scienza politica', in N. Bobbio, N. Matteucci and G. Pasquino, *Dizionario di politica*, Turin: Utet, 1983, p. 1025.

36  Cf. O. Neurath, *Foundations of the Social Sciences*, pp. 26–8.
37  Norberto Bobbio has drawn a 'map' of political philosophy which has been widely discussed in Italy. See 'Dei possibili rapporti fra filosofia politica e scienza politica', in N. Bobbio et al., *Tradizione e novità della filosofia della politica*, 1, *Annali della Facoltà di Giurisprudenza dell'Università di Bari*, Bari: Laterza, 1971, pp. 23–37. See also C. Taylor, 'Political Theory and Practice', in C. Lloyd (ed.), *Social Theory and Political Practice*, Oxford: Clarendon Press, 1983; A. MacIntyre, 'The Indispensability of Political Theory', in D. Miller and L. Siedentop (eds), *The Nature of Political Theory*.
38  See P. Laslett and W. G. Runciman, Introduction, in P. Laslett and W. G. Runciman (eds), *Philosophy, Politics and Society*, Oxford: Basil Blackwell, 1967, pp. 1–5; P. Laslett and J. Fishkin, Introduction, in P. Laslett and J. Fishkin (eds), *Philosophy, Politics and Society*, pp. 1–5; A. Brown, *Modern Political Philosophy*, Harmondsworth: Penguin Books, 1986, pp. 11–22.
39  On this subject an old book of mine may still retain some philological value: *La teoria comunista dell'estinzione dello Stato*, Bari: De Donato, 1974.
40  See the two classic volumes: *Rehabilitierung der praktischen Philosophie*, ed. M. Riedel, Freiburg: Rombach, 1972–4; see also M. Riedel, *Metaphysik und Metapolitik. Studien zu Aristoteles und zur politischen Sprache der neuzeitlichen Philosophie*, Frankfurt a.M.: Suhrkamp Verlag, 1975.
41  Cf. J. G. A. Pocock, *The Machiavellian Moment: Florentine Political Thought and the Atlantic Republican Tradition*, Princeton (NJ): Princeton University Press, 1975, pp. 156–218; see A. MacIntyre, *After Virtue*, Notre Dame (Ind.): University of Notre Dame Press, 1981; M. Walzer, 'Philosophy and Democracy', *Political Theory*, 9 (1981), 3. 379–99.
42  See R. Dworkin, *Taking Rights Seriously*, Cambridge (Mass.): Harvard University Press, 1977; R. Nozick, *Anarchy, State and Utopia*, Oxford: Basil Blackwell, 1974; B. A. Ackerman, *Social Justice in the Liberal State*, New Haven (Conn.): Yale University Press, 1980; for a general criticism of the ethical versions of liberalism see R. Bellamy, 'Defining Liberalism: Neutralist, Ethical or Political?', in R. Bellamy (ed.), *Liberalism and Recent Legal and Social Philosophy*, Suppl. 36 of *Archiv für Rechts- und Sozialphilosophie*, Stuttgart: Franz Steiner Verlag, 1989.
43  According to a broad conception of power as 'social discipline' it is difficult to distinguish between prescriptions in a rigorous sense – for instance legal prescriptions, guaranteed by the possible use of force – and other sorts of 'evaluative' communication that may have the effect of influencing and fashioning people's behaviour. In this respect family, school, hospitals, scientific institutions, mass media and especially psychiatric hospitals should be conceived of as 'linguistic games' which are asymmetrical and prescriptive in nature, over and beyond and strictly linguistic structures of the communication and the conscious motivations of social agents. I am indebted to Emilio Santoro for a stimulating discussion on this point, which does, however, deserve further research. See M. Foucault, *Surveiller et punir. Naissance de la prison*, Paris: Gallimard, 1975, Eng. trans. New York: Vintage Books, 1979.

44  By evaluative, but not prescriptive, propositions I mean assertions of the following kind: 'This song is sad'; 'Mary is a nice girl'; 'The smell of these flowers is good'; 'This is a boring book'; 'That wall is yellow'; by prescriptive propositions (which are obviously also evaluative ones) I mean assertions of the kind: 'Abortion is a crime'; 'Life is inviolable'; 'Lying is immoral'; 'private property is a natural right'; 'There is a duty to obey political authorities.'

45  For a more analytical discussion see my 'Theoretical Language, Evaluations and Prescriptions: A Postempiricist Approach', in E. Pattaro (ed.), *Reason in Law*, Milan: Giuffrè, 1988, vol. 2, pp. 371–81.

46  Cf. my *Reflexive Epistemology*, pp. 147–53.

47  See J. Rawls, *A Theory of Justice*, Cambridge (Mass.): Harvard University Press, 1971. For a recent general assessment of Rawls's political philosophy see the 'Symposium on Rawlsian Theory of Justice: Recent Developments' in *Ethics*, 99 (1989), 4. 695–944.

48  J. Rawls, *A Theory of Justice*, pp. 40–5, 46–8, 580.

49  Ibid., pp. viii, 11; see in addition J. Rawls, 'A Well-Ordered Society', in P. Laslett and J. Fishkin (eds), *Philosophy. Politics and Society*, pp. 6–20.

50  J. Rawls, *A Theory of Justice*, p. 256.

51  When the Roman *plebs* had withdrawn to the Aventine in 494 BC, the former consul, Menenius Agrippa, is said to have successfully persuaded them to return by means of his fable about the Belly and the Limbs: There once was a body, whose limbs refused to continue feeding the belly, which appeared to them only to take and never to give. When the limbs themselves began to waste away, they finally saw, too late, that the belly had been nourishing them just as much as they had been nourishing it. In the same way, neither could the Senate function without the people, nor the people without the Senate (cf. Livy, II. 32. 8–12).

52  J. Rawls, *A Theory of Justice*, p. 4.

53  However, the axiomatized theory of social choice itself suggests the impossibility of collective decisions that are consistent and justified from a deontological standpoint; i.e. a theory of distributive justice cannot be founded on the principle of ethical cognitivism; see A. K. Sen, 'The Impossibility of a Paretian Liberal', *Journal of Political Economy*, 78 (1970) 1. 152–7; K. J. Arrow, *Social Choice and Individual Values*, New Haven (Conn.): Yale University Press, 1963.

54  See C. Offe, *Contradictions of the Welfare State*, London: Hutchinson, 1984; id., *Disorganized Capitalism*, Cambridge: Polity Press, 1985.

55  Cf. J. Rawls, 'A Well-Ordered Society', pp. 6–8.

56  Cf. J. Rawls, 'Justice as Fairness: Political, not Metaphysical', *Philosophy and Public Affairs*, 14 (1985), 3. 223–50; id., 'The Idea of an Overlapping Consensus', *Oxford Journal of Legal Studies*, 7 (1987), 1. 1–25.

57  Cf. P. Laslett and J. Fishkin, Introduction, pp. 4–5.

58  Some writers accept Rawls's level of discussion and then focus on the internal tensions of his theoretical construction, but this holds little interest from the point of view of the criticism of political moralism; see J. C. Harsanyi, 'Can the

Maximin-Principle Serve as Basis for Morality?', *American Political Science Review*, 69 (1975), 2. 594–606; R. M. Hare, 'Rawls' Theory of Justice', in N. Daniels (ed.), *Reading Rawls*, Oxford: Basil Blackwell, 1975, pp. 81–107; T. Scanlon, 'Rawls' Theory of Justice', ibid., pp. 169–205; B. Barry, *The Liberal Theory of Justice*, Oxford: Oxford University Press, 1973.

59 See M. Seliger, *The Marxist Conception of Ideology*, Cambridge: Cambridge University Press, 1977; N. Bobbio, 'Pareto e la critica delle ideologie', in N. Bobbio, *Saggi sulla scienza politica in Italia*, Rome–Bari: Laterza, 1977, pp. 79–107; N. Bobbio, 'L'ideologia in Pareto e in Marx', ibid., pp. 109–22.

60 Cf. D. Hume, *Of the Original Contract*, in *Essays: Moral, Political, and Literary*, Oxford: Oxford University Press, 1974, pp. 452–73.

61 Cf. J. Habermas, *Zur Rekonstruktion des Historischen Materialismus*, Frankfurt a.M., Suhrkamp Verlag, 1976, pp. 276–81.

62 This is clearly stated by Cicero in *De Re Publica*, III. xv; cf. his *De Re Publica, De Legibus*, with Eng. trans. by C. W. Keyes, Cambridge (Mass.): Harvard University Press, 1970, pp. 202–5.

63 The expression was used by Cardinal Reginald Pole.

64 Cf. J. Habermas, *Moralbewußtsein und kommunikatives Handeln*, Frankfurt a.M.: Suhrkamp Verlag, 1983, pp. 53–125, Eng. trans. Cambridge: Polity Press, 1990; J. Habermas, *Die nachholende Revolution*, Frankfurt a.M.: Suhrkamp Verlag, 1990.

65 I personally agree with Nicola Matteucci's opinion that *The Prince* is 'the most fascinating and deepest of Machiavelli's works'; cf. N. Matteucci, *La ricerca dell'ordine politico*, Bologna: Il Mulino, 1984, p. 63. Consequently, I do not share the tendency, promoted by F. Gilbert and J. G. A. Pocock, to see Machiavelli's *Discorsi*, in which he founds the modern republican tradition, as the most important of his works. This does not of course prevent me from recognizing the scientific interest of this kind of interpretation. See F. Gilbert, *Machiavelli and Guicciardini*, Princeton (NJ): Princeton University Press, 1965; J. G. A. Pocock. *The Machiavellian Moment: Florentine Political Thought and the Atlantic Republican Tradition*; Q. Skinner, *Machiavelli*, Oxford: Oxford University Press, 1981. David Held also follows this interpretation; cf. D. Held, *Models of Democracy*, Cambridge: Polity Press, 1987, pp. 43–7.

66 N. Machiavelli, *Il Principe*, ed. L. Firpo, Turin; Einaudi, 1974, ch. xvii, Eng. trans., ed. by Q. Skinner and R. Price, Cambridge: Cambridge University Press, 1988, p. 59.

67 Cf. C. K. Rowley, *Democracy and Public Choice*, p. 3.

68 Cf. A. Gehlen, *Der Mensch. Seine Natur und seine Stellung in der Welt*, Eng. trans., pp. 24–37.

69 On the relationship between fear and politics in Hobbes see, e.g., J. Freund, 'La thème de la peur chez Hobbes', *Ress-Cahiers V. Pareto*, 49 (1980), 1. 15–32. Among the essays devoted by Guglielmo Ferrero to the subject of political fear see especially *Pouvoir. Les génies invisibles de la Cité*, New York: Putnam, 1942. According to Ferrero, 'power is the supreme manifestation of fear

which man produces to himself, despite the efforts at freeing himself from it.... while people always feel fear of power to which they are subjected, power always feels fear of people under its control.... The inner nature of the principles of legitimation is the ability to exorcise fear: the mysterious and reciprocal fear between power and people subjected to it' (ibid., pp. 38, 41, 46).

70  Cf. F. Neumann, 'Angst und Politik', *Recht und Staat* (1954), 178–9, Eng. trans. in F. Neumann, *The Democratic and the Authoritarian State*, New York: The Free Press, 1957, pp. 270–300.

71  See K. Lorenz, *Das sogenannte Böse. Zur Naturgeschichte der Aggression*, Vienna: G. Borotha-Schöler, 1963, Eng. trans. New York: Harcourt, Brace and World, 1966. On the relationship between ethology and political theory see R. D. Masters, 'The Impact of Ethology on Political Science', in A. Somit (ed.), *Biology and Politics. Recent Explorations*, Mouton: Publications of the ISSC, 1976, pp. 197–233.

72  See I. Eibl-Eibesfeldt, *Liebe und Hass. Zur Naturgeschichte elementarer Verhaltensweisen*, Munich: Piper Verlag, 1970, Eng. trans. New York: Holt, Rinehart and Winston, 1972.

73  Cf. A. Gehlen, *Der Mensch. Seine Natur und seine Stellung in der Welt*, Eng. trans., pp. 54–64.

74  Cf. A. Gehlen, *Die Seele im technischen Zeitalter*, Eng. trans., p. 59.

75  On the modern notion of 'risk' cf. N. Luhmann, 'Familiarity, Confidence and Trust: Problems and Alternatives', in D. Gambetta (ed.), *Trust. Making and Breaking Cooperative Relations*, Oxford: Basil Blackwell, 1988, pp. 123–40; see also J. F. Short, 'The Social Fabric of Risk', *American Sociological Review*, 49 (1984), 6. 711–25.

76  Cf. A. Gargani, *Il sapere senza fondamenti*, Turin: Einaudi, 1975, pp. 94–6.

77  See N. Luhmann, *Vertrauen. Ein Mechanismus der Reduktion sozialer Komplexität*, Stuttgart: Enke Verlag, 1973, Eng. trans. in N. Luhmann, *Trust and Power*; B. Barber, *The Logic and Limits of Trust*, New Brunswick: Rutgers University Press, 1983; D. Gambetta (ed.), *Trust. Making and Breaking Cooperative Relations*.

78  Cf. N. Luhmann, *Rechtssoziologie*, pp. 24–49. See also N. Luhmann, *Macht*, Stuttgart: Enke Verlag, 1975, Eng. trans. in *Trust and Power*; N. Luhmann, *Legitimation durch Verfahren*, Neuwied and Berlin: Luchterhand, 1969.

79  For an interesting, if questionable, list of the risks covered by modern paternalistic legislation see G. Dworkin, 'Paternalism', in P. Laslett and J. Fishkin (eds), *Philosophy, Politics and Society*, pp. 78–96.

80  On the relationship between fear and aggressive behaviour there is a wide psychological, ethological and biological literature; socio-anthropological works are less numerous: among these see D. L. Scruton (ed.), *Sociophobics. The Anthropology of Fear*, Boulder (Colo.) and London: Westview Press, 1986. Research concerning the relationship between social insecurity and aggressive political behaviour is virtually non-existent.

81  Cf. E. E. Schattschneider, *The Semisovereign People*, New York: Holt, Rinehart and Winston, 1960, pp. 30ff.

82  See P. Bachrach and M. S. Baratz, *Power and Poverty. Theory and Practice*, New York: Oxford University Press, 1970. See also my introduction to the Italian translation: P. Bachrach and M. S. Baratz, *Le due facce del potere*, Padua: Liviana Editrice, 1986, pp. 7–27.

83  Cf. S. Lukes, *Power. A Radical View*, London: Macmillan, 1974, pp. 21–5.

84  F. Neumann ('Angst und Politik', Eng. trans., pp. 278–87) has rightly included 'conspiracy theories' within this phenomenology and has drawn up a precise typology of them. He lists the following five conspiracy theories: the Jesuit, the freemasonry, the communist, the capitalist, and the Jewish conspiracies.

85  Cf. R. Dahrendorf, 'Amba, Amerikaner und Kommunisten. Zur These der Universalität von Herrschaft', in R. Dahrendorf, *Pfade aus Utopia. Arbeiten zur Theorie und Methode der Soziologie*, Munich: Piper Verlag, 1967, pp. 315–36; see also R. D. Masters, 'The Impact of Ethology on Political Science', in A. Somit (ed.), *Biology and Politics. Recent Explorations*, pp. 197–233.

86  See M. Stirner, *Die Einzige und sein Eigentum*, Leipzig: Otto Wigand, 1845, Eng. trans. New York: Libertarian Book Club, 1963; R. Nozick, *Anarchy, State and Utopia*.

87  Cf. V. Pareto, *Trattato di sociologia generale*, Milan: Comunità, 1964, paragraphs 842–1396, pp. 507–877, partial Eng. trans. in V. Pareto, *Sociological Writings*, ed. D. Mirfin, Oxford: Basil Blackwell, 1966, pp. 215–50.

88  Examples of 'caesarist identification' in representative democracies come to mind; cf. F. Neumann, 'Angst und Politik', Eng. trans., pp. 274–8.

89  Naturally, celebration of the rite also has a marginally reassuring effect for citizens who do not personally take part in it, but do expect to obtain some benefit as 'free riders'. A. Pizzorno stresses the aspect of the search for collective identity: cf. 'Sulla razionalità della scelta democratica', pp. 3–46; cf. also D. Miller, 'The Competitive Model of Democracy', pp. 146–50.

90  See C. Schmitt, *Der Begriff des Politischen*, Berlin: Verlag Walther Rothschild, 1928, Eng. trans. New Brunswick (NJ): Rutgers University Press, 1976.

91  Cf. J. Freund, *Sociologie du conflit*, Paris: Presses Universitaires de France, 1983, p. 85.

# 3 Complexity and Democratic Theory

Cesare Borgia was considered cruel, yet his harsh measures restored order to Romagna, unifying it and rendering it peaceful and loyal.

Machiavelli, *Il Principe*

## Fear and democracy

The central concern of this book, as I have indicated in the preface, is with the relationship between democratic institutions and the increasing complexity of post-industrial societies. In this and the succeeding chapters I shall attempt to argue that our present theories of democracy fail to offer us conceptual instruments sufficiently complex[1] to permit a realistic interpretation of that relationship. As we prepare to enter the third millennium, Western political theory appears increasingly unable to cope with the massive transformations which the 'information revolution' is bringing about in the primary subsystems of industrialized society. These transformations seem certain to speed up the processes of functional specialization and consequently, following the logic of one of the general hypotheses I advanced in chapter 1, to bring about still further large-scale growth of social complexity.

The impact this process is bound to have on the mechanisms of political representation will, I shall argue more specifically, call into question the very premises of democratic theory, whether in its classical or in its revisionist versions.[2] For it is the democratic encyclopedia as a whole that seems destined for obsolescence, along with its most basic paradigms: participation, representation, competitive pluralism. Above all, the danger seems greatest for two assumptions which modern democratic doctrines have drawn from the classico-Christian tradition and which have often been redeveloped in European political thought from Locke to Kant, de Tocqueville and John Stuart Mill: first the liberal-bourgeois idea that individual agents are the constitutive elements and effective political actors in a democratic regime, and second the puritan conviction that the basis of democratic life lies in the autonomy of the individual, understood in terms of the sovereignty, rationality and responsibility of the moral person. Thus the present revival of political moralism may be seen, in both its neo-Benthamite and neo-Kantian versions, as an attempt to respond to the powerful stresses to which the pillars of the Western liberal-democratic tradition are being subjected.

In the light of these circumstances, the theme 'complexity and democracy' will clearly not be approached without a philosophical discussion which is broadly based, radical and free from bias. Such a discussion, as I see it, should aim to profit not only from the contemporary epistemological debate, but also from the contributions which are offered by anthropological and sociological research. It is not sufficient for it merely to exclude the wishful thinking of academic moralists who, as a matter of professional course, choose to close their eyes to the 'severity of politics'.[3] In addition the discussion should aim to break out of the positivist constraints of both political science and the neo-classical doctrine of democratic pluralism. These are each concerned, though of course on different levels, with accrediting as 'purely descriptive' an image of the Western democracies which is essentially based on the desire to confirm the absolute superiority of that system.[4]

The upshot of this, as seen from my theoretical position, is that the idea of democracy needs to be rethought in the light of the realistic approach I have attempted to frame in the preceding chapter. Once it is accepted that the general function of a modern political system is that of reducing fear through a selective regulation of social risks and a competitive distribution of 'security values', and once it is accepted that the central categories of the political code are the inclusion/exclusion principle and the asymmetric power/subordination relation, then one is bound to ask what connection exists between these political categories and theories of the forms of government.

The first step is suggested by Thomas Hobbes and Robert Michels: a form of government which involves a monocratic (or, at most, an oligarchic) leadership answers to the protective functions of the political system in an appreciably more linear and effective way than any democratic system, if by democratic is meant, in broad terms, a form of government which aims to include in its decisional channels a designedly high number of agents. The political system which exercises the power of coercion according to the despotic and totalitarian model of sacerdotal or paternal authority is the one which succeeds in fulfilling its elementary and essential role, which is that of protecting citizens against disorder, anarchy, open conflict or civil war. As Bobbio puts it, the state which exercises power 'without curbs or restraints', in the words of Montesquieu, 'is the state in its essence, the state at the moment of its ideal origin from the chaos of the state of nature'.[5] And this is still true for political institutions within societies with a relatively low level of differentiation.

If fear is mankind's basic impulse in response to the dangers of an environment to which we are excessively exposed, and if the political system is a social structure which reduces fear by selectively reducing the complexity of the environment, then political power must be the more effective, the greater the 'reduction of complexity' it is able to bring about. It is able to guarantee very high levels of security when it removes a wide range of expectations of disappointment. Clearly the simplest and most effective mechanism for obtaining this protection is a drastic reduction in social complexity.[6]

By issuing orders binding on all, and by the use of symbolic disciplining structures, political power is able to achieve an extensive restriction of the range of possible experiences both conceived and actualized by members of a group. In this way it renders less likely chances which are perceived by each member as negative, and therefore obtains more manageably a peaceful coordination of the behaviour of individuals and a reassuring state of social balance. It is then obvious – as Hobbes was once again the first to point out – that the greater the reduction of social complexity for which a political system must make provision, the wider and more concentrated its power must be. In the extreme case, for example under conditions of the 'extraordinary state' envisaged by Carl Schmitt, a situation of unusually great danger must be matched by the maximum concentration and intensity of power and by the requirement of unconditional obedience.[7]

The more serious and uncontrollable the dangers by which a social group feels threatened (as a result either of external or of internal factors), the more widespread is its fear and the more intrusive and extensive must the Leviathan's power of intervention become. The Leviathan must be active in its use of the 'sword', because it is the fear which this instils – i.e. the sovereign right of life and death over citizens – which succeeds in neutralizing the fear diffused throughout the social body. It could reasonably be argued that in the model of the 'geometry of fear' so central to Hobbesian political theory there is an implicit statement of a law of the conservation both of power and of fear.[8] With respect to the first, the original power which individuals abdicate by making their pact of subjugation (*pactum subjectionis*) is found to reappear in a concentrated form in the absolute power (*potestas absoluta*) of the Leviathan. And with respect to the second, the fear which is absorbed by the protective function of the Leviathan is, so to speak, neutralized, but not removed: it reappears as the capability of the 'mortal god' to bring about discipline by instilling fear. Fear of humanity and fear of the state – *metus hominis* and *metus reipublicae* – interconnect and condition each other in turn.[9]

The threat of a sovereign sanction is the only means by which it is possible politically to reduce social complexity and to confirm expectations of order and security. In this capacity to reduce fear by the exercise of fear, as was well appreciated in terms of political realism by both Hobbes and Machiavelli, lies the essential paradox of power. A prime example of the paradox is seen in Remirro de Orco, one of the most dramatic characters of *The Prince*, who skilfully united and pacified Romagna on the orders of the Cesare Borgia.[10] Having deputed his lieutenant full powers over the region when it was 'full of thefts, quarrels and outrages of every kind', Borgia then decided to suppress him, both through fear of the 'formidable reputation' he had acquired and also in order to placate popular resentment. The mutilated body which was exhibited in the Renaissance piazza of Cesena 'with a block of wood and a blood-stained sword at his side' summed up all the ambiguity inherent in power: its indispensable function of control matched by its unavoidable violence and dangerousness.[11]

In these circumstances there can be little doubt that the regulation of social risks is better guaranteed the more efficaciously the political system exercises its systemic function of exclusion/inclusion, i.e. the more it succeeds in making the internal bond of political fidelity both organic and exclusive and in introducing it into the consciousness of its subjects. Such is its capacity for doing this that it can create a collective opinion virtually equivalent (or even, as in the case of ancient Israel or modern Islamic states, exactly equivalent) to a religious belief.

The same is true of the relation of subordination. The more a power is concentrated in institutions of authority, and the more its orders enjoy the privileges of asymmetry and heteronomy with respect to the powers and wishes of its subjects, so as to become the object of their 'obedience', the more efficacious it is in playing its essential role of reducing insecurity.

If things were not so, it would be difficult to explain why – leaving apart instances of purely military power – the monarchic-theocratic has been by far the most prevalent type of regime in the history of mankind. Nor would it be clear why, for almost two millennia and up to the beginning of modern times – before, that is, the sudden surge of consensus in its favour in the twentieth century – democracy has been unanimously held, within the European philosophical tradition, to be the least perfect and least reliable form of government.[12]

In reality, despite the imposing mass of opinion to the contrary, democracy has to be considered, as it was by Weber, to be a wholly modern phenomenon arising from the beginnings of the industrial revolution and not before that time. In spite of the profusion of rhetoric devoted to arguing for the continuity of the democratic tradition within Western culture – from the Greek *polis* to the 'electoral polyarchy',[13] from the Roman Republic to Florentine republicanism and American federalism,[14] from the Athens of Pericles to Rousseau's Geneva and communard Paris[15] – it is in fact true to say that the idea of democracy has arisen in modern Europe in opposition to a quite different millennium-long tradition. It has even arisen against the classical conception itself, both Aristotelian and Platonic, of politics, i.e. against the organicistic and naturalistic model of the political city – the *polis*, to be precise – which was central to both ancient and medieval political thought.[16] Not unnaturally, this is the model which contemporary proponents of the 'rehabilitation of practical philosophy' inspired by Leo Strauss and Hannah Arendt contrast nostalgically with modern forms of liberal democracy.[17]

The totalitarian obligarchies which ruled the city-states of classical Greece, Athens included[18] – not to mention the institutions by which republican Rome was governed – can in no way be held to form a significant precedent for modern liberal-democratic constitutions. (Of course, this is true only if one does not intend to maintain that representative democracy does not differ in substance from an oligarchic and totalitarian form of government and its social framework is not markedly different from the illiberal, anti-feminist and slave-based framework of antiquity.) Nor is it any more plausible, to my mind, to see representative democracy as a reformulation of the principles of Athenian democracy – envisaged as direct or assembly democracy – which was supposedly made by Montesquieu, Madison and John Stuart Mill in the face of the need technically to adapt those principles to the changed geographical and demographic conditions of the nation or federal states.[19]

Instead, a realistic approach to the question of democracy must succeed in keeping two things distinct: first, the process of differentiation and development towards autonomy of the political system which is so typical of modern times in Europe – that is, the transition from the organicistic and corporative models of the 'class state' to the formalism of the 'representative state'; and second, the enlightenment values with which the liberal-democratic and radical-democratic doctrines have viewed this process.

As it is, theories of liberal democracy have presented themselves as a radical and even, to use Bobbio's term,[20] a 'subversive' challenge, to the very criteria of the political code. They have set out to reject in principle any restriction of citizenship or extension of the state's sphere of influence, and have argued for the inviolable autonomy of the individual agent and, at the extreme limit, for negation of the heteronomous, descendent and asymmetric nature of the power relation. In this sense the *Contrat social* stands as the democratic paradigm *par excellence*, given Rousseau's overriding concern to urge the need for the removal of the distinction (and inequality) between governors and governed as well as the eradication of the heteronomous nature of political command. In this sense, as we shall go on to see, the communist theory of the withering away of the state, with the tragic ambiguity of its anarchic radicalism, has emerged in our own time as the logical end of Rousseau's utopianism.[21] Even in its more moderate forms, paradoxically even in Plamenatz and the recent work of Robert Dahl,[22] democratic theory radically opposes the principle which James Burnham, Robert Michels and Max Weber have defined, following Machiavelli, as 'the necessarily oligarchic nature' of any non-elementary political system.[23]

What, historically, lies behind this rejection by democratic theories of the functional code of politics? Looking beyond the ideological emphasis and ingenuousness of the natural-law position, there appears to be a historical realization that the protective aspects of the political system present high costs in terms of the reduction of social complexity, and that these costs can be markedly disproportionate to the advantages they are supposed to achieve. As one would expect, this discovery transforms itself historically into wide political awareness, and then into revolutionary demands, only within social environments which display an already high level of social differentiation, such as in the bourgeois European societies of the seventeenth and eighteenth centuries.

The great flowering of liberal-democratic thought was not only connected with the process of differentiation of the political subsystem from the framework of religious universalism and corporate organicism, but also presupposed a clear functional distinction between the normative and bureaucratic structures of the nation-state and 'civil society'.[24] For it was within the rich network of business, industrial, financial, scientific, cultural and family relations of civil society that the growth of bourgeois political individualism was fostered. The European bourgeoisie was in fact the first political and economic class in human history to demand for itself *qua* a social group, and for its members *qua* free and equal citizens, a freedom which was not so much, according to Hannah Arendt's critical definition, a political freedom as a 'freedom from politics'. It was, in other words, a freedom both conceived of and claimed as the differentiation of social functions and individual roles *vis-à-vis* the political body, and was no longer understood in Aristotelian terms as an organic adherence to the ethical and rational forms of collective life. This has been clearly (though, in ideological terms, somewhat naïvely) expressed by Benjamin Constant by means of the contrast he draws between ancient and modern freedom.[25]

In the same way the need for a more defined functional specification of the political system was next to become clear, to be realized through its procedural 'uncoupling' from such subsystems as the economic, religious, family, parental, etc., in the form of secret ballots and the equality of citizens before the law.[26] Hand in hand with this went the demand for the functional autonomy of the economic subsystem which was then to be entrusted, after a comprehensive reduction of the 'protective' restrictions of a political nature, to the risks of the free play of market forces. In order to justify these functional needs both ethically and politically, democratic doctrines have even had recourse to the old theological and metaphysical doctrine of natural law. On the basis of this, or of a contractualistic variant of it, the attempt has been made to establish the original and universal nature of individual rights, the sanctity of private property and the freedom of economic initiative.

What, then, are the consequences for the political system of this process of functional differentiation and the associated demand for autonomy on the part of the civil society and its individual members? If the political regulation of fear requires a reduction of social complexity which is itself guaranteed by fear and if extensive reduction of complexity leads to high levels of the 'dangerousness' of power, then the request made by differentiated social agents – i.e. free and equal citizens who possess private property – can only, within a society which has become more complex, be that political power, inasmuch as it is a creator of risk and a source of fear, should itself become subject to political procedures for the collective regulation of social risks. The sovereignty of the Leviathan, to which functionally there exists no alternative, will need to be balanced, and in some way controlled and limited, by another sovereign element. This will have to be the sovereignty of a parliament capable of 'representing', in the strongest sense of the term, the demand for autonomy from citizens who are free, equal, and possess private property. The principle of 'no taxation without representation' will have to be both the basis and the symbol of a general freedom. A constitutional system will therefore need to play a, so to speak, secondary 'protective' function – that of (circularly) protecting the members of the 'civil society' from the dangers of political protection.[27]

The power of deciding the methods and levels of political regulation will therefore itself need to be subjected to political regulation through a recursive procedure by which a requirement for 'retro-action' (i.e. participation in – or at least control over – the sovereign decision) exists to benefit the recipients themselves of the sovereign decision. Democracy will thus function as a negative feedback on the operation of political power, which has a natural tendency to expand in threatening ways. In this lies the force of the principle of the division of power, which is to be understood not simply as a segmentary differentiation of power functions, but, in somewhat more complex terms, as recursivity and functional self-limitation.

The extreme 'dangerousness' inherent in the severe curtailment of possibilities of experience for members of civil society by coercion from the courts or police, or of the restriction of the range of their economic activities by the outlawing of certain forms of behaviour or by the confiscation of part of their private resources, means that these powers will need to be subjected to the same ritualization and procedural limitations as govern the powers of individual agents. This is all the more the case, given that the monopoly of the Leviathan has deprived members of political society of the possibiliy of 'thinking for themselves' in their dealings either with other agents or with the institutions of authority. The result will be the general limiting of the intensity and scope of the power of state intervention, an increase in the 'legitimized' complexity of individual choices and, correlatively, a contraction of the protective functions of the political system which will leave to individual agents the task of absorbing a greater proportion of social disappointments, including economic ones. In other words, therefore, democracy will mean the preservation of higher levels of social complexity and, at the same time, the collective acceptance of a larger quantity of social risks and insecurity.[28]

But in order that the recursive mechanisms of democracy can function effectively – a factor which liberal-democratic theorists appear not always to take into account – a far-reaching alteration of the institutions of authority will be necessary and a substantial alteration of the very logic of the political code. In place of the linear simplicity of the traditional mechanisms for reducing fear, it will be necessary to substitute a nexus of interdependencies within which the need for order and security would be held constantly in balance with the opposite need for the preservation of complexity and political and economic 'freedoms'. In place of the structures of vertical power there will need to be political mechanisms of a reflexive type, capable of subordinating, through a powerful retroactive circle, both the sovereign political will to the will of the citizens (i.e. the limitation and democratic constitutional legitimizing of power) and the will of the citizens to the sovereign will (i.e. the guarantee by bureaucratic administration of security and order). Herein lies the great challenge in defence of social differentiation which the bourgeois requirement of a democratic constitutional state makes against the power of unlimited political protection, i.e. against the unlimited reduction of complexity.

While the protective function of a political system demands a regulation of social risks of an asymmetric and essentially oligarchic (if not strictly hierarchic) nature, the democratic constitutional requirement will aim to dissolve the pyramidical structure of political power according to a hypothesis of recursive transitivity, diffusion and symmetry of the relations of power. Taking the ideology of radical democratism to its extreme, Rousseau, as we shall see, demands the complete coincidence in a perfect democracy of the sovereignty which disciplines with the sovereignty which is disciplined, and of protective power with legitimizing power. Thus the pool of each citizen's original complexity remains intact in his hands, and each political reduction of this complexity neither is, nor is seen as, 'heteronomous' coercion imposed from outside, but as the result of a perfectly 'autonomous' choice, a realization – not a restriction – of liberty.[29]

Seen in such realistic terms as these, the danger the doctrine of liberal democracy holds for the structure and functions of the political system comes through very clearly, over and beyond the functional requirements themselves which have led in bourgeois Europe to the downfall of the despotic organicism of the *ancien régime*. This view of liberal democracy also shows the reasons why the democratic-constitutional model proves to be the most improbable, most fragile and least realistic form of government of a state – so improbable and so unrealistic that today, after two centuries of experience and despite the universal agreement it currently commands, democracy still appears as a wholly unattainable objective, desired all the more, according to John Dunn's paradox,[30] the more unattainable it is.

My own view suggests that this paradox might be formulated in the following terms: the increase of differentiation and social complexity is responsible for modern demands for democracy and is still continuing to foster the need for it, but it is the self-same increase of differentiation and social complexity which means that such demands cannot in the end succeed. This is the central functional antinomy contained within the relation between complexity and democracy, an antinomy which, as I shall argue in the next chapter, our present-day theories of democracy seem wholly unable to perceive and consequently cannot even begin to resolve.

The increasing differentiation of spheres of experience and hence of individual experiences – i.e. the process which Arnold Gehlen has called 'subjectivization'[31] – engenders a growing demand in advanced industrial societies for autonomy from the organic aspect of politics and its 'protective' criteria for the reduction of complexity. In addition, the growing complexity of information-based societies, with the vast range of possibilities for experience which they offer, render individual agents ever more sensible of the political mutilations of their existence and ever less prepared to put up with them. Given the growing contingency of the human condition and the instability of even the anthropological characteristics of our species (which now extend to the sexual dimension and our reproductive functions), agents seem increasingly guided by the desire for individual expression and action, but ever less confident of envisaging political ideas which go beyond the everyday experience of their lives as they know them, and ever less willing to allow themselves to participate in the rituals of homologation and collective integration which are such a vital necessity for politics. The feminist movement in the West is, despite mixed success, a notable expression of this process of social defferentiation and auton-omization of individuals from the romantic dimension of politics.[32]

But it is the very increase both in differentiation of the political system and, more broadly, in social complexity brought about by the rapidity of scientific and technological development which serves to make democracy improbable on account of the evolutionary risks which threaten it. The increasing differentiation and autonomy of the political system, the tech-nical difficulty of administrative problems, the steep rise in inter-dependencies and negative externalities, the multiplication of factors of risk and of situations of emergency, the variety and mobility of social interests, the increasing sense of social discontinuity and personal uncer-tainty all come together to make the government of post-industrial coun-tries difficult by democratic means.[33] Problems continue to emerge which are less amenable to political handling, while political solutions require a consensus which is increasingly difficult to obtain through formal pro-cedures under conditions in which the 'general will' dissipates and frag-ments itself into a confused multiplicity of particularisms and localized interests. Individualistic fragmentation of the social fabric tends in fact to reformulate itself along lines of particularistic solidarity, of a purely 'ascriptive' sort, based on type, age, health, ethnic, regional or family characteristics, forms of employment and leisure etc.[34] The very desire for solidarity and for communion tends to express itself in esoteric, intimate and neo-religious ways, which remove legitimacy from, rather than provide it for, the collective dimension of political life. Once again Hobbes's model of the 'natural state' as being a condition of profound insecurity and uncontrollable contingency comes to the fore, as Jean-François Lyotard has well seen, to describe the fundamental anthropological characteristic of a 'post-modern' society in which the legitimating power of the great universalistic and emancipative stories has long since undergone a process of irreversible erosion.[35]

Under such conditions, the political reduction of insecurity cannot avoid requiring the exercise of an increasing quantity of power, at the same time as the growth in social complexity, with its close intertwining of powers of veto and the fragmentation of political wishes, makes 'positive power' an increasingly scarce commodity.[36] For this reason post-industrial societies are constantly exposed to the danger of 'power inflation', and may even reach the extreme of decisional paralysis. At the same time they are threatened by the pressure of the centrifugal tendencies and negative externalities of functionally differentiated areas which only strong political regulation would seem to be able to coordinate.

In post-industrial societies it is not the traditional institutional alternatives of left and right which seem to threaten the future of democracy. On the contrary, these seem less credible or practicable now than at any time in the past. Rather, it is an evolutionary force inherent in 'democratic' political systems – by which expression I have 'evolutionary risks' in mind – which seems to impose, in the name of the efficiency of political decision, security of the society, technological growth or, above all, expansion of consumption schemes for the drastic reduction of social complexity which are quite separate from the traditional problems of participation, representation and freedom.[37] In this sense recent legislative developments in Europe and the United States which aim to criminalize acts of individual behaviour which are not directly injurious to the interests of others (e.g. in areas such as the use of narcotics or alcohol, or some sexual activities, or new scientific developments) may be cited as an example, as yet still restrained, of the illiberal solution to which a democratic political system will have recourse in order to remedy its own inability to control an increasingly complex and risk-filled environment. The same too may be said of the illiberal and discriminatory rules contained in national laws (or in international agreements in Europe and the West) for the containment of migratory flows from the poorer countries of the Third World, and for the control of terrorism or of traffic in arms and drugs.

Individuals and social groups within societies dominated by high technology do not seem to be in a position to cope with social risks or to be able to 'reduce fear' without the help of a concentrated and specialized political system. There is no justification for thinking that it will be possible to realize through 'unpolitical' paths the ideal 'political communication freed from domination' which Hannah Arendt and Jürgen Habermas have hoped for, or that the ethical dimension of community life can be recovered within the new city-states adumbrated by Alasdair MacIntyre,[38] or that it will be possible to recover the sort of naturalistic 'state of naure' which contemporary trends in ecological romanticism call for as an alternative to the consumer society and the domination exercised by the multinational companies. In post-industrial societies the possibility that spontaneous social groupings will succeed in dealing locally and autonomously with social risks becomes on the contrary an increasingly less credible hypothesis, if for no other reason than the planetary scale which factors of risk have now assumed in such areas as, for example, ecological disequilibrium, nuclear disasters, demographic pressure, problems of food supply, the disposal of waste, the interconnection of financial systems, terrorism and the world-wide circulation of drugs.[39]

## The classical doctrine of democracy

Advanced industrial societies, both in the East and in the West, make use of what are essentially two theoretical models of democracy, both of them derived from the political tradition of Europe. The first model can, broadly speaking, be identified with what, following Max Weber, Joseph Schumpeter[40] defined fifty years ago as the 'classical doctrine' of democracy.[41] The second, which I intend to call the 'neo-classical', has dominated Western political theory in the second half of the twentieth century (from Schumpeter onwards) and has given birth to an entire school of thought. This is the model known as democratic pluralism or, as others prefer to call it, 'democratic elitism'.

Schumpeter's 'classical doctrine' is of course only a summary description and one which bands together several different models (e.g. the utilitarian and that of Rousseau) which are not wholly compatible with one another.[42] Graeme Duncan and Steven Lukes have shown with some truth that Schumpeter's criticism of the classical doctrine as unrealistic rests on a confusion by which he considers the ideal scope and the normative structure of the democratic theories developed by such writers as Locke, Bentham or Rousseau to be analytical fallacies.[43] Indeed there can be no doubt whatever that these classic writers, not least Rousseau himself, understood full well, even though they did not themselves draw any distinction between the realistic and the idealistic sides of their thinking, that democracy has to be conceived of as a regulative ideal far more than as any realized or realizable political regime. Despite all this, however, I cannot share with Carole Pateman the idea that Schumpeter's purpose was to construct in the classical doctrine a convenient target for his conservative and anti-democratic critique. Nor would I follow her in denying the existence of any such doctrine as being an out-and-out myth.[44]

Instead, the charge which I believe can be levelled against Schumpeter, apart from the effect of his personal ideological preferences, concerns the conflation he makes of the two fundamentally different versions of the classical doctrine, the participative and the representative. He directs his criticisms against aspects of the theory of representation which are perhaps more characteristic of the theory of participation, while he appears not to have developed any particular critique of participation *per se*. But this, as

I see it, is a marvellously happy error. In making this mistake of overall definition, Schumpeter has hit upon an essential aspect which runs behind both theories and in fact makes the classical theory of political representation a simple institutional variant of the theory of participation. This is the idea that not only does democracy necessarily involve the notions of 'common good' and 'popular will', but its realization is the more complete the more the agents, content and criteria of political decision coincide with the agents, content and criteria of the 'popular will'. In other words, democracy, insofar as it is the direct or indirect expression of the 'popular will', is in fact the realization of the 'common good'. For, by definition, the 'common good' and the general will of the *demos* come to the same thing.

In the most radical version of the classical doctrine (which leads from Rousseau to Babeuf and then to Marx, the sovietism of Lenin, the workers' councils of Rosa Luxemburg, the 'self-government of the producers' in Gramsci and ends ideally in the Marxist theory of the withering away of the State) the amalgam of notions of democracy, popular will and common good is complete.[45] In Rousseau the metaphysical assumption of the irreducible, indivisible and unerring nature of the popular will leads to the denial of democratic legitimacy to any form of institutional delegation of power. Democratic power is identical with the direct and ever-present expression of the general will, which pre-exists any institutional exercise of power. Moreover this exercise of power is legitimate only in the form of a commissarial or imperative mandate and under the constraint of a public vote and submission to a final check. In accordance with these premisses, a political decision is the more democratic the closer the majority which passes it comes to unanimity, because at that point the coincidence between the will of each citizen and the will of the generality is at its height.

Democracy is therefore completely realized only when the will of individuals, in being adapted to political command, becomes aware that the *ratio* of the heteronomous general will coincides with the *ratio* of their own autonomous self-disciplining will. In these ideas the organicistic model of the ancient *polis* and the myth of the *Ekklesia* as the perfect realization of direct democracy[46] cast so powerful a spell that they actually overturn and annul the requirement of bourgeois individualism which animates Rousseau's political theorizing. Here also the circular structure of the (radical-)democratic utopia reveals itself in its true colours: in Rousseau political command loses all distinction and directionality because, as a result of this fiction of the direct coincidence between general will and individual will, the very agents of the power relationship are abolished, being absorbed in the absolute inclusivity and symmetry of the 'democratic' power relation. More than any other democratic utopian, Rousseau shows himself unable to see that the primary function of political power – i.e. that of ordering and protecting – is inseparable from the discriminatory and heteronomous nature of political command.[47]

In Marx too, both in his early criticism of Hegel's philosophy of public law and in his later acclamation of the Paris Commune, exposition of the antinomies of representative democracy leads, just as in Rousseau, to outright negation of the modern political code.[48] It leads to the idea that any political form other than the direct self-representation or self-government of the *demos* is a pure institutional formalism concealing the classist, bureaucratic and despotic nature of the modern state.[49] 'True democracy' for Marx meant the suppression, following the anarchic-Proudhonian model of the Paris Commune, of all stable bureaucratic and parliamentary structures. Administrative functions, without any distinction between legislative and executive power, should in part be discharged by officials elected by universal suffrage, directly responsible to those who elected them and recallable at any time; the remaining part (especially in areas such as justice, policing, military defence) should be entrusted to direct popular management.[50] His aim was clearly the removal of any separation between civil society and political State in accordance with a community ideal which in practice countered the process of differentiation in modern society with the organicism and universalistic conception of politics of classical and medieval times. Undoubtedly the anthropological idea behind this was the originally Aristotelian one of the 'total citizen', i.e. the denial in principle of any distinction between *bourgeois* and *citoyen*.

Engels and Lenin, for their part, took over a central aspect of Saint-Simon's apolitical and industrialist ideology and developed a theory of the 'withering away of the State' as the withering away of 'proletarian democracy'. For them the realization of communism meant the disappearance of man's power over man, democratic power included. All political functions would become superfluous and the state would wither away spontaneously when, once all forms of capitalist production had been suppressed and the social classes generated by it had disappeared, social development could be secured through simple process of 'the administration of goods and the direction of the processes of production'.[51]

For Lenin and the Soviet jurists of the 1930s, such as P. I. Stučka and E. B. Pašukanis, who drew on the theses of *State and Revolution*, the 'drowsiness' of the State meant a situation in which all citizens would spontaneously observe 'the elementary rules of social intercourse' without the need for any intervention from regulative and corrective structures.[52] This stage of universal self-discipline would be reached through processes of maximum socialization and an expansion of politics involving large masses of people in a continuous process of change and self-education. Representative procedures and the guarantees provided by a legal framework were the inheritance of bourgeois constitutionalism and would accordingly be set aside.

Engels's and Lenin's version of Saint-Simon's apolitical utopia was also shared by Gramsci, as his *Prison Notebooks* make clear. But he added to it a stronger instructional and organicistic emphasis. For him the socialist State would be an ideological instructor and would therefore have to show itself capable of the moral and physical moulding of new generations through the pedagogic use (involving encouragement as well as correction) of legal apparatuses and scholastic institutions.[53] Little by little, as the consensus and self-discipline of the citizens became established, the State and the law would gradually wither away, having come to the end of their functions, and so give way to the 'regulated society' or 'ethical State'. In this process the place of 'the divinity or the categorical imperative' in the consciousness of the citizens would be taken by the 'modern prince', i.e. the communist party, since 'any given act is seen as useful or harmful, as virtuous or as wicked, only in so far as it has as its point of reference the modern prince himself, and helps to strengthen or to oppose him'.[54]

The Soviet jurist A. V. Vyšhinskij, one of the most faithful interpreters of Stalin's wishes, highlighted the true nature of this regressive utopia when he used it as a basis to justify the need for 'a gigantic system of provisions designed to discipline the new socialist society and instruct it in the norms'. Only at the height, as he saw it, of a process of growing repression would the state be turned dialectically into its opposite, the communist society without law and without state. For at that point the citizens, long accustomed to compliance with socialist prescriptions, would have come to respect the rules of social coexistence without any need for prevention and penal coercion.[55]

As a result of this analysis it is possible for at least the following three general assumptions behind the radical-socialist model to be identified:[56]

1   The political system is conceived along Aristotelian lines as the one general social system which includes in itself all possible dimensions of experience. Political action is the condition of the rationality and morality of the citizens, and politics is an 'architectonic science' assigned to the moulding of every aspect of individual and social life according to an ideal of the 'good life' which reflects the rationality of a universal *nomos* and the objective order of the world. This means, in brief, a metaphysical conception epitomized by an organicistic and strongly expansive idea of politics.

2   It is assumed that the participation of the greatest possible number

of citizens in the decisional process is a moral good in itself. The reason for this, as John Stuart Mill also thought and as Carole Pateman continues to think,[57] is that political participation has an educationally beneficial effect on its practitioners. But also, above all else, political participation is the condition and guarantee of the realization of the 'common good', i.e. the affirmation of values connected with the original freedom, goodness and equality of human beings. Democracy, to the extent to which it is the political form through which the overcoming of the heteronomous nature of political command becomes possible, is the proof that power is a dispensable social function. A human community is therefore conceivable in which social relationships would no longer possess connotations of the exclusivity and asymmetry which belong to the political relationship.

3  The Enlightenment idea that civil progress and social emancipation will lead not to levels of greater complexity and specialization in social, political and economic relations, but to their progressive simplification, dominates all else. Marx early on outlined the idea of a society without division of labour, either social or technical. Lenin then argued that industrial societies, once freed from capitalism, would be able to reach such levels of transparency and simplicity that even a cook could discharge the role of head of state. The task of managing and controlling society, for which no special skills would be necessary, could then rotate among all citizens.

If this is, in all essential aspects, a plausible analysis of the political themes and philosophical assumptions which lie behind the radical-social-ist version of the 'classical doctrine', then there can surely be no doubt as to the limitation of its relevance to differentiated and complex societies of the post-industrial West. The model of social coexistence it presents is one based on the direct interaction between members of a group whose rationality, as Weber wrote, 'is intimately bound up with the hierarchic or patriarchal primitive community'.[58] This runs entirely counter to the assumptions and hypotheses behind the realistic view of the relationship between 'complexity and democracy', which I have so far attempted to set out.

Above all, the Aristotelian idea of the centrality, universality and total inclusivity of the political system seems to me wholly insupportable in the context of societies which are by no means elementary and undifferen-tiated – as was in fact never entirely the case even in Periclean Athens and was certainly not so in Geneva at the time of Rousseau. In modern societies, and especially in advanced industrial societies, the political system does not occupy a central position in the strategy of social repro-duction. Rather, it is a functional subsystem on the same level as others and carrying out functions which are differentiated from those of the other primary subsystems. Also, as we shall find, it is in large part afflicted by a certain looseness and by functional antinomies from which other subsystems – principally the scientific-technological one – appear to be entirely free.

Secondly I see the Aristotelian and Thomist idea of the 'common good' which Rousseau made so central to his thought – as indeed do many of our own latter-day Aristotelians – as a kind of ethico-metaphysical residue of the view based on the organicism and solidarity of the classical *polis* or medieval city. As Schumpeter has persuasively argued, the idea of the existence of a 'common good' as an object of popular will (and so as an essential postulate of participative democracy) presupposes that every normal adult citizen is able to see without difficulty what is good both for himself and for others. It also assumes (as Rawls, Apel and Habermas continue to do) that by means of reasoning, discussion and rational persuasion it is possible to arrive, if not exactly at a general political consensus, then at least at a moral agreement on the fundamental postulates of justice or of social equity.

This solidaristic notion of democracy implies furthermore the idea that all citizens, seeing what the 'common good' is, are directed towards its stable pursuit by virtue of their natural sense of justice. There is also implicitly present Rousseau's fiction of the natural coincidence, in a complete democracy, between the common good and the concrete expectations of social gratification possessed by each member of the political community. By definition, acceptance on the part of citizens of the requirements of the 'general interest' implies no conflict with their own particular interests. Where it does, they will normally be inclined to self-sacrifice. If, in exceptional circumstances, they are not, they will then be 'forced to be free'.

What this radical-democratic vision appears to me to lack most of all is a perception of the variety, particularism and mutual incompatibility of social expectations in non-elementary societies. It fails to consider the structurally scarce nature both of social resources and of the instruments of power responsible for the allocation of politically distributable resources. Social resources – security, ownership, prestige, money, power, time, inforation, etc. – are structurally scarce because they cannot satisfy corresponding expectations in absolute terms, according to cardinal values, but only in terms relative to the context of conditions appropriate to other agents or social groups. There is no stage therefore at which demand for a social benefit can be considered to have been met in full.

In reality politics belongs very much to the 'agonistic' sphere of disagreements, conflicts and antagonisms which cannot be removed by means of discussion and argument, still less by the standard of universal criteria of impartiality or of distributive justice. Insofar as exclusiveness and the asymmetry of power are the basic principles of the political code, no political system can, short of its own destruction, satisfy all expectations or give free rein to all competing points of view.[59] Faced with a multiplicity of conflicting social expectations, the political system makes imperative choices by virtue of pure decision. This decision is a political command precisely to the extent to which it is justified not by moral or rational criteria, but by contingent and opportunistic requirements of the stability of the system – *auctoritas, non veritas, facit legem*. It is clear, in sum, that the radical-democratic position clashes with the basic assumption of political realism, which is that political conflict may be mediated and neutralized, but not removed. And it may be neutralized not by logic, reason or justice, but by a power capable of 'absorbing fear' through the exercise of its protective functions, i.e. by producing order, security, stability and trust.[60]

Thirdly, I believe that Rousseau's equation and that of the radical socialist by which more participation is taken, absolutely, to mean more democracy, and vice versa, should be rejected without hesitation. In saying this I do not by any means espouse the opposite thesis, following Berelson or Lipset, that a certain substantial element of apathy and political non-participation is the best proof of the good functioning of a democratic regime.[61] But, to my mind, Rousseau's equation turns out, in conditions of intensified social complexity, to be an ideological formula which is not simply unrealizable, but also deeply counter-productive.

Once it is established that in modern societies the political subsystem is differentiated and specialized with regard to the other subsystems, then expansion of its functional range will, if it goes beyond certain limits, produce two types of dysfunction: dysfunctions within the political system itself and dysfunctions affecting the other primary subsystems.

The expansion and the socialization of the political system under normal conditions require a corresponding reduction in the centrality of decisions and the injection of a very large number of deciders into the decisional processes. Clearly, this can easily lead to an explosion in the length of time it takes for a political decision to be made, and can create forms of functional sluggishness and of power 'inflation'.[62] It can reduce to dangerously low levels the information available to the deciders, so diminishing their competence and responsibility, as well as introducing paralysing interdependencies between contrary and diffused powers of veto.[63] It can lead, finally, to phenomena indicative of the corporate fragmentation of decisions and the side-tracking of power into blind alleys.

Rather than increasing the stock of legitimacy enjoyed by the political system and involving large masses in processes of political socialization and self-education,[64] an excessive attempt to achieve democratic participation can instead induce widespread phenomena of frustration and a drop in political motivation as a result of the lack of gratification felt by the deciders when they participate in a hotchpotch of emasculated decisional processes.[65] It can also stimulate, instead of attitudes of solidarity, the unscrupulous pursuit of personal interest, which may well have the effect of leading to cynicism and political corruption, as is to be seen even in cases of democratic political militancy.[66]

As for the dysfunctions which affect the other primary subsystems – the economy, science, culture, information, the spheres of private life such as the emotions, free time, etc. – these can be calculated in terms of the time, energy and attention lost from other areas of experience, as well as in terms of the superimposition of diverse and mutually incompatible functional logics.[67] Obvious instances of this are the dysfunctions of an economy rigidly planned by an administrative authority, or the impoverishment of cultural life and scientific research brought about by political standardization, or the severe reduction of forms of spontaneous association caused by the presence of monolithic and expansive public apparatuses, or the suffocation of indigenous cultural traditions beneath the invasive cultural models brought in by mass-communication media. The totalitarian regimes of our time clearly provide many examples (e.g. Lysenkoism in the Soviet Union, the suppression of all intermediary groups by fascist regimes, the 'cultural revolution' in China, the monopoly of power of the communist party in the countries of Eastern Europe). But democratic regimes are by no means themselves immune, witness the dulling effects of television in the Western democracies and the excessive political power of religious organizations. Alongside such phenomena may also be placed the debilitating effects brought about by the excessive economic interventionism of the Welfare State in certain European countries, including Italy, to which political forces of both right and left have drawn attention in recent years.

Lastly it should be noted that it is from enlightenment culture and utopian socialism that democratic progressivism and historicism have drawn the idea that pluralism and complexity result from the disorder and anarchy of the capitalist system. From Saint-Simon to Engels, Weitling to Gramsci, Lenin to Vyshinskij, the democratic or socialist society of the future has been thought of as linear and 'transparent', the natural result of the final resolution of social conflict and the simplification of political institutions, administraive procedures and legal forms which inevitably follows from the abolition of the private ownership of the means of production. But, once it is recognized that modernization and the development of technological applications bring about phenomena of exactly the opposite type, then a theme emerges which is crucial to any philosophical and political thought on democracy. This is the necessity, not just of accommodating the claims of democracy with the need for 'the conservation of complexity', but of understanding the ways by which, within advanced industrial societies, the democratic requirement comes in the end to the same thing as the conservation of complexity and social differentiation on a political level.[68] It is easy to predict that no future political regime will be able to keep the 'promises of democracy' – to use Norberto Bobbio's well-found phrase[69] – if it is unable to equip itself with increasingly more complex and differentiated legal procedures and politico-administrative institutions, i.e. ones which are richer in specialized skills, more flexible, and prompt to react to the variability and growing interdependencies of the environment with reflexive strategies of self-correction and self-programming.

Under such circumstances, I think we may well doubt whether the model of direct democracy still preserves, in itself, any relevance at all to evolved societies, for all the sense of aristocratic nostalgia it continues to evoke in writers such as Leo Strauss, Hannah Arendt and, at least in part, Jürgen Habermas, for whom the *agora* still embodies the ideal of perfect political communication and the exercise of civil virtues. But this model, to my mind, will now not even serve as a simple regulative ideal for the development of progressive schemes for the participative or referendary strengthening of the strictly representative forms of parliamentary democracy.

In saying this, I have very much in mind theorists of the New Left in Britain and America such as Crawford Macpherson, Carole Pateman and Perry Anderson or, on the continent of Europe, the views expressed by Nicos Poulantzas or by Pietro Ingrao.[70] John Burnheim and Benjamin R. Barber also come to mind. With rationalistic optimism worthy of the best utopian tradition, these writers have recently developed alternative models of political theory whose concern with 'democracy by lot' and 'strong democracy'[71] ought perhaps to inject new life into the Western democracies. But it is unfortunately all too easy to see how such initiatives as these, notwithstanding the good intentions, ingenuity and, at times, astuteness which have gone into them, are most unlikely to remain anything more than academic exercises incapable ever of making the transition from paper to reality.

## The myth of political representation as 'adaptation'

In his critique of what he called the 'classical doctrine' of democracy, Schumpeter referred explicitly only to the classical conception of representative democracy. His main concern was to exclude the 'strong' meaning of political representation as an electoral procedure which facilitates the transmission and realization of the 'popular will'. At heart his aim was to show that the conception of representative democracy, in its strong sense, is just as rudimentary and unrealistic as the idea of participative democracy proposed by Rousseau.

For Schumpeter the idea that the wishes of individuals tend to converge towards a common 'popular will' and thereby attain to higher ethical and rational values was entirely without foundation. This belief he attributed to the founders of modern democratic theory and the moralism which arose from their naïve puritan and utilitarian faith. It was equally illusory, he thought, to imagine that members of elective assemblies – the political specialists – are disposed to act disinterestedly in order to realize the will of the people in the way that, for instance, a doctor works to realize his patient's wish to be cured.[72]

Consequently it only made sense within restricted communities with a very simple social structure to suppose the existence of a 'general will' which could be transmitted and 'represented' by deputies entrusted with the execution of collective decisions. As soon as a social group becomes numerically substantial, with its internal functions differentiated and more complex, the illusoriness of the representative scheme becomes apparent. The 'general will', he argued, then amounts to no more than the casual result of isolated individual volitions which lack either autonomy or rationality. For the average citizen is capable of only limited attention and an equally limited independence of mind. Often he or she is the prisoner of irrational preconceptions and is subject to vague and emotional impulses influenced by propaganda slogans and ambiguous impressions. Under normal circumstances they show none of the unity of mind and capacity for coherent planning which puritan moralism presupposes and which Freud's findings have in fact shown to be totally unfounded.[73] Not only are they little inclined to observe and interpret facts with objectivity and precision, but, as soon as they find themselves in a collective situation, their sense of responsibility seems to diminish, their level of intellectual energy drops, with the mind lying open to irrational suggestions.[74] This is most noticeable, by a kind of law of diminishing efficiency, when the citizen moves away from questions to do with family or profession and finds him- or herself confronted with the large-scale problems of national and international politics.[75]

Another difficulty Schumpeter found is that the political professionals tend to group themselves in a power elite and to locate themselves within a wider constellation of political, economic and professional groups motivated by quite different interests from those of the majority of average citizens. Political parties do not conform to the picture classical doctrine paints of them as groups of people anxious to advance the public good on the basis of principles approved by all. Rather, a party is an association whose members propose to act in concert in the competitive struggle for political power and who behave no differently from agents in the economic sphere when they seek to win or to control economic competition.[76] Parties and other economic or professional groups set out to use the means of pressure and propaganda manipulation at their disposal in order to model the popular will and even to create it in accordance with their own wishes. Despite the view of theorists of classical democracy, including even Jefferson and Lincoln, it has to be acknowledged that the people *qua* political agent is not capable of posing, or of deciding, any particular question.[77]

Of course it could be argued that these views of Schumpeter's, put in so broad and summary a manner, require more specific argumentation than he and his followers have given them. But it makes even less sense, to my mind, to claim that their content was purely 'mythological'. If the word myth is at all relevant, it should be applied not to Schumpeter's notion of a 'classical doctrine', but to Rousseau's theory of participative democracy and the Athenian archetype which lies behind it. Consequently, it should also be applied to what I intend to call the 'adaptation theory', by which I mean the theory which sees (and justifies) political representation in terms of an adjustment or up-dating of the Athenian model or, further still, as the combination of this model with elements progressively added from the classical republican tradition of Rome, the medieval Italian city-states and the Renaissance.[78] This theory has been advanced, with many different gradations of thought, by a long series of classic authors from Montesquieu to James Mill, John Stuart Mill, Bentham and Destutt de Tracy, and has still not relaxed its hold even on contemporary authors such as Hans Kelsen and Robert Dahl.[79]

According to Dahl, representation, although not originally a democratic institution, has become the essential element of modern democracy. It is the necessary result of the application of the principle of the equality of all citizens to modern political systems. The seventeenth- and eighteenth-century shapers of the liberal-democratic institutions of the nation-state were, he argues, perfectly aware that, for the logic of political equality to be applied to the changed historical conditions of their day, it was necessary for direct democracy to be transformed into representative democracy.[80]

The two reasons behind this were, he finds, the growth both of the territorial extent and of the population density of the nation-states compared with the *polis* or Italian communes. He is quick to point to the well-known fact that the population of Athens was numbered only in thousands, of whom only a small part effectively met in assembly, with women, slaves, metics, and perhaps other groups, excluded from citizenship.[81] In the light of this he expresses surprise that, in the course of the so-called 'democratic tradition' over the two millennia which separate the Athenian *ekklesia* from the English parliaments of the seventeenth century, the idea never surfaced that a legislative assembly could be constituted by elected representatives rather than the entire body of citizens.[82]

According to the 'adaptation theory', the institutions of political representation *indirectly* fulfil the same functions which were previously exercised by direct democracy in the context of the *polis*. The evident changes are owed to the fact that, for reasons of scale, the methods and forms of representation are *procedurally* different from the methods and forms of participation.[83] Meeting of the whole people in a deliberative assembly becomes physically impossible within political entities which are territorially and demographically extended. Moreover, the scope and complexity of administrative tasks within a modern state demand a wide network of political institutions which can only reduce the centrality of the popular assembly. Over-numerous assemblies would in any case find it impossible to discuss complex political problems and come up with rational, ordered and timely decisions. It becomes inevitable therefore that, rather than participate directly in deliberative bodies, a populace will carry out self-selection by entrusting a small number of its 'representatives' with the responsibility of meeting in an elective parliament. These elected members will be the people's 'representatives' in a sense not easily defined, but including the idea of a significant relationship (albeit falling short of perfect correspondence) between the wishes of the citizens and the wishes expressed by their representatives in parliament. The extent of this correspondence will be an accurate indication of the democratic nature of electoral systems and of elected assembles.

In the mid-1950s this thesis was reiterated by even so disenchanted and formalistic a theorist of democracy as Hans Kelsen, whose allegiance was in other respects closer to the 'neo-classical' school. In direct criticism of Schumpeter, he found the most democratic type of election to be based on proportional representation, since this offers 'the greatest possible approximation to the ideal of popular self-determination within a representative democracy'.[84] For him competition for the popular vote was, if anything, a wholly secondary aspect of democracy, for:

The primary criterion of democracy is that the power of government is with the people. In a direct democracy there are no elections at all. If the people cannot or will not exercise this power directly, they may delegate it by free election to representatives and thus, instead of governing themselves, create a government. Hence free election and its consequence, the competitive struggle for the people's vote, is a secondary criterion. Only by reversing the relationship between the two criteria and making the creation of a government by free election the primary criterion can democracy be defined as government established by competition. But such reversion is inconsistent with the essence of democracy.[85]

In my own view it should be stated quite clearly that this doctrine of political representation as an adaptation of assembly-democracy not only confirms the validity of Schumpeter's notion of a 'classic doctrine of democracy', but also justifies the criticism he made of it – that it is both elementary and unrealistic. It takes no account of the historical precedents (which are medieval and not classical) behind modern forms of electoral representation or of the effective functions which electoral procedures and parliamentary institutions have gradually come to exercise in the course of the long process of development of the liberal-democratic State.

There are, to my mind, three lines of argument in support of this idea that the adaptation theory is both elementary and unrealistic.

1 Principally there is the historical argument. Representation has no connection with the political institutions of antiquity. The institution of representation, unknown either in the Greek *polis* or in republican and imperial Rome, emerged in the late middle ages, especially in England and Sweden, with distinct characteristics of a corporative and organic nature. Medieval representation was based on the assumption that the political agents summoned to a solemn audience of the king – high-ranking lay and ecclesiastical dignitaries, the lower nobility and lower clergy, villages, towns, etc. – either were in a position to represent themselves or else should have themselves represented by others. In the latter case the representatives stood for their communities by virtue of personal prerogatives which owed nothing to any formal conferral of authority on the part of those they represented. The mechanisms of designation were principally those of co-option, inheritance or nomination from above.

The typical function of medieval representation was to give authorization to the actions not only of those able to represent themselves, such as the higher nobility and higher clergy, but also of those acting in the name and interests of those whose inability to act for themselves was taken for granted. The institution required the authority of the representative to be recognized (exclusively) by the one holding the power to call the assembly, even though this could naturally not rule out that the representative might bring demands, and even protests, from the collective body he represented. Nor did it rule out that in some cases his mandate might be fully 'imperative' rather than of an open fiduciary type.

In addition, the representative roles within the medieval political assembly were conceived of as the stones in a mosaic which reproduced organically the interests and social conditions of the various classes which made up the world of the people. The right to be represented did not therefore belong to single individuals, but only to towns, classes, corporations, collegiate bodies and so forth.[86] These collective agents aimed to use the institution of representation to defend their own interests and autonomy against the centralist pressure and incursions of monarchial power. Nothing could be further than this from the model of market-place democracy based on the *isegoria* (equal right to speak in the assembly) and *isonomia* (equality before the law) of all individual members, as such, of the *demos*.

Once, then, the process of electoral and parliamentary formalization of the modern state is shorn of the doctrinal colouring given to it by theorists of representative democracy, it emerges quite clearly that the puritan, bourgeois and proprietarial origins of the institutions of representation were signalized far more by medieval corporative logic than by any of the universalist aspirations of the natural law and contractualist schools. This is evident in the constitutionary history of England, a history which was to have a decisive influence on the representative constitutions of both the old and the new world, especially of Australia and New Zealand.

In practice, as Marx was early to appreciate,[87] modern representation functions as an instrument for the formalization and autonomization of the political system thanks to an institutional mechanism which works on two levels: first, the fragmentation of the *demos* via an electoral procedure which presupposes the individual sovereignty of each voter (and this, in the context of the growing differentiation of individuals, was beyond doubt the real innovation of the bourgeois revolutions), and second, the successive recomposition of assemblies of representatives in the form of organic bodies of the State. In just the same way as in medieval representation, the legitimacy of the parliamentary organ depends much less on a popular investiture or on the relations of individual representatives with their electors than on their assumption of power (within the sphere of the powers of the State) in the service of the general interest of the country.

Bourgeois parliaments do not arise in order to represent the people in any sense approaching that of the classical *agora*, i.e. to provide a general instrument, however indirect, of self-government. They arise in order to protect the autonomy of the civil society and its individual members from the 'protective' invasion of political power. Their job is to limit the executive power of the monarchy by imposing respect for the interests presented by the members of a particular stratum of the citizens, i.e. the holders of 'active citizenship' identified essentially on the basis of property and wealth. Members of the English parliament, for example, saw themselves as so much of a privileged class that for a large part of the nineteenth century the work of parliament was conducted under close secrecy with severe fines imposed on writers or journalists who dared to breach it.

Furthermore, parliament represents much less the interests and will of individual members of the bourgeoisie than the interests and general will of a countrywide bourgeois class concerned to emancipate itself from the hegemony of the old classes linked to the Crown. It may well be doubted, with Weber, whether the subsequent introduction of universal suffrage really succeeds in changing, at any deep level, the original 'oligarchic-corporative' structure of bourgeois parliaments or in involving them in a process of 'democratization' or popular diffusion of power. Extension of suffrage has probably only led to a modification of the selection procedures of political elites, aiding the process of the transformation of bourgeois democracy into modern party democracy.[88]

2 Second, there is a consideration of a functional kind. Political representation preserves only a vague analogy with the classical institution, originating in Roman private law, of legal representation.[89] In particular the relationship between representatives and represented entails no precise form of political – and still less legal – responsibility of the former for the latter. The latter have no control over the actions of their representatives on the basis of any requirement for them to render account, nor can they recall them or apply for any form of redress in cases where they have not acted correctly or in furtherance of the tasks they have undertaken or the promises they have made. Citizens can only attempt to avoid the same error in future by entrusting themselves to other (equally uncontrollable) representatives. Alternatively they can refuse to participate in the representation procedure, even if they will not by these means escape being represented altogether.

It is significant how quickly theorists of democratic representation, such as Burke and Siéyès, have asserted the incompatibility of parliamentary functions with any form of imperative mandate and how this negation has since become a fundamental rule of liberal-democratic constitutions.[90] In practice, political representatives become responsible not to their own electors, but to the nation or, rather, to public opinion, which expresses the general interests of the nation. Public opinion, as we shall find, means the rational opinion which emerges from the civil society and does not therefore mean the same as the opinion of particular groups of voters or the opinion of the electorate globally considered.[91]

The nation's general interest requires that delegates refuse to follow any kind of sectional interest. They therefore hold a general open mandate which carries no requirement that they should account to any particular mandator. The essence of representation does not reside, then, in any handing over of power, but rather in the ability of the deputy to interpret and protect the interests and views of the nation. Only those who show that they possess these qualities can become *partners* in a fiduciary relationship which involves, as Montesquieu maintained in *Esprit des lois*, a precise 'designation of ability'. This is an ability which, according to Burke, Kant and Constant, a calls for intellectual and moral gifts which may only be obtained under conditions of private property.

When seen in this manner, it is clear that the electoral function is not that of giving a mandate to representatives, but that of appointing certain agents to a general and autonomous political function. The electoral procedure does not properly involve the notion either of popular sovereignty or of representation, even in its weakest sense. The mechanism of election is the formalized procedure for the constitution of an organ of the State and, at the same time, the specific form of its legitimization on the basis of the participation of a large number of citizens in the appointment of its members. It differs from other procedures for the creation of state organs by the particular complexity of the process and by the fact that, unlike the handing over of power through bureaucratic co-option, the organ created by this election takes precedence over the organs which have contributed to its creation.[92]

3    Lastly there is a sociological aspect which has been given prominence especially by Max Weber and, following him, by Hans Kelsen.[93] From a sociological standpoint, modern democracy is a system of producing universally binding commands which entrusts the task of producing these commands to one specific organ, the parliament. The mechanism of election has the simple purpose of applying to the political system the general criterion of the division of labour in that it demands of a body of specialists – the politicians by profession – a function which requires high professional abilities and which works according to the specific logic of the 'parliamentary dialectic'. Parliamentarism expresses itself through the criterion of the majority vote and various forms of relation and interaction between majority and minority, including the 'parliamentary compromise'. Parliament functions also as a mechanism for the selection of political

leaders, and provides their training and advancement on a career in government. Thus it is a state organ for the expression of autonomous acts of will and the playing of specific functions which have little in common with the idea of an assembly which 'represents' the will of the people. For these reasons Schumpeter even argues that any attempt to influence members of parliament and to infringe their freedom of action by means of pressure from below – for instance by sending them letters or telegrams – should be rigorously proscribed as being an attack on the rationale of the division of labour in the political sphere. Parliament, Kelsen affirms, represents the people in just the same way as, according to monarchic theory, the person of the hereditary sovereign or his/her nominees used to 'represent' the people, country or State. The will of parliament takes the place of the will, institutionally presumed to exist, of the 'sovereign people'. The doctrine of popular sovereignty serves only as a 'totemic mask'.[94] For Kelsen democratic parliamentarianism means universal suffrage, the existence of a plurality of parties, the principle of majority decision and – antinomic residuum of the classical idea of representation – the system of election by proportional representation.

What the attributes and functions of a democratic parliament should be or, in other words, what the relation should be between representation and democracy, has become one of the central themes for over two centuries now in the debate in political theory on the institutions of the modern state. It is interesting to see how, in the course of the long and laborious process of transition from the classical-liberal State to the various forms of liberal democracy and then of social democracy and of the social State, the connection between representation and democracy has received increasingly weaker interpretations. The more suffrage has been extended so as to become 'universal', the more have liberal-democratic theorists become aware of the need progressively to attenuate the 'representative' link between the preferences of the electorate and the decisions of elective assemblies. The interpretations of both Kelsen and Schumpeter, each influenced by Weber, may well be considered the last chapter in this process. Going well beyond the negation of the 'imperative mandate' found in the first theorists of liberal democracy, Kelsen and Schumpeter both refuse to accept a connection of any kind between 'the fiction of representation' and the democratic method.

In the end, as we shall see in chapter 4, the political system within the pluralistic-corporative structure of advanced industrial societies attempts to recover yet more plainly the features of medieval representation through the complete neutralization of the individualistic and universalist presuppositions of classical democratic theory. According to Norberto

Bobbio, one of the 'unkept promises' of representative democracy is precisely this prevalence of the representation of interests over political representation, extending over and beyond electoral procedures and parliamentary institutions.[95]

## The 'neo-classical' doctrine of democracy

In place of the classical doctrine of democracy, Schumpeter proposed, as is well known, 'another theory of democracy'. His aim in doing this was to translate the requirements of the democratic tradition into realistic terms and to adapt the tradition to the levels of complexity and differentiation which had been reached by modern societies. According to his reformulation, democracy could not be defined as a political regime which allows its citizens to participate, directly or indirectly, in the determination of political questions and to control the activity of the rulers.[96] In enlarged communities of complex structure, participation, representation and, beyond a certain stage, even political control are illusory aspirations.[97] Democracy is more simply a 'method' which involves citizens in the formal process of designating agents who will determine political questions.

The position which Schumpeter assigned to the voters, therefore, shares many of the characteristics of the institution of medieval representation. The citizens' role is to contribute to the designation of authoritative agents who will 'represent' them in exactly the medieval sense that decisions taken by the representatives are ascribed to a collective agent, the people, which is assumed to be incapable of self-representation. For Schumpeter, democracy was therefore a procedural stratagem to provide for the fact that within evolved and differentiated societies the people, although formally designated as the holder of political sovereignty, is not in fact able to exercise it. The democratic method is a nexus of procedures and institutions which allows popular sovereignty to express itself in the only manner in which it is capable, that is, by co-operating in the production of a government and, by extension, of political decisions. This production is 'democratic', Schumpeter argued, because the conferral of power upon certain individuals takes place through 'a competitive struggle for the people's vote'.[98]

The prime elements of Shumpeter's reformulation of the concept of democracy can perhaps be expressed analytically under the following three headings:

1   In order to define a political regime as democratic, it is necessary to consider not the values it protects and the objectives it pursues, but solely the procedures of the 'production of government' which lead to the

realization of certain objectives and values. The democratic method is therefore at root compatible with any objective and with any value.[99]

2   In democratic, as opposed to autocratic or despotic, regimes the production of government takes place through a competitive struggle.

3   This struggle is aimed at winning the people's vote and is decided by an election.

But the following further points emerge with equal clarity, even though Schumpeter's formulation of them is not wholly explicit and is in some cases marred by evident inconsistencies:

1   The democratic method is preferred by Schumpeter, despite the epistemological assumption of its mere 'procedurality', because to his mind it subordinates all other political objectives – especially administrative efficiency – to the single value of individual liberty. The link between democracy and freedom, he declared, though not rigorous, is still extremely important: a lower level of efficiency in government is distinctly preferable to 'dictatorial efficiency', especially from the standpoint of the 'intellectual'.[100]

2   Competition for the vote implies the existence of a plurality of groups interested in winning political leadership. It supposes a situation of social and political pluralism, but does not identify itself exclusively with this. Democracy not only involves the freedom of every political group to formulate its own programmes and to compete for the vote, but also implies an effective rivalry between political alternatives which are submitted to the people's judgement. The need for each group to submit to competition for the winning of political leadership is the essential element which distinguishes the democratic from the despotic regime.[101]

3   Not all types of competition are compatible with the democratic method. A competition is democratic only when it is a 'free competition for a free vote'.[102] Evidently this implies that the contestants will renounce violence and the use of armed force. But the fact that in a democracy all groups are free to announce their candidature for political command means above all that there will be a conspicuous level of freedom of speech for all and, in particular, a wide freedom of the press.[103]

4   In a democratic regime, just as in any other, the leadership function plays a primary role. Political groups act almost exclusively by expressing or taking on leadership. It is up to the leaders, and not the masses, to be the protagonists in democratic life because it is their actions which determine whether latent collective expectations will be transformed into instruments of political action, according to whether or not they are included in the political bid launched against competitors in the 'political market'.

For Schumpeter there were no proofs of a general and absolute validity either for or against democracy, but there were simply social conditions and contingent reasons of a practical nature which both make democracy expedient and guarantee its success. In the extended and highly differentiated societies of the capitalist West, the democratic method is preferable to others because it is the instrument best adapted to the regulation of the relationships of competition between the political elites who aspire to command. It is also preferable because it aims to regulate the political market, using criteria analogous to those which govern the relations between entrepreneurs and consumers in a freely competitive economic market.

Just as there are no alternatives to the capitalist market in conditions where the aim is to achieve rational regulation of the flow of economic resources within differentiated and complex societies, so too there are no alternatives to the democratic method when the objective is one of 'producing a government' compatible with a high level of differentiation of the political system and of freedom of the citizens. This is the reason why the democratic method remains preferable despite its limited administrative efficiency, the inadequate technical competence of the political personnel it is normally able to select, and, above all, the enormous wastage of resources brought about by its open and competitive nature.

It is clear from this that Schumpeter came nowhere near his avowed aim of achieving a pure empirical analysis of politics, rigorously *wertfrei* in respect of its object of study. Schumpeter's 'empirical theory of democracy', lovingly handed on in recent decades by 'neo-classical' political scientists,[104] turns out to be no more than an epistemological fiction. It is in no way the product which had been hoped for of a rigorous inductive conceptualization of the 'facts', with its theoretical statements susceptible to equally rigorous empirical verification. Sartori affirms that Schumpeter has quite simply defined 'the necessary and sufficient conditions' of a purely descriptive theory of democracy.[105] If one followed his example, democracy could be straightforwardly defined in purely descriptive terms, and its system of technical rules and formal procedures could be kept distinct from the evaluative and prescriptive areas belonging to political ideology. But, as we have already established in broad terms in chapter 2, this neo-positivist claim is nowadays shown to lack any epistemological foundation.

Schumpeter's view of democracy as competitive leadership has, as is well recognized, given rise to an entire school of thought and has deeply influenced what in the West has been understood for the last forty years by the term democracy. The main features of Schumpeter's model provide the prototype of what I have called the 'neo-classical paradigm' of pluralistic democracy as elaborated by authors such as Nelson Polsby, William Kornhauser, Raymond Aron, Giovanni Sartori, Ralf Dahrendorf and, especially, Robert Dahl.[106] It may well be said that this paradigm now plays the leading role in Western political philosophy, having substantially ousted the models of classical democracy, above all the radical-socialist one.

The leading characteristic of the neo-classical school, which has led its enemies to call it 'democratic elitism', is the attempt to avoid any contradistinction between elitist theses and the classical-democratic tradition.[107] For writers such as Mosca, Michels and Pareto elitism was a realistic and conservative (even at times openly authoritarian and anti-democratic) rejoinder to radical-democratic and socialist progressivism, but for exponents of the neo-classical school the function of elites seems to have become far from something opposed to democracy, but rather its primary content. In Dahl, and still more in Aron and Sartori, democracy is identified with the indispensible function of 'representation' which political elites are called upon to exercise in competition with one another.[108] Democracy is not different from despotism because it is a 'government by a majority': rather, Dahl argues, democracy is a 'government of the minorities', which is quite different from the government of a (single) minority.[109] This point of view has found its most succinct and emblematical expression in Sartori's definition of democracy as 'a system based on the fictitious will of the majority and in fact devised and sustained by a minority government' and his argument that 'it is not possible to force initiative on the large number of those who find it easier and more restful to be carried along in tow'.[110]

In analytical terms the neo-classical paradigm may be said to rest on the following three conceptual axioms:

1   A democratic regime distinguishes itself from non-democratic regimes through the pluralistic and competitive nature of the (electoral) procedure for access to political power.

2   Democracy does not lead either to extensive participation by citizens in the decisional process[111] or to their 'representation' (in any sense other than the organico-corporative one of medieval assemblies).

3   Democracy is a by-product of electoral competition between minorities, in the sense that the procedural demands of competition entail a high degree of freedom of speech and freedom of the press, and force contestants to take account of the condition of the political market in presenting their own offerings to the public.[112] Political entrepreneurs act in just the same way as economic entrepreneurs who, although they are in no sense representatives of the consumers, often being, on the contrary, the mouthpiece of opposite interests, are compelled by the logic of competition to take account of the demands which emerge from the market. Dahl defines democracy as the 'system of decision-making in which leaders

are more or less responsible to the preferences of non-leaders'.[113] The concept of the 'responsiveness' of the complex of public decisions to the expectations of the political consumers is central:[114] only in this very weak sense is democracy a political system based on the consensus of the citizens.[115]

From these three basic axioms, the neo-classical school draws at least the following corollaries:

1   In modern (extended, differentiated and complex) societies, democracy entails no form of political equality which goes beyond the holding of political rights, i.e. of citizenship in a legal sense;[116] it requires only the formal equality of adult citizens and their freedom to vote and to compete for elective offices.[117]

2   Representative assemblies, including parliament, are organs of the State which do not differ from other organs of power except in the particular procedure for their constitution and legitimation, which allows for the intervention of a large number of agents who are not hierarchically superior to the organ which is to be constituted.

3   The political system is a structure, analogous to that of the economic market, within the organism of the social division of labour. The function of parliament is of a substitutive kind in the sense that its members perform a task for which the other citizens have not the time, the ability or the desire. It therefore calls for professional specialization and interests specific to the political persons who form a differentiated 'political class'.[118]

4   The need for pluralism and competition between political groups is not contradicted by the oligarchic character of the structures within those groups. In the political market, just as in the economic market, competition between oligarchic groups produces a result which is not oligarchic, but pluralistic. Dahl has argued against Michels that inter-party competition, despite non-democratic organization within the parties, ensures that 'the rulers' political decisions give a timely response to the preferences of the majority of the voters'.[119] Democracy, Schattschneider adds, does not consist *in* the parties, but *between* the parties.[120]

5   The request for proportional representation in voting systems is compatible only with a classical view of the function of elective assemblies.[121] The competitive view of democracy sees the true function of the vote as being the acceptance of a leadership, not the reproduction on the level of the elective assembly of the profile of the voters' differing interests and opinions. The majority system is therefore preferable, in that it introduces an element of efficiency into a system which is in other respects only scantily efficient.

Given these elements, the neo-classical model of democracy as competitive leadership is found to contain, alongside its distinct merits of clarity and realism, aspects of theoretical inconsistency and analytical weakness which render it unsuitable in my view for understanding the effective conditions under which democratic regimes function in modern complex societies of the post-industrial period.

By taking economic competition as an explanatory metaphor of the democratic process, the neo-classical theorists implicitly commit themselves to an evaluation which commends the general rationality of the mechanisms of the market. For it is clear that democracy can be thought of as a by-product of the political market only on condition that this market operates with an effective freedom of choice for the 'political consumers' and as a furtherance of their preferences. The political market must function as a mechanism for the utilization of (political) resources and the distribution of (political) goods capable of achieving a satisfactory, if not exactly optimal, balance between the interests of the 'political producers' and of the 'political consumers'. It has to be assumed therefore that the pluralism of elites provides the opportunity for effective political competition and effective differentiation of the offerings made by the political parties, because it is precisely in this respect that the rationality of the market counters the irrationality of oligopoly or monopoly. The very sovereignty of the political consumer and the democratic responsiveness of the complex of political decisions to the expectations of the public in fact depends in large measure on the accuracy with which the political producers respect the market's rules and play their parts within them.

Secondly, a specific rationality has to be assumed on the part of the political consumer, who has to be credited with the ability to evaluate the offerings of the market and to make a choice between them with a view to his own particular preferenes. The neo-classical theory envisages a model of the political market whose overall rationality continues to depend on the rationality (i.e. the intellectual and moral autonomy) of the individual voters, and not simply on their 'negative liberty', understood as the absence of external physical constraints.[122] Schumpeter's insistence on the liberty of the press and on 'freedom of expression for all' as necessary implications of democracy seems to refer to the need for the autonomous and rational political persuasion of citizens. Despite his critique of the metaphysical assumptions behind the classical doctrine and despite his censure of the shortfalls of information, will-power and political responsibility possessed by the average citizen, the neo-classical model continues to grant a decisive role to the undifferentiated public of electors who have the job of pronouncing on the attribution of political leadership.

Thus a number of elements in neo-classical theory must be considered instances of a mere *non sequitur*, such as Schumpeter's open admission that political entrepreneurs, just like economic ones, have the ability to break the rules of the game by operating forms of covert or fraudulent competition,[123] or his pessimism over the real differentiation of offerings contained in parties' manifestos and their fidelity to them,[124] or his candid admission that a decisive role in influencing voters' choices is played by the psychological techniques used by parties in their political propaganda.[125]

Here there is a kind of excess of practical realism in Schumpeter which surmounts and contradicts the theoretical realism of his definition of democracy, which thereby ends by appearing paradoxically elementary and utopian. Schumpeter and the neo-classical theorists are not wrong, as I see it, to argue that an unbiased examination results in the classical notions of participation, representation and popular control appearing unrealistic and elementary. For myself, I have no doubts on the absolute unsuitability of democratic procedures for reducing economic and social disparities and I believe that 'representative' functions have a place in the processes of the division of labour and of functional differentiation which are characteristic of modern societies. I am also convinced that pro-portional representation voting systems are less compatible than majority or mixed systems with the need for an increase in 'positive power', a need which has become dramatically urgent in modern 'risk societies' of heightened complexity. I believe also, and shall attempt to show in chapter 4, that the relationship between democracy and the party system is now-adays beset by extreme problems.

But if, to pursue this line further, we admit that the functioning of the representative institutions in post-industrial societies operates according to rules which are incompatible with those of free pluralistic competition, that a large part of political power is exercised within invisible circuits removed from any logic of the market, that citizens are at the mercy of uncontrollable forces, that they are subject to apathy and lack of infor-mation and responsibility, and are incapable of self-motivation, even if they are physically and legally free, then it would be licit to ask ourselves wherein lies the difference, if it is not at root at least contingent and prag-matic, between democratic elitism and elitism *tout court*, or else between democracy and its opposite. It would in the end no longer be clear in what resides the 'freedom for all' and the 'responsiveness' to citizens' political demands that competition is presumed to impose as democratic side-effects on the will for power of groups struggling for political command. It would be reasonable for us to ask, finally, what reasons there could be to make us prefer this type of democracy to its overtly non-democratic (but indeed more efficient and reassuring) variants. From the standpoint of the relationship between complexity and democracy, it is precisely here, in this deep *aporia* of Schumpeterian political realism, that the need arises, as I see it, for a reconstruction of democratic theory.

# Notes

1  By 'complex' I here mean 'adequate to the complexity of the environment' from a cognitive, adaptive and projectual standpoint.

2  By 'revisionist' I mean, along with John Plamenatz (*Democracy and Illusion*, London: Longman, 1973, p. ix) and Crawford Macpherson (*Democratic Theory: Essays in Retrieval*, Oxford: Oxford University Press, 1973, p. 78), versions of democratic theory belonging to the 'Schumpeter–Dahl axis'. Cf. also H. S. Kariel (ed.), *Frontiers of Democratic Theory*, New York: Random House, 1970 pp. 31–94.

3  I draw the expression from Nicola Matteucci's work on Machiavelli's demonstration in *Il Principe* of the 'severity of politics'; cf. N. Matteucci, *Alla ricerca dell'ordine politico*, pp. 57–65.

4  Cf. D. Held, *Models of Democracy*, pp. 186–201.

5  Cf. N. Bobbio, 'La crisi della democrazia e la lezione dei classici', in N. Bobbio, G. Pontara and S. Veca, *Crisi della democrazia e neocontrattualismo*, Rome: Editori Riuniti, 1985, pp. 15–16.

6  This is the strategy normally adopted both in the exercise of paternal and patriarchal authority and in the exercise of paternalistic and patriarchal political power.

7  See G. Schwab, *The Challenge of the Exception*, Berlin: Dunker and Humblot, 1970.

8  My reference here is predominantly to the most famous pages of Hobbes's *Leviathan*: ch. 13 of the first part and ch. 17 of the second part; cf. T. Hobbes, *Leviathan*, Parts I and II, ed. H. W. Scheider, Indianapolis (Inf.): The Library of Liberal Arts, 1982, pp. 104–9, 130–60.

9  With less penetration, on the other hand, Montesquieu opposes 'virtue', envisaged as the principle of democracy, to 'fear', envisaged as the principle of despotism; cf. N. Bobbio, *Il futuro della democrazia*, Eng. trans., p. 35.

10  N. Machiavelli, *Il Principe*, VII, Eng. trans., p. 26.

11  Ibid., Eng. trans., p. 26: 'This terrible spectacle left the people both satisfied and amazed' is Machiavelli's final comment; Machiavelli explicitly refers to the relationship between politics and fear in ch. XVII of *Il Principe*, Eng. trans., p. 59.

12  The surprisingly delayed and inflated character of the contemporary success of the democratic model is stressed by many authors; cf. e.g.: C. B. Macpherson, *The Real World of Democracy*, Oxford: Clarendon Press, 1966, p. 1; D. Held, *Models of Democracy*, pp. 1–9.

13  Cf. G. Sartori, *The Theory of Democracy Revisited*, p. xiii.

14  See e.g. J. G. A. Pocock, *The Machiavellian Moment: Florentine Political Thought and the Atlantic Republican Tradition*, Princeton (N.J.): Princeton University Press, 1975.

15  Cf. e.g. A. Arblaster, *Democracy*, Milton Keynes (Bucks.): Open University Press, 1987, pp. 13–25. Arblaster explicitly states that democracy begins in Athens and 're-emerges', after two millennia, with the movement of Diggers and Levellers in seventeenth-century Great Britain.

16   On the distance which separates the modern bourgeois conception of politics
     from the communitarian *pathos* of the Greek *polis* and the Italian city-state
     see C. Meier, *Die Entstehung des Politischen bei den Griechen*, Frankfurt
     a.M.: Suhrkamp Verlag, 1980.
17   See M. Riedel (ed.), *Rehabilitierung der praktischen Philosophie*, Freiburg:
     Rombach, 1972–1974.
18   Cf. D. Held, *Models of Democracy*, pp. 13–35.
19   This thesis appears as the central structure of Robert Dahl's latest book: in
     his view democracy has developed from ancient Greece to the present by
     virtue of successive transformations. For him, the third and final trans-
     formation might lead from simple polyarchy to 'polyarchy I' and 'polyarchy
     II', namely to higher levels of political participation; cf. R. Dahl, *Democracy
     and Its Critics*, pp. 13–33, 213–24, 311–41.
20   Cf. N. Bobbio, *Quale socialismo?*, Turin: Einaudi, 1976, Eng. trans. Cam-
     bridge: Polity Press, 1987, p. 74: 'Democracy is subversive in the most radical
     sense of the word, because, wherever it spreads, it subverts the traditional
     conception of power, one so traditional it has come to be considered natural,
     based on the assumption that power – i.e. political or economic, paternal or
     sacerdotal – flows downward'.
21   I share, at least from this point of view, Talmon's commendable thesis;
     see J. L. Talmon, *The Origins of Totalitarian Democracy*, Boulder (Colo.):
     Westview Press, 1985.
22   Cf. J. Plamenatz, *Democracy and Illusion*, pp. 52–93; R. Dahl, *Democracy
     and Its Critics*, pp. 265–79.
23   Cf. R. Aron, *Democracy and Totalitarianism*, London: Weidenfeld and
     Nicolson, 1965, pp. 81–94; D. Beetham, *Max Weber and the Theory of
     Modern Politics*, Cambridge: Polity Press, 1985, pp. 102–112.
24   On 'civil society' cf. N. Bobbio, 'Sulla nozione di "società civile"', *De
     Homine*, 7 (1968), 24–5 19–36; id., *Stato, governo, società*, Turin: Einaudi,
     1985, pp. 23–42; my *La teoria comunista dell'estinzione dello Stato*, pp. 86–
     9, is also relevant.
25   See B. Constant, *De la liberté chez les modernes: écrits politiques*, ed. M.
     Gauchet, Paris: Le livre de poche, 1980; S. Holmes, *Benjamin Constant and
     the Making of Modern Liberalism*, New Haven (Conn.): Yale University
     Press, 1984.
26   Cf. N. Luhmann, *Soziologische Aufklärung*, I. 154–77.
27   The 'protective' function of the 'democratic franchise' identified by the
     first liberal-democratic and utilitarian thinkers – James Madison, Jeremy
     Bentham and James Mill – has been stressed by Crawford Macpherson and,
     following him, by David Held; cf. C. B. Macpherson. *The Life and Times of
     Liberal Democracy*, Oxford: Oxford University Press, 1977, pp. 23–43; D.
     Held, *Models of Democracy*, pp. 60–71.
28   The development of bourgeois society breaks through the constraints of the
     organicistic and protective structure of the medieval city. Marx, for instance,
     stressed that the social condition of hired workers within capitalist society

is much less protected in comparison with the situation of feudal serfs, and even of ancient slaves.

29  Cf. N. Bobbio, *Quale socialismo?*, Eng. trans., p. 75.

30  'Today, in politics, democracy is the *name* for what we cannot have – yet cannot cease to want'; cf. J. Dunn, *Western Political Theory in the Face of the Future*, Cambridge: Cambridge University Press, 1979, p. 27.

31  Cf. A. Gehlen, *Die Seele im technischen Zeitalter*, Eng. trans., pp. 73–91.

32  On the relationship between democracy and feminism see C. Pateman, 'Feminism and Democracy' in G. Duncan (ed.), *Democratic Theory and Practice*, pp. 204–17; cf. D. Held, *Models of Democracy*, pp. 79–85, 97–100, and see also the recent contribution of S. Rowbotham, 'Feminism and Democracy', in D. Held and C. Pollitt (eds), *New Forms of Democracy*, London: Sage Publications, 1986, pp. 78–109.

33  On the increasing feeling of insecurity which goes hand in hand with the growth of complexity within post-industrial societies and on the connected political expectation of 'psychic reassurance' see the interesting analyses of Californian society in T. R. La Porte and C. J. Abrams, 'Alternative Patterns of Postindustria: The Californian Experience', in L. N. Lindberg (ed.), *Politics and the Future of Industrial Society*, New York: David McKay, 1976, particularly pp. 37, 40–8; cf. also T. R. La Porte, 'Complexity and Uncertainty: Challenge to Action', in T. R. Laporte (ed.), *Organized Social Complexity*, ch. 10.

34  Cf. C. Offe and U. K. Preuss, 'Democratic Institutions and Moral Resources', Zentrum für Sozialpolitik, Universität Bremen, Working paper No. 5, 1990, pp. 4, 31.

35  See J.-F. Lyotard, *La condition postmoderne*, Paris: Les Éditions de Minuit, 1979, Eng. trans. Manchester: Manchester University Press, 1984; J.-F. Lyotard, *Le différend*, Paris: Les Éditions de Minuit, 1983.

36  By 'positive power' I mean the power of doing, constructing, and planning with the aim of 'solving problems'. It is analytically distinguished from 'negative power' which consists of prohibiting, preventing, repressing.

37  On the future of democracy see my debate with Niklas Luhmann: D. Zolo, 'Il futuro della democrazia: domande a Niklas Luhmann', *Il Mulino*, 36 (1986), 6 565–72; N. Luhmann, 'Il futuro della democrazia: delusioni e speranze', ibid. 573–83.

38  See A. MacIntyre, *After Virtue*, London: Duckworth, 1981.

39  The question of spontaneous social initiatives (*die Bürgerinitiativen*) as possible alternatives to representative party democracy (*repräsentative Parteiendemokratie*) has been widely discussed within German political philosophy; see B. Guggenberger and U. Kempf (eds), *Bürgerinitiativen und repräsentatives System*, Opladen: Westdeutscher Verlag, 1978.

40  G. Roth and D. Held stress the dependence of Schumpeter's concept of democracy as 'competitive leadership' on Weber's notion of 'plebiscitarian leadership democracy'; cf. G. Roth, 'Introduction' to M. Weber, *Economy and Society*, 2 vols, Berkeley (Calif.): University of California Press, 1978,

p. xcii; D. Held, *Models of Democracy*, pp. 164–85; see also D. Beetham, *Max Weber and the Theory of Modern Politics*, pp. 111–12; T. Bottomore, *Theories of Modern Capitalism*, London: Allen and Unwin, 1985; id., Introduction to J. A. Schumpeter, *Capitalism, Socialism and Democracy*, London: Allen and Unwin, 1987.

41    Cf. J. Schumpeter, *Capitalism, Socialism and Democracy*, pp. 235–302. Despite its extraordinary success, there is still no complete monograph devoted to Schumpeter's political thought. There are, however, numerous essays which indirectly refer to Schumpeter's conception of democracy. Among them the following at least repay attention: M. Kessler, 'The Synthetic Vision of Joseph Schumpeter', *Review of Politics*, 23 (1961), 3. 334–55; E. Schneider, *Joseph A. Schumpeter*, Lincoln: Bureau of Business Research, University of Nebraska, 1975; A. Heertje (ed.), *Schumpeter's Vision: 'Capitalism, Socialism and Democracy' after 40 Years*, New York and Eastbourne (Sussex): Praeger Publishers, 1981; W. C. Mitchell, 'Precursor to Public Choice?', *Public Choice*, 42 (1984), 1. 73–88; id., 'Democracy and the Demise of Capitalism: The Missing Chapter in Schumpeter', ibid. 42 (1984), 1. 161–74; G. Urbani, 'Schumpeter e la scienza politica', *Rivista italiana di scienza politica*, 14 (1984), 3. 383–412; M. Ferrera, 'Schumpeter e il dibattito sulla teoria "competitiva" della democrazia', ibid. 413–32; R. D. Coe and C. K. Wilber (eds), *Capitalism and Democracy: Schumpeter Revisited*, Notre Dame (Ind.): University of Notre Dame Press, 1985.

42    For an accurate critical analysis cf. C. Pateman, *Participation and Democratic Theory*, Cambridge: Cambridge University Press, 1970, pp. 16ff. Schumpeter calls 'classical doctrine' the complex of theories that he holds to be the eighteenth-century conception of the democratic method. According to that conception, he maintains, 'the democratic method is that institutional arrangement for arriving at political decisions which realizes the common good by making the people itself decide issues through the election of individuals who are to assemble in order to carry out its will' (*Capitalism, Socialism and Democracy*, p. 250); According to D. Held, Schumpeter's definition 'represents a curious amalgam of theories combining elements of a variety of quite different modes' (*Models of Democracy*, p. 171).

43    Cf. G. Duncan and S. Lukes. 'The New Democracy', *Political Studies*, 11 (1963), 2. 156–77. repr. in the useful anthology: H. S. Kariel (ed.), *Frontiers of Democratic Theory*, New York: Random House, 1970; see also G. Parry, *Political Elites*, London: Allen and Unwin, 1969.

44    Cf. C. Pateman, *Participation and Democratic Theory*, p. 17; cf. also H. Held, *Models of Democracy*, pp. 164–85; W. N. Nelson, *On Justifying Democracy*, pp. 34–52. I agree with D. Miller's stance in 'The Competitive Model of Democracy', pp. 150ff.

45    On the Marxist theory of the State see my anthology *I marxisti e lo Stato. Dai classici ai contemporanei*, Milan: Il Saggiatore, 1977.

46    It may be worth mentioning that the *ekklesia* was rigidly separate from the vast majority of the population which did not belong to the *demos* and that

the *ekklesia* used to work in secret. Also, effective power was largely exercised through indirect forms within the complex political and administrative organization of the *polis* (in Athens the *Boule*, civil magistrature and the courts).

47  For a criticism of Rousseau's democratic utopianism see, in addition to J. L. Talmon's masterly essay, L. G. Crocker, *Rousseau's Social Contract: An Interpretative Essay*, Cleveland (Ohio): Press of Case Western Reserve University, 1968; J. W. Chapman, *Rousseau Totalitarian or Liberal?*, New York: Columbia University Press, 1956.

48  Cf. K. Marx, *Kritik des Hegelschen Staatsrechts*, in K. Marx and F. Engels, *Werke*, Berlin: Dietz Verlag, 1956–69, vol. 1, pp. 229–234, 320–9, Eng. trans. in K. Marx and F. Engels, *Collected Works*, London: Lawrence and Wishart, 1975, pp. 29–33, 115–24; K. Marx, *The Civil War in France*, in *Archiv Marxa i Engelsa*, III (VIII), Moscow, 1934; see also K. Marx, *Zur Judenfrage*, in K. Marx and F. Engels, *Werke*, Berlin: Dietz Verlag, 1956–69, vol. 1, Eng. trans. New York: Philosophical Library, 1959. In my opinion, Lucio Colletti is correct in maintaining that Marx's political thought was already completely contained within Rousseau's conception of popular sovereignty and direct democracy; cf. L. Colletti, *Ideologia e società*, Bari: Laterza, 1969, pp. 250–1, 261. More generally Norberto Bobbio argued for the non-existence of any Marxist theory of the State; cf. *Quale socialismo?*, Eng. trans., pp. 31–64.

49  Cf. K. Marx, *Kritik des Hegelschen Staatsrechts*, pp. 229–34, 246–53, Eng. trans., pp. 29–33, 44–50: 'In democracy the constitution, the law, the state, so far as it is a political constitution, is itself only a self-determination of the people, and a determinate content of the people', ibid., p. 231, Eng. trans., p. 31; H. P. Kainz, *Democracy East and West. A Philosophical Overview*, London: Macmillan, 1984, pp. 86ff.

50  Cf. K. Marx, *The Civil War in France,* pp. 328ff. On the utopian character of Marx's political thought, despite the realistic nature of his conception of the State, see Norberto Bobbio's lucid pages in *Quale socialismo?*, Eng. trans., pp. 62–4.

51  Cf. C.-H. de Saint-Simon, *Cathéchisme des industriels*, in *Œuvres*, Paris: Dentu-Leroux, 1869, vol. IX, p. 131; F. Engels, *Antidühring*, in K. Marx and F. Engels, *Werke*, vol. 20, pp. 261–2.

52  Cf. V. I. Lenin, *Selected Works*, vol. 3, New York: International Publishers, 1943, pp. 81–3, 89, 92–4; on Stučka's and Pašukanis' legal philosophy see J. N. Hazard (ed.), *Soviet Legal Philosophy*, Cambridge (Mass.): Harvard University Press, 1951.

53  Cf. A. Gramsci, *Note sul Machiavelli, sulla politica e sullo Stato moderno*, Turin: Einaudi, 1966, pp. 83–4, 87–9, Eng. trans. London: Lawrence and Wishart, 1971, pp. 242, 246–7; L. Ferrajoli and D. Zolo, 'Marxism and the Criminal Question', *Law and Philosophy*, 4 (1985), 1. 71–99.

54  Cf. A. Gramsci, *Note sul Machiavelli, sulla politica e sullo Stato moderno*, pp. 8, 128, 131–2, Eng. trans., pp. 133, 257–8.

55   Cf. A. J. Vyšinski, 'Voprosy prava i gosudarstva u Marksa', in *Voprosy teorii gosudarstva i prava*, Moscow: Gosudarstvennoe izdatel'stvo juridičeskoij literatury, 1949, pp. 43ff.; cf. also my *La teoria comunista dell'estinzione dello Stato*, pp. 36–43.

56   For a more analytical reconstruction of the diverse models of the radical version of what I agree should be called the 'classical doctrine' see D. Held, *Models of Democracy,* particularly pp. 4–5.

57   Cf. C. Pateman, *Participation and Democratic Theory*, pp. 22–44.

58   Cf. M. Weber, *Wirtschaft und Gesellschaft*, Tübingen: Mohr, 1922, Eng. trans. Berkeley (Calif.): University of California Press, 1978, p. 290.

59   Cf. O. Neurath, 'Das Problem des Lustmaximums', *Jahrbuch der Philosophischen Gesellschaft an der Universität zu Wien 1912*, pp. 89–100, now repr. in O. Neurath, *Gesammelte philosophische und methodologische Schriften*, pp. 47–55; cf. also my *Reflexive Epistemology*, pp. 153–8.

60   This function does not rule out the possibility of political compromise, if by this expression is meant a practical transaction that is not based on a general rule for solving the conflict or on any actual agreement, but that leaves the reasons for the conflict intact by regulating the conflicting political demands through reciprocal 'opportunistic' concessions.

61   Cf. J. B. Berelson, P. Lazarsfeld and W. McPhee, *Voting*, Chicago: University of Chicago Press, 1954, pp. 306–7; S. M. Lipset, *Political Man,* New York: Doubleday, 1963, p. 32.

62   Cf. N. Luhmann, *Macht,* pp. 87–9, Eng. trans. in N. Luhmann, *Trust and Power*, Chichester: John Wiley and Sons, 1979, pp. 164–6.

63   Cf. C. Offe and U. K. Preuss, 'Democratic Institutions and Moral Resources', pp. 28–9.

64   The following passage from Pietro Ingrao may stand as a typical example of this expansive and 'processual' conception of politics: 'The incorporation of political knowledge and of the planned direction of productive and social activities must become diffuse and pervasive, i.e. a *mass process* which involves and transforms millions of men and women and realizes itself on many different levels and in many different dimensions. This diffuse process of the *socialization of politics* is the way not only actually to realize democracy, but also to arrive from the present confusion at a "new order", namely, to realize a true discipline in the face of the enormous risks of social disaggregation and corporative fragmentation' (*Crisi e terza via*, Rome: Editori Riuniti, 1978, p. 100).

65   Cf. N. Luhmann, *Politische Planung*, p. 39. His pessimistic thesis seems to have been confirmed by the Italian experience of 'quarter councils' and 'school councils'. During the 1970s and the 1980s initial enthusiasm has given way to widespread scepticism and apathy towards participatory institutions which people realize to be marginal and ineffective.

66   Cf. C. Offe and U. K. Preuss, 'Democratic Institutions and Moral Resources', pp. 22–3.

67   Bobbio rejects Rousseau's idea of the 'total citizen' and stresses its natural

connection with the concept of the 'total State'. He also finds elements of transitivity between Rousseau's political philosophy and totalitarian conceptions of democracy; cf. N. Bobbio, *Il futuro della democrazia*, Eng. trans. p. 44.

68　Pietro Ingrao seems to recognize the crucial nature of this problem. He admits that the development of industrial societies leads to an increasing complication of social patterns, to the fragmentation of functional roles and the differentiation, specialization and sectorialization of political structures; cf. *Tradizione e progetto*, Bari: De Donato, 1982.

69　Cf. N. Bobbio, *Il futuro della democrazia*, Eng. trans., pp. 26–42.

70　See P. Ingrao, *Masse e potere*, Rome: Editori Riuniti, 1977; P. Ingrao, *Crisi e terza via*, Rome: Editori Riuniti, 1978. For a complex and conscious, even if in my opinion problematical, effort to integrate elements drawn from the libreral and Marxist traditions, see the last chapter of David Held's book, *Models of Democracy*, pp. 267–99; he also has a good discussion of the neo-Marxist positions maintained by authors such as Nicos Poulantzas, Ralph Miliband and Claus Offe (ibid., pp. 205–14); see also K. Graham, *The Battle of Democracy*, Brighton (Sussex): Wheatsheaf Books, 1986; D. Held, *Political Theory and the Modern State*, Stanford (Calif.): Stanford University Press, 1989, pp. 174–88.

71　See J. Burnheim, *Is Democracy Possible?*, Cambridge: Polity Press, 1985; J. Burnheim, 'Democracy, Nation States and the World System', in D. Held and C. Pollitt (eds), *New Forms of Democracy*, pp. 218–39; B. R. Barber, *Strong Democracy*, Berkeley (Calif.): University of California Press, 1984; see also B. Holden, 'New Directions in Democratic Theory', *Political Studies*, 36 (1988), 2. 324–33.

72　Cf. J. Schumpeter, *Capitalism, Socialism and Democracy*, p. 250.

73　Ibid., pp. 256–7.

74　Ibid., pp. 257–8.

75　Ibid., p. 261.

76　Ibid., p. 283.

77　Ibid., p. 264.

78　Cf. R. A. Dahl, *Democracy and Its Critics*, pp. 13–33.

79　Cf. H. Kelsen, 'Foundations of Democracy', *Ethics*, 66 (1955–56), 1. 1–101; R. A. Dahl, *Democracy and Its Critics*, pp. 28–30, 215–7.

80　Cf. R. Dahl, *Democracy and Its Critics*, pp. 215–16, 225–31. For an opposite thesis see A. Levine, *Liberal Democracy. A Critique of Its Theory*, New York: Columbia University Press, 1981, pp. 139–52.

81　Cf. R. Dahl, *Democracy and Its Critics*, pp. 18–23; D. Held, *Models of Democracy*, pp. 15–23; N. Bobbio, *Il futuro della democrazia*, Eng. trans., p. 53.

82　Cf. R. A. Dahl, *Democracy and Its Critics*, p. 28.

83　Cf. H. Kelsen, 'Foundations of Democracy', p. 3: 'Participation in the government, and that means in the creation and application of the general and individual norms of the social order constituting the community, must be considered as the essential characteristic of democracy. Whether this participation is direct or indirect, that is to say, whether there is a direct or a representative democracy, it is in both cases a *procedure*, a specific method of creating and applying the social order constituting the community which is the criterion of that political system which is properly called democracy.'

84    Cf. H. Kelsen, 'Foundations of Democracy', p. 85.
85    Ibid., p. 84.
86    See M. V. Clarke, *Medieval Representation and Consent*, London: Longman, 1936.
87    Cf. K. Marx, *Kritik des Hegelschen Staatsrechts*, pp. 327–9, Eng. trans. pp. 122–4.
88    Cf. D. Beetham, *Max Weber and the Theory of Modern Politics*, pp. 102ff.
89    Cf. H. Kelsen, *General Theory of Law and State*, Cambridge (Mass.): Harvard University Press, 1945, pp. 294–7.
90    Cf. H. F. Pitkin, *The Concept of Representation*, Berkeley (Calif.): University of California Press, 1967; J. R. Pennock, *Democratic Political Theory*, Princeton (N.J.): Princeton University Press, 1979, pp. 309–62.
91    On the notion of 'public opinion' see chapter 5 below.
92    Cf. G. Mosca, *Elementi di scienza politica*, Bari: Laterza, 1953, vol. 2, p. 96, Eng. trans. New York: McGraw-Hill Book Company, 1939, pp. 394f; H. Kelsen, *Vom Wesen und Wert der Demokratie*, Tübingen: J. C. B. Mohr, 1929, p. 85.
93    Cf. D. Beetham, *Max Weber and the Theory of Modern Politics*, pp. 95–118.
94    Cf. H. Kelsen, *General Theory of Law and State*, p. 296; id., *Vom Wesen und Wert der Demokratie*, pp. 29, 86.
95    Cf. N. Bobbio, *Il futuro della democrazia*, Eng. trans. pp. 28–30.
96    Cf. J. Schumpeter, *Capitalism, Socialism and Democracy*, pp. 245–6, 269, 273, 284–5, 294–5.
97    Ibid., p. 272.
98    Ibid., p. 269: 'The democratic method is that institutional arrangement for arriving at political decisions in which individuals acquire the power to decide by means of a competitive struggle for the people's vote.'
99    On this thesis of Schumpeter's cf. Hans Kelsen's lucid criticism in 'Foundations of Democracy', pp. 4ff.
100   Cf. J. Schumpeter, *Capitalism, Socialism and Democracy*, pp. 271–2, 288.
101   Ibid., p. 280.
102   Ibid., p. 271.
103   Ibid., p. 272.
104   For a typical example of this kind of interpretation cf. G. Urbani, 'Schumpeter e la scienza politica', pp. 386ff.
105   Cf. G. Sartori, *The Theory of Democracy Revisited*, pp. 152–6.
106   According to some interpreters, Robert Dahl's recent books, such as *A Preface to Economic Democracy* (Cambridge: Polity Press, 1985) and *Democracy and Its Critics*, show his detachment from the previous model of democratic pluralism. David Held, for instance, describes Dahl's new posi-

tion as 'neopluralism'. In so doing he intends to stress that today Dahl agrees with some important radical-democratic and socialist theses, such as economic democracy and social equality (cf. *Models of Democracy*, pp. 201–5). Without denying the evolution of his political philosophy, I shall consider Robert Dahl as a typical exponent of 'democratic elitism' and I shall continue – correctly, I believe – to include his recent works within this perspective.

107 See P. Bachrach, *The Theory of Democratic Elitism*, Boston (Mass.): Little, Brown and Co., 1967; J. L. Walker, 'A Critique of the Elitist Theory of Democracy', *American Political Science Review*, 60 (1966), 2. 285–95.

108 See R. Dahl, *A Preface to Democratic Theory*; R. Aron, 'Social Structure and the Ruling Class', *British Journal of Sociology*, 1 (1950), 1. 1–16; G. Sartori, *The Theory of Democracy Revisited*, pp. 131–80.

109 CF. R. Dahl, *A Preface to Democratic Theory*, p. 133.

110 Cf. G. Sartori, *Democrazia e definizioni*, Bologna: Il Mulino, 1957, p. 98 and p. 74.

111 Cf. R. Dahl, 'Hierarchy, Democracy and Bargaining in Politics and Economics', in H. Eulau (ed.), *Political Behaviour*, Glencoe (Ill.): The Free Press, 1956, p. 7.

112 Cf. E. E. Schattschneider, *The Semisovereign People*, p. 141.

113 Cf. R. Dahl, 'Hierarchy, Democracy and Bargaining in Politics and Economics', p. 7.

114 On the concept of 'responsiveness' and its difficulties cf. H. Eckstein and T. R. Gurr, *Patterns of Authority*, New York: J. Wiley and Sons, 1975, pp. 216ff, 318ff, 381ff; J. R. Pennock, *Democratic Political Theory*, pp. 261ff; H. Eulau and P. D. Karps, 'The Puzzle of Representation: Specifying Components of Responsiveness', *Legislative Studies Quarterly*, 2 (1977), 3. 233–54.

115 CF. P. Birnbaum, 'Consensus and Depoliticisation in Contemporary Political Theory', in P. Birnbaum, J. Lively and G. Parry (eds), *Democracy, Consensus and Social Contract*, pp. 176ff.

116 Cf. H. Kelsen, *Vom Wesen und Wert der Demokratie*, p. 93.

117 Cf. R. Dahl, *Democracy and Its Critics*, pp. 220–2.

118 Cf. J. Schumpeter, *Capitalism, Socialism and Democracy*, p. 285; H. Kelsen, *Vom Wesen und Wert der Demokratie*, pp. 27ff.

119 Cf. R. Dahl, *Democracy and Its Critics*, p. 276; cf. also G. Sartori, *The Theory of Democracy Revisited*, p. 156.

120 Cf. E. E. Schattschneider, *Party Government*, New York: Holt, Rinehart and Winston, 1942, ch. 3.

121 Cf. J. Schumpeter, *Capitalism, Socialism and Democracy*, pp. 272–3.

122 On the classical distinction between 'negative freedom' and 'positive freedom' see I. Berlin, *Four Essays on Liberty*, Oxford: Oxford University Press, 1969; cf. also N. Bobbio, *Politica e cultura*, Turin: Einaudi, 1953, pp. 160–94.

123 Cf. J. Schumpeter, *Capitalism, Socialism and Democracy*, pp. 283 and 271.

124   Ibid., p. 283.
125   Ibid.; cf. C. B. Macpherson, *The Life and Times of Liberal Democracy*.
      Oxford: Oxford University Press, pp. 90–1.

# 4 The Evolutionary Risks of Democracy

> Experience shows that in our times the rulers who have done great things are those who have set little store by keeping their word, being skilful rather in cunningly confusing men. One could give countless modern examples of this, and show how many promises have been rendered null and void.
>
> Machiavelli, *Il Principe*

## Broken promises and unforeseen obstacles

In a series of essays which attracted much attention in Italy and Spanish-speaking countries (and have also, more recently, appeared in English translation) Norberto Bobbio set out what he called a 'minimal definition' of democracy. His aim was the relatively modest one of assembling a collection of procedural rules whose adoption assures a 'minimum' political content. This content, which Western liberal democracies have always, in his opinion, been successful in providing, may be summed up as protection of the rights of liberty.[1] Conversely, the constitutional guarantee of basic rights – i.e. freedom of assembly, opinion, speech, etc. – represents what he considers to be the condition *sine qua non* of democracy, in both its moderate and its radical forms.[2] Thus for Bobbio, as for Kelsen, the democratic system coincides substantially with the 'rule of law'. Democracy is in effect a functional surrogate for the use of force to resolve social conflicts. Its fundamental principle is that

> in each conflict the winner is not the one who has more physical force, but the one who has more persuasive force, that is to say the one who by the force of persuasion (or of clever propaganda or even of cunning manipulation) succeeds in winning the majority of the votes.[3]

The formal rules which together make up this 'minimal definition' of democracy have been expressed by Bobbio in a number of variously overlapping formulations. They may, however, be satisfactorily presented under the following five headings:

1    Political elections should take place with equal and universal (or at least 'very broad') suffrage, and recur with a reasonable degree of periodicity.

2    Individuals should be free to vote according to their own judgement, formed as freely as possible in the context of open competition between rival political groupings.

3    'Real alternatives' should be put before the voters in order to give them a choice between genuinely different political solutions.

4    The principle of majority decision should be followed in the resolutions of elective assemblies (or of compromise decision in the case of the 'consociational' or 'neo-corporatist' democracies).

5    Some limit should be set to the legal extent of majority decisions, in the sense that no decision should violate the political rights of a minority and prevent it from itself becoming, given equal opportunity, a majority.[4]

These rules leave me in no doubt that Bobbio's 'minimal definition' of democracy is in essence a more sophisticated version of Schumpeter's doctrine of democracy as competitive leadership. But, in addition to his employment of Schumpeter's realistic theories, Bobbio has also profited from the formalism of the Kelsenian conception of democracy. In the same way as Schumpeter, he locates the defining feature of a democratic government not in the absence of political elites, but in the presence of a number of political élites competing with one another.[5] And, as is shown by his censure of Rousseau's ideal of the 'total citizen' and of the 'fetish' of direct democracy,[6] he also sees democracy as not necessarily implying extensive participation by citizens in the decisional processes, although this will not, of course, be excluded. Nor, for him, does democracy demand 'representation' of individuals in any strong sense. In this respect he agrees with Kelsen, taking up his idea of the radical incompatibility between the legal nature of a mandate and the scheme of political representation whose essence lies in non-recognition of the 'binding mandate'.[7] Along with Kelsen and Weber, he recognizes that contemporary democracy is party democracy – that it is the parties and not the undifferentiated public of voters that are the effective agents in so-called 'popular sovereignty'.[8] Quoting Kautsky's famous critique of 'doctrinaire democratic theory', he acknowledges that parliamentary government is subject to the logic of the social division of labour and that political activity demands levels of professionality and competence. The radical-democratic idea of government of the people by the people is, for him, a retrograde and anti-democratic utopia if it means political affairs being entrusted to unpaid amateurs working in their free time rather than to salaried officers of the State.[9]

What Bobbio has been at pains to make clear, avoiding Schumpeter's conspicuous theoretical ambiguity on this point, is that the nature of the democratic system is not purely procedural. It is not the case that any decision which respects certain procedures – the principle, for instance, of majority decision – can for that reason alone be defined as democratic. Schumpeter is able to envisage cases in which democratic procedures can be followed and yet still lead to religious oppression, as in witch-hunts or the persecution of Jews. But this is explicitly excluded by Bobbio. The use of an electoral procedure or of a formally correct parliamentary decision in order to suppress the individualistic assumptions of representative democracy can in no sense, according to Bobbio, be called democratic, as was classically shown by the 'democratic' end of the Weimar Republic.[10] For Bobbio, as for Kelsen, democracy does not exist outside the tradition of the European *Rechsstaat* or 'rule of law' in its strong sense, i.e. in its guaranteeing, rather than simply legal-bureaucratic, form.

But Bobbio's main addition to Schumpeter's doctrine lies in his development of one of its less obvious facets. He emphasizes the requirement that competition between political élites should lead not only to citizens' freedom of choice, but also to a significant diversification of political offerings. Indeed, pluralism and competition do not, to Bobbio's mind, guarantee effective political freedom except insofar as they are successful in putting before the voters a range of differentiated political alternatives between which there is a significant choice to be made.[11]

By arguing in this way, Bobbio is thinking principally of those regimes which, while claiming to be democratic and adopting electoral procedures and parliamentary institutions, still employ a single-party structure. But his thesis is, as I shall attempt to show, equally meaningful when applied to the multi-party regimes of the Western democracies. If it is true that the democratic system can only operate where there is a reasonably high level of homogeneity of the interests diffused throughout the social body, it is also true that an excessive reduction of conflict within the political system runs the risk of reducing democracy to nothing. The sovereignty of the citizen as 'political consumer' is exercised in vain when the range of the right of choice to which the electoral system formally entitles an individual is either restricted to marginal questions or has no bearing on the political problems of greater moment. This restriction can occur either when a pre-emptive, and naturally monopolistic, consensus on important matters exists between the political forces which are legitimated within the party system and which are represented in parliament, or when the political system as a whole is unable to submit anything more than marginal questions to political decision.[12]

At this point – i.e. with a minimal legitimacy established for democracy inasmuch as it is an *elitist and liberal* regime – Bobbio declines to produce any wider defence of the values or institutions of democracy, admitting instead that democracy is a regime capable of operating only within highly specific historical and social contexts and is thus deprived of any prescriptive universality.[13] In fact he then goes on to draw up his condemnatory list of the 'broken promises' of modern democracy. In talking of the broken promises and paradoxes of democracy, his aim becomes one of drawing attention to the gap which exists between democratic ideals and 'actually existing democracy', a term he uses to mirror the sense of 'actually existing socialism'.[14]

The comparison between the 'promises' of liberal and democratic thinkers such as Locke, Rousseau, de Tocqueville, Bentham and Mill and the effective functioning of democratic institutions is, according to Bobbio, an especially sad one, a deceptive, and for many dispiriting, reality. This is not simply the result of the 'degradation of public life, the shameful spectacle of corruption, of sheer ignorance, careerism and cynicism which the bulk of our [democratic] professional politicians present us with every day.'[15] More serious still is the process of the 'transformation of democracy',[16] which is causing the development of Western democratic institutions to be paradoxical and riddled with 'perverse effects'. It is paradoxical and perverse, Bobbio argues, because the failure of the democratic regimes to keep faith with the commitments made by the theoreticians and ideologists of democracy is to a large degree a consequence of the very evolution of Western societies which have been governed by representative institutions.

Bobbio's 'broken promises', variously expressed over the years,[17] amount principally to the following:

1   The first, and most general, is the promise of popular sovereignty. This promise has been completely drained of effect by the growth of the public bureaucracies. The functional logic of the large-scale organizational bureaucracies is, as a result of their unrestrainable hierarchical and oligarchical tendencies, quite opposite to the logic of democracy. The spread of bureaucratic structures is, however, closely related to the increased pressure which the democratic organizations and the 'mass parties' in particular have imposed upon public structures, especially within Welfare State societies.[18]

2   The emergence of a pluralistic society, abetted by the open and tolerant nature of democratic institutions, has resulted in the suffocation of the postulate of individualism which was held to be so essential by the

theorists of democratic contractualism, the utilitarian philosophers and above all, by the bourgeois economists for whom the idea of the *homo oeconomicus* supplanted that of the *zoon politikon*. As it is, individuals have been progressively succeeded as principal agents in the political life of modern democratic societies by groups, large-scale public and private organizations, parties, trade unions and professions. If autonomy still has any force as a postulate of democratic life, it can now only be looked for in groups rather than in individuals. The individual who is affiliated to no organization is in effect deprived of any autonomous political agency. Even those individuals who operate within politically autonomous groups are subjected to functional restraints imposed by the organizational logic of large-scale systems. The result is that 'we require increasingly high levels of democracy under conditions which are, in objective terms, increasingly less favourable to it.'[19]

3    A third paradox, which leads to the annulment of another fundamental postulate of democracy, is the increasing gap between the individual's lack of competence in the face of ever more complex problems and the need for technical solutions only accessible to (and verifiable by) specialists. The technical and scientific growth which typifies the Western democratic countries has led increasingly to the protagonists in political life being scientists, experts or professional consultants, especially those belonging to powerful and prestigious organizations. Meanwhile, the 'theoretical' protagonist of democratic society, the average citizen, whose decisions have to be made less on the basis of competence than on the basis of personal experience and preferences, is increasingly marginalized. 'Is it not therefore a contradiction in terms', asks Bobbio, 'to ask for more and more democracy in a society increasingly shaped by technology?' Such a request can only be satisfied by an extension of the ability to decide to a growing number of those incompetent to do so.[20]

4    'Education for citizenhood', i.e. active participation in political life, has been a central concern of democratic thinkers from Montesquieu to Mill, de Tocqueville and the American political scientists who, since the 1950s, have given the concept fresh impetus in the form of 'political culture'. Despite all this theorizing, however, democratic countries have in fact experienced the widespread diffusion of mass conformity and political apathy amongst voters. The growth of both of these phenomena, far from being hindered, has been decisively advanced by the development of instruments of mass communication and by the intensive use of commercial and political propaganda. Nor is it the totalitarian regimes alone that have seen the establishment, alongside the 'cultural industry', of a 'political industry' based on sophisticated techniques for the organization and manipulation of consensus.[21]

5   Democracy, despite all the aims of its founding fathers, such as the French Constituent Assembly of 1791, has never succeeded in dispensing with oligarchic power. Not only, as the theorists of democratic elitism have argued, do modern democratic regimes necessarily entail the presence of 'democratic elites'. There have also become established alongside these, as leading agents in democratic life, groups explicitly devoted to the 'representation' of what can only, by their nature, be particular 'interests'. Never has a constitutional norm been more violated than the veto on binding mandates, and never has a principle been more disregarded than that of the 'political' (i.e. general) nature of representation (*qua* something opposed to the 'corporatist' principle). It is no mere coincidence, Bobbio observes, that we have begun to hear the European democratic systems being talked of as a new type of system going by the name, rightly or wrongly, of 'neo-corporatism'.[22]

6   Far from shaping the entire range of social relationships, the principle of democracy has established itself solely within certain limited areas. The acquisition of universal suffrage has made no dent at all in the two 'great blocks of descendent and hierarchical power', public bureaucracy and big business. As for the last in particular, the sovereignty of citizens is immediately 'cut in half' by the limitations which the capitalistic conduct of business puts on the possibility of their agreeing with decisions which affect economic growth. But even everyday institutions such as the family, schools or hospitals are run on substantially non-democratic lines.[23]

7   The last, and by far the most serious, broken promise of 'actually existing democracy' is its failure to eliminate 'invisible power'. For theorists of liberal democracy, from the philosophers of the French Enlightenment to Kant, the aim of making power visible, of 'illuminating' it, has been identical with democracy itself, understood in this context as 'the rule of public power in public'. Democratic power is diametrically opposed to the uncontrollable secrecy of the *arcana imperii*. Its rule is publicity, a rule which will allow only few passing exceptions. But in the Western democracies, the elimination of invisible power would require a wholesale assault on the structures of the 'double State' – double in the sense that hand in hand with the visible State goes an 'invisible State' coexisting alongside it in democratic, and not solely in totalitarian, regimes.[24] This invisible area extends both to the public government of the economy and to the system of mass communication. For in both these sectors, the political parties operate covertly and even, in some countries, illegally, in order to finance their activities and increase their own influence. Through the use of electronic technology, the holders of power are so enabled to gather and manipulate information that even democratic institutions tend to assume the structure of Bentham's model prison, the *Panopticon*, with an all-

seeing and invisible power on one side and, on the other, an exposed public made up of citizens deprived of any personal outlook.[25]

The licidity and intellectual strength which lie behind this catalogue of woes can hardly be denied. They amount to the most powerful list of the delusions and self-deceptions of democratic doctrine so far amassed by any liberal-democratic thinker. They also represent a far-seeing analysis of the dangers which threaten the future of democracy in the advanced industrial countries. From this point of view Bobbio's political philosophy goes considerably further than being a lucid and self-aware development of Schumpeter's realist theories of politics: in fact it shows how political realism can be successfully dissociated from the conservative tradition of thought.

Realism and far-sightedness in theoretical analysis are accompanied, however, in Bobbio's work by the practical exhortation not to ask for too much from 'actually existing democracy', to accept it as it is, as a lesser evil. Its future, that is to say its stability, depends precisely on the ability of citizens to accept it as it is without wishfully pursuing improbable alternatives which, as has catastrophically become the case with Marxism, turn out to be unsustainable and fraught with danger.

If the gap between the reality of democracy and its ideals is so broad, the fault is assuredly less that of the politicians than that of the theoreticians. In reality, with the sole exception, perhaps, of the survival of invisible power,[26] the promises of democracy can only be considered, restrospectively, as having been hardly worth the paper they were written on. They could not be – and therefore 'ought not' to be – maintained. They were, right from the beginning, as Bobbio now warns us, illusions, or hopes which were badly misplaced. Nor can the phenomena which gave rise to them appropriately be called the degeneration of democracy: it is better instead to speak in terms of the natural consequences of adapting abstract principles to reality, or of the inevitable contamination of theory when it is forced to submit to the demands of practice.[27]

'The project of political democracy', Bobbio argues, again in full agreement with Schumpeter, 'was conceived for a society much less complex than the one which exists today.'[28] The project has never been realized because of the arrival of 'unforeseen obstacles', incapable of being foreseen, since they were brought about by transformations which have made industrial society far more complex than it was. The classical writers on democratic thought never predicted, nor were they ever in a position to do so, that technological development would lead almost unavoidably to a rule of technicians, in direct contrast with the underlying principle of democracy which hypothesizes that 'all are in a position to make decisions about everything.'[29] The extreme technical difficulty of present-day political problems cannot avoid recreating once more a removal of the *arcana imperii* away from the cognizance of the general public composed of citizens who possess insufficient scientific or technical information to understand them.

The same may also be said, Bobbio continues, of the uncontainable growth of public bureaucracies within the 'social State'. It is a response, as Weber well appreciated, to technical and 'rational' demands which, like it or not, naturally accompany the 'democratization' of modern society. As to the 'ungovernability' of modern democracies caused by the inability of the democratic institutions to 'satisfy demand', Bobbio's views in this area appear to approximate best to those of authors such as Rose, Huntington and Crozier who attribute the crisis of democracy to an excess of democracy.[30] It is to be expected that democratic governments, given the inevitable slowness of their procedures, will be unable to respond to the pressures of demands emanating from a free and emancipated society. These demands come at such a speed and in such quantity that no political system, however efficient it may be, would ever be able adequately to provide for them.[31]

Despite all the broken promises, the paradoxes and the perverse effects to which they give rise, Bobbio still finds that the political systems of the West deserve the title to which they lay claim. They are still recognizably 'democratic' and, as such, preferable to all other regimes, either present or past. Not coincidentally, he argues, the last forty years have seen the extent of democracy progressively increased both in Europe and in the rest of the world.[32] One substantial difference between democratic and non-democratic regimes has always remained untouched: the guarantee of basic freedoms. This guarantee has been preserved by the existence of competing parties periodically submitting themselves to the judgement of the electorate under conditions of universal suffrage.[33]

It emerges quite clearly, therefore, that Bobbio's political philosophy, for all the acuity of its analysis and the moral vigour of its criticisms, still stands within what I have termed the 'neo-classical paradigm of pluralist democracy'.[34] For Bobbio, as for Schumpeter, 'actually existing democracy' is democratic because it is an elitist regime which is, at the same time, *pluralist and liberal*. Despite revealing the systematic incongruity between the theoretical principles and the reality of democracy, and despite laying responsibility for the incongruity on the theory rather than on the practice, Bobbio still fails to address the problem of the revision or reconstruction of democratic theory, and even seems to rule out the need for it.

In practice, however, as I shall attempt to show in the course of the following pages, even the basic categories of the 'political market' upon which Bobbio too appears to rely, such as pluralism, inter-party competition, sovereignty of the 'political consumers' in the choice between competing elites,[35] become inoperative in modern complex and differentiated societies, or they operate according to functional logics very far removed from the original theory. There are also serious problems inherent in the alternative presented by Schumpeter (and implicitly accepted by Bobbio) between the protection of individual freedoms and the efficiency of administration. This alternative proposes that a democratic regime is preferable on account of its ability to guarantee a reasonable level of 'liberty for all' notwithstanding its inability to satisfy demand, the slowness of its decisional procedures and the enormous waste of resources inherent in its pluralistic and competitive structure.

Bobbio, like Schumpeter, appears to undervalue the link between the defence of liberties and the 'protective' efficiency which even a democratic regime must possess in giving a timely response to the pressures emanating from the demands of a complex and differentiated society involved in a process of extremely rapid transformation, with all its attendant 'evolutionary risks'. Here Bobbio's position, in just the same way as that of the theorists of democratic pluralism, is today in danger of appearing theoretically and politically weak. Its main fault, as I see it, is the less than adequate perception it has of the problems and challenges – the 'unforeseen obstacles' of social complexity in Bobbio's own vocabulary – with which the institutions of democracy are currently faced as a result of the revolution in information and technology. These problems and challenges are above all evident – to a far greater extent even than in Bobbio's predictions – in the extreme unlikelihood that the information society will guarantee the preservation of the procedural mechanisms of democracy and the rule of law. Instead, these mechanisms appear to be in increasing danger of being replaced by more efficient forms of the exercise of power, attractive as a result of their ability to 'manage complexity' with a more economical use of money, time and attention.

One further fact which appears not to have had great impact on Bobbio is the significant loss of evolutionary direction and growth which has, notwithstanding the 'conversion' of Eastern European regimes, become visible in the democratic model in recent times. The evolution of democratic institutions had, for at least the last 200 years, maintained a steady progression – from the revolutionary assertion of the rights of man and of the individual to the acquisition, somewhat later, of general suffrage, and then to the constitutional protection of social rights. This historical curve, which was destined, in the minds of European progressives, to lead to the gradual establishment of socialism – i.e. of social equality, generalized political participation and the withering away of the State – has now ground to a sudden halt at an evolutionary bottleneck whose dangers are manifest in the contemporary crisis of the Welfare State and in the involutions of authoritarian, technocratic and neo-liberal democracy.

It may also be added, quite separately, that the theory of 'broken promises' would be open to the risk of grave disappointment – of being to some extent itself a broken promise – if its sole purport had to be that of absolving the democratic regimes of all their inadequacies with regard to the abstract principles of theory or if it had to amount to no more than a clear exhortation to patience. For, according to Bobbio, the citizens of democratic countries ought sensibly to resign themselves, just as they would to the 'natural adaptations' of theory to practice, to the loss of popular sovereignty, the eclipse of individual political subjectivity, the monopoly of technicians and bureaucrats, the hegemony of the cultural and political industries and the superpower of big business. They ought even, it appears, to have few illusions about the possibility of escaping the onset of the information *Panopticon* into which post-industrial democracy is silently transforming itself.[36] But at the same time they should continue to believe in the ideals and values which underlie democratic procedures and historically gave birth to them: tolerance, non-violence, free discussion of ideas, fellowship and fraternity.[37]

Clearly Bobbio is hardly wrong in finding many of the classical assumptions of democracy to be unrealistic and in finding the common origin of those 'unforeseen obstacles' that have prevented their actualization to lie in the growth of social complexity. On this point I would be the last to disagree. But it is remarkable that he attempts to justify actually existing democracy on the basis of its 'minimum content' – the guarantee of basic liberties – when he has drawn the margin between it and non-democratic regimes so narrowly as to risk compromising the very reasons behind his argument. How is it possible to be sure that the 'minimum content' of democracy will be in any sense firmly guaranteed when we grant everything that Bobbio grants? What meaning does it have to talk of the 'protection of the rights of freedom' at the same time as recognizing that there is taking place 'an inversion of the relationship between controllers and controlled, since an unscrupulous use of the means of mass communication has now led to the elected controlling the electors'?[38]

In what sense can we continue to call a regime 'democratic' when it is based on the 'inversion' of the democratic relationship between citizen electors and the institutions of authority? Can a regime be termed democratic in which the autonomy of the citizens is sacrificed to a rudimentary notion of liberty defined as an absence of physical coercion and the presence of a plurality of sources of multi-media persuasion? Does this notion of 'liberty' and the related one of 'rights of liberty' retain any significance in the context of the 'information society' in which manipulative pressure focuses increasingly on individuals' acts of volition rather than on their external behaviour?

Perhaps the same kind of answer may reasonably be given to Bobbio as to Schumpeter. If 'actually existing democracy' is necessarily what he honestly believes it to be, then there is a distinct danger of its having no future. For the 'minimum content' it possesses is so slender and hazardous that this can only be perceived less and less as a 'general good' to be preserved in the face of the despotic involutions occurring in democratic regimes. Perhaps, therefore, one of the deepest causes of the spread of political apathy in Western democracies lies precisely here – in the conviction, however right or wrong it may be, that none of the 'broken promises' of democracy could, without exception, ever have been kept. In a proposal for the reconstruction of democratic theory it is necessary, as I shall argue in the concluding pages of this book, for a clear distinction to be maintained between those democratic promises that had no chance of being kept and those that ought to have been kept – and should still be kept today – even within a rigorously realistic conception of democracy.

## Polyarchy and social complexity

According to the neo-classical doctrine, the closest modern equivalent to the Athenian ideal of popular self-determination arises from the pluralism of the social and political agents who compete with one another to shape the political agenda. Pluralistic democracy, Robert Dahl has written in a recent summation of his political philosophy, *Democracy and Its Critics*, is 'one of the most extraordinary of all human artifacts'.[39] But, in order to justify this statement, Dahl, who has been somewhat over-hastily labelled as 'neo-pluralist' by some,[40] turns once more to the rehearsal, unfortunately without alteration or qualification, of the traditional theses of the neo-classical doctrine. He repeats that 'the modern, dynamic and pluralistic societies' – i.e. the advanced industrial societies of the capitalist West – are typified by a broad social diffusion of political resources, 'strategic locations', and 'bargaining positions';[41] also that, in the systems of 'corporate pluralism' (or of 'democratic corporatism'), the dynamics of the market are constantly bringing into being a variety of powers and counter-powers, thereby hampering the formation of public or private autocracies in favour of a multiplicity of relatively independent and competing decisional centres.[42] And, further, that competition between elites causes regroupings to take place – the 'circulation of elites' in Pareto's phrase – given that there is always some group amongst those in power which is interested in supporting the introduction of new groups, which have been either excluded or are less strong, in exchange for their political support.[43]

Equal distribution of opportunities between politically active groups, he argues, allows the coordination of interests, the allocation of resources, and the transactive solution of conflicts to occur with the minimum recourse to direct coercion.[44] Any group can appeal, in accordance with the logic of the market, to the principle of its equal freedom to take bargaining positions, in order to achieve its own admission into the political arena. Nor are there any reasons which can be invoked by others to justify any group's exclusion from pursuing their own particular interests.[45]

The network of polyarchic transactions, protected and legitimized by the party system, is thus held to be in a position to bring about a good level of 'general advantage'. This effect is normally guaranteed by the fact that in the sphere of the polyarchies, policy-making is the result (which is filtered, arbitrated and enforced by the political system) of negotiation and reciprocal accommodation between the groups. It reflects 'partisan mutual adjustment', to cite Lindblom's famous definition.[46] These groups, embedded in the most diverse social sectors, know how to interpret and express better than any 'numerical democracy' the diffused requirements of a modern industrial society in which all the primary interests and a large proportion of legitimized interests are in a position to organize themselves. Thus Dahl asserts:

> Associational pluralism, combined with a good deal of decentralization of decisions to local governments, would help to ensure that the interests of citizens in the different publics would be given more or less equal consideration. In that sense, the public good would be achieved in a pluralist democracy.[47]

In this sense, the pluralist system of groups and parties is believed to guarantee, over and above the protection of fundamental freedoms, a high level of 'responsiveness' of political decision to the expectations of citizens.

Such a sketch of a political system may well appear to be merely the last in a long line of simplistic and stereotyped representations of North American society. But this does not mean that Dahl, in proclaiming that corporative polyarchy is an 'extraordinary invention', is not perfectly conscious of its limitations compared to the ambitions and 'promises' of both Rousseau's and Locke's versions of classical democratic theory. In common with Schumpeter and Bobbio, he recognizes that these limitations derive in general from the growing complexity of modern societies. By complexity he means, in accordance with a typically systemic stance, 'the increase in the variety and number of relatively independent subsystems and the increase in the extent of variation in the possible relations between the subsystems'.[48]

Most importantly, in the concluding pages of his political *summa*, which he dedicates to an evaluation of the future prospects of democracy, he recognizes that the development of contemporary (modern, dynamic and pluralist) societies and the growing internationalization of problems

> brought about the adoption of increasingly complex policies. Not only did policies within a particular issue-area grow more complex, but the increase in the sheer number of policies, as governments expanded the scope of their concerns, was itself a source of complexity. The management of this growing complexity in policies led in turn to greater complexity in the policy-making process. Just as the extension of the democratic idea to the scale of the nation-state required a radical adaptation and innovation in political institutions – the creation of polyarchy – so new institutions were now required in polyarchies to meet the demands of complexity in policy and policy-making.[49]

Nevertheless, he still argues that, even in conditions of heightened social complexity, the democratic process, albeit in the limited form of polyarchy, favours individual and collective self-determination, encourages moral independence, promotes human development and provides citizens with effective instruments for the protection of their common interests.[50] It is true, he grants, that the 'conditions of extreme complexity' in which modern political systems find themselves threaten to replace democracy with variously disguised forms of technocracy. Indeed, the excess of complexity generates 'a drift toward government by de facto quasi guardians'.[51] But there can be no doubt, to his mind, that in information-based societies democracy will survive to the extent to which it succeeds in preserving as its pivotal point the pluralism and reciprocal autonomy of groups, especially those that will provide the new social management, i.e. the various technical, scientific and professional associations. The growth of the means of mass communication brought about by the new information technologies, along with the possibility of interactive, rather than unidirectional, communication, offers a decisive impetus in favour of the creation and development of an 'attentive public', or at least of active, informed minorities who are capable of political control and intervention.[52] It will thus be possible to advance, thanks to a third 'great transformation', towards progressively more complete forms of democracy, towards the goals of 'Polyarchy II' and 'Polyarchy III'.[53]

The portrait of (North American) pluralistic society which Dahl depicts today is, in spite of his basic optimism, decidedly more toned down and open to consideration of the deeper problems than the pictures he has previously painted in the course of over thirty years of pluralistic apologia, from his *Preface to Democratic Theory* onwards. But, notwithstanding his significant reference to the problem of social complexity, this current representation seems to me to possess no more credibility than the ones that have attracted close criticism over this period from a multitude of philosophers and political scientists, particularly in England, America[54] and Germany.[55]

Since the early 1960s, left-wing critics – i.e. those of radical-democratic, socialist, and Marxist persuasion – have been strong in their criticism of the ideological and apologetic nature of pluralism. The case has not been difficult to make against the pluralists that, even if the mechanisms of political bargaining guarantee advanced industrial societies a good level of 'systemic balance', and thus of stability and growth, they also have the effect of stabilizing social disequalities by standing in the way of innovation and social mobility. The circuits of polyarchic transactions, it has been argued by this school, operate a systematic discrimination between the interests of those groups that possess great organizational and bargaining powers, the interests of associations which occupy no strategic positions in the system of the technological division of labour[56] and, finally, the great majority of average citizens, the simple economic and political consumers who possess no powers of organization or bargaining and to whom no affiliations (other than those of a clandestine or, more effectively, criminal kind) can offer the slightest advantage. Thus, it comes about that the circuits of polyarchic transaction are firmly occupied, if not by a 'power elite', as Wright Mills somewhat simplistically maintained, then at least by a narrow concentration of strategically stronger groups, who locate themselves at levels which are decisive for the allocation of collective resources, ranging from economic and fiscal politics to foreign affairs, defence spending, town-planning and transportation.

It is evident that this mechanism cuts out any possible representative connection between voters and elective bodies. Its systematic interference with the formal procedures of political decision-making through the practices of lobbying, 'log-rolling' and, worst of all, corruption, effectively destroys 'sovereignty' on both sides and markedly distrusts the rule of the majority, so dear to Kelsen and Bobbio. Here Schumpeter's scheme of the rigid division of labour between private citizens and parliamentary representatives – he would, as we have already seen, ban even the practice of sending telegrams to members of parliament – runs up against a disastrous historical contradiction. But the most serious aspect, it is further argued, is that 'democratic corporativism' even tends to nullify the 'presumption of personal independence' on the part of the individual – i.e. all individuals are, until proved otherwise, the best judges and the best representatives of their own interests – whose irreplaceable democratic function Dahl loses no opportunity to exalt.[57]

In theory these criticisms seem to me well founded. It is possible that some of them may even be subscribed to today by Dahl himself. They show quite unassailably that a pluralistic society is orientated by none of the principles of political participation, social equality or the parliamentary representation of interests. And this, it may be added, reveals the wholly academic nature of the distinction drawn by political scientists such as Arend Lijphart between pluralistic regimes based on the Westminster (or majority) model and those based on the 'consociative' model.[58] Under current conditions, however, there is a danger that these criticisms have lost not only their theoretical focus, but also their political teeth. Their insufficiency from both the theoretical and the political aspect arises from the fact that the analytical scheme they presuppose is still bounded by a 'representative' horizon and fails to take account of the systemic logic which increasingly governs the relation between the political subsystem and its environment. Directly or indirectly, these theories appeal to a classical model of democracy whose relevance they defend against 'democratic revisionism', without noticing that in complex societies all the postulates of its possible application are steadily diminishing.

It cannot, of course, be denied that Dahl's pluralism has in the past remained relatively unscathed by this sort of criticism. It seems likely to fare even better today after the disastrous failure of 'actually existing socialism' and the emergence of serious difficulties, not only for radical-democratic political positions in the West, but even for more moderate social-democratic ones.

The iconography of polyarchy keeps the reasons for the low level of its theoretical reliability well concealed until it finds itself confronted with the classical ideals of democracy or with the postulates of socialism. With respect to the first, Dahl is a sufficiently lucid realist to concede that polyarchy is an 'adaptation' of, and a simple approximation to, the classical models. With respect to the other, he explicitly argues – not incorrectly – that, from the liberal-democratic standpoint, pluralism is a preferable alternative to socialist 'guardianship'.

A more effective reply to Dahl's theses (as indeed to those of Schumpeter, Sartori and, in part, of Bobbio) is provided, to my mind, by drawing attention to the insufficient realism of the 'revisionist' reinterpretation of the democratic process. In the post-industrial societies typified by growing complexity and functional differentiation, political systems are simply no longer able to function – and tend therefore to function increasingly less – in accordance with the model of the polyarchic political market. This model is still, even if to a reduced degree, a 'representative' model. It continues to be based on the ideas of 'respondence' and 'consensus', i.e. that there is a significant relation between the expectations of the voters and the satisfying of political interests. Nor has it in any sense abandoned the premiss of the cognitive and moral autonomy of individuals, or released itself at all, especially in Dahl's more recent work, from the grip of the category of the 'common good'. The idea that the rules of this model are still effectively operative in post-industrial societies is to my mind a supposition no less ingenuous and unrealistic than the touching democratic faith shown by the puritan founding fathers against whom Schumpeter directed the full force of his irony.

A rigorously realist outlook, in contrast, would start from the hypothesis that in complex societies a systemic (rather than 'representative') logic governs not only the relations between the party system and its 'social environment', composed of the undifferentiated public of citizens, but also the relations between the political system and the other subjects of polyarchy. Above all, the nature of these relations can only be grasped fully once certain obsolete categories closely linked with the classical idea of representation have been put aside. The distinction has to be abandoned between the State, understood as the 'public sphere' of general interests, and 'civil society', the area of private and particular interests. The classical idea of power should also, as Niklas Luhmann proposes, be removed, as should that of consensus, if by this term, following Habermas, is meant a 'rational approbation' of the forms and contents of political decision by the subjects of the *demos*.[59]

In this realist outlook the problem of the 'evolutionary risks' of democracy becomes central. To an extent far byond that cautiously admitted by Dahl, the increase of differentiation and social complexity is in danger of producing in modern post-industrial societies a radical *dispersal of the public sphere*. This dispersal extends even to the removal of the horizon of the 'political city' itself as the domain of 'citizenhood'. In its place, the 'protective' functions of prescription and social integration are coming to be exercised by a network of 'private governors' – the political parties and the other agents of corporative polyarchy – who are becoming increasingly more autonomous and increasingly less responsible, but who are at the same time devoid of any capacity for the efficient and timely solution of complex problems. The dispersal of the public sphere, as I shall now attempt to argue in the succeeding sections of this chapter, assumes the threefold morphology of *the self-reference of the party system, the inflation of power* and *the neutralization of consensus*.

# The self-reference of the party system

Theorists of democratic elitism – such as Dahl, Sartori, and even Bobbio – have identified competitive pluralism as the condition and defining characteristic of democracy understood as an *elitist and liberal* regime which 'responds', according to the logic of the political market, to the expectations of 'political consumers'. First, however, it ought to be made clear what is meant, within differentiated and complex societies, by 'political pluralism'. Evidently, the term does not refer to a purely numerical plurality of political, social and economic organizations. For this plurality could not be the sociologically and politically most important, and certainly not the decisive, criterion for distinguishing a democratic political system from one which is not.

For Schumpeter, the notion of pluralism indicates the multiplicity of groups – i.e. essentially the parties – which compete at the electoral level for the winning of political leadership. Economic market and political market thus remain clearly distinguished concepts in his theory. For neoclassical theorists, however, the notion of pluralism is decidedly broader, especially from the sociological aspect. It denotes the plurality of the groups which compete both formally and informally in the determination of policy-making. This definition extends well beyond the parties to include trade unions, large economic and financial concerns, ethnic, cultural and religious organizations, professional and solidaristic associations, etc. In sum, it comprehends all those groups that are in a position, at least potentially and with some level of stability and legitimacy, to see that their demands get onto the political agenda.

Taking the formalized political system as a point of reference, it is possible to discern two types of pluralism – 'intrasystemic' and 'extrasystemic'. In both cases the agents of pluralism are not individuals, but groups. And in both cases groups, rather than citizens, are to be conceived of as the primary conveyors of political demand, whether or not they are affiliated to politically significant organizations. It is groups that supply input to the system, while the political institutions proper preside over the output, i.e. the functions of administration and control.

In both cases it is presumed that the classical scheme of democratic political legitimation, even in the weak form implied by the notion of 'responsiveness', is at work within the political market. The general interests of society – or, which comes to the same thing, the sum of the particular interests of each group – are taken to be expressed, via the channels of political exchange, by the highest echelons of the organized groups. These then transmit it in their turn, through electoral competition or functionally equivalent circuits, to the heights of the political-administrative system: parliament and government. These organizations translate the requests into responses, in the form of universally binding decisions, and these decisions form the point of departure for the process of administrative execution. The executive process (that is to say, implementation) operates in conjunction with the complex bureaucracies of the national and local administration until the point is reached where it impinges on the interests of individual citizens. Insofar as this 'reflexive' circuit functions effectively, political command – both when it favours the interests of the individual citizen and when it obstructs them – is democratically legitimated. That is to say, it follows the correct market logic in 'responding' to the expectations of the political consumers.

Arguments against this scheme of collective legitimation through democratic pluralism are provided first of all by an analysis of the 'self-reference' mechanisms of the party system and of the counter-circuits of self-legitimation which it sets in motion. This analysis shows, as we shall see, that in post-industrial societies pluralistic competition between political groups is far from constituting a fulcrum for the reflexive circulation of the democratic will. The party system cannot be seen as the collecting and propulsive mechanism of a political will which emerges from the social base, giving 'prospective' legitimation to the procedures of delegated representation and 'retrospective' approval (or disapproval) to the results of administrative decision-making. The party system is rather the source, prospective and retrospective at the same time, both of its own procedural and institutional (self-) legitimation, and of the legitimation of bureaucratic-administrative output. Its 'self-referential' quality consists precisely in its capacity to establish and reproduce itself, *qua* differentiated system, through the continuous production of consensus and political legitimation. The parties do not merely collect the political demands which emerge from society and give them organizational and competitive power, because it is by overcoming the competition of other political demands that they succeed in establishing themselves in the political arena. Nor do they stop at the demarcation line traced by Kelsen, for whom the influence of the parties had to be rigorously contained within the sphere of legislative power, competing at most in the appointment of the supreme executive organs of the State.[60] On the contrary, the parties are constantly at pains to reinvest their power in order to reconstitute the bases on which it rests. This is a short circuit in which, largely outside the legitimated procedures, they distribute resources, advantages and privileges in order recursively to feed the flow of solidarity, shared interests and shared involvement which form the substance of their power.[61]

Given this self-referentiality of the political system, the social environment is not, as political moralists imagine, the space in which the universal values of politics, such as the 'common good', the 'general interest' or justice, are to be found. Rather, the social environment, with its growing mobility and complexity, represents a permanent challenge to the stability of the system, a potential for crisis which threatens the security and authority of the political institutions and, above all, of the parties. Self-reference is the immunizing response which guarantees the party system an acceptable level of homeostatic balance with the social environment.

The neo-absolutist nature of the 'self-reference' of the political system and the reasons why it creates serious *aporia* for 'intrasystemic' pluralism and constitutes one of the gravest dangers for the future of democracy are best seen through a historico-sociological view of the process which in the last two centuries has led to the establishment of the modern liberal-democratic State. Once the veil of natural-law ideology has been removed, as was suggested in chapter 3, the liberal-democratic State essentially distinguishes itself from the political forms which preceded it through the high level of its differentiation and autonomy as against other functionally differentiated subsystems: e.g. religion, ethics, the economy, science, the family, private life, etc. Its differentiation and autonomy manifest themselves both in the establishment of specific political roles – such as the secret, general and equal vote, the veto on binding mandates, parliamentary sovereignty, etc. – and in the definition of a precise, legally fixed, limit to the sphere of political activity. In the context of diversified and complex societies, the political subsystem can no longer be identified *tout court* with the general social system. Politics is simply one subsystem alongside many others, possessing no pre-eminence or functional centrality of its own.[62] Recognition of social complexity and definition of the limits of politics are matched with perfect functional symmetry by the constitutional establishment of certain fundamental rights of the individual and citizen. Thus individuals differentiate themselves and establish their autonomy *vis-à-vis* the social dimension both as private and as public agents.[63]

The mechanism of representation allows administrative structures to keep the decision-making process free from any too immediate or concrete reference to the interests of the citizens, and to avoid local or corporative pressures. Without the restriction of a binding mandate, representatives are able to operate within wide margins of freedom, referring only to an abstract 'general interest' of the people and the country. Strange though it may seem, the liberal-democratic system has, even more than preceding types of regime, a high potential for selectivity in meeting political demands. It is able to 'regulate fear' through the *peaceful* absorption within its own formalized procedures of frustrations and social conflicts and can manage crises by means of 'opportunistic' strategies which *legitimately* omit any direct reference to particular interests or to diffused requirements. In this way, it is able to give its untrammelled attention, in the name of the 'general interest', to the pursuit of its own stability as a representative political system.[64]

Especially since the end of the second world war, Europe has witnessed a process of the gradual transformation of parliamentary democracy into what Leibholz at the end of the 1920s perceptively called the 'party State' (*der Parteienstaat*).[65] This process has developed within – and has itself given acceleration to – a widespread and, *rebus sic stantibus*, irreversible evolutionary trend towards the differentiation and autonomization of the representative system. The parties originally came into existence as private associations, open to spontaneous allegiance from citizens who shared certain interests or ideologies. Once the parties had got over the initial hostility of the monarchic-liberal oligarchies, who saw them as a threat to their own 'general interest', they came to be viewed as the primary expression of the right to political association. As a direct emanation of 'civil society' and its growing complexity, they stand outside the bureau-cratic-administrative logic of public institutions. They are even potentially in conflict with the State and its constituent powers. For they show a strong tendency to oppose the powers of the State and also, equally strongly, to evade any control of a public nature. Their character is rather closer to that of a 'movement' (including even the revolutionary movement) than to that of bureaucratic structures.

Following the introduction of universal suffrage and the arrival into the parliamentary arena of the mass parties, the post-war period has seen a gradual functional transformation taking place both of the political parties and, consequently, of the very functions of parliament. Mass parties, whether arising as the expression of religious organizations or springing directly from the workers' movement, tend in the early stages to take on 'semi-governmental' tasks of the organization and moral and intellectual education of the masses in pursuit of social, rather than politi-cal, emancipation. Subsequently they tend to assume progressively more institutional roles and prerogatives until they reach a bureaucratic status which assimilates them almost entirely to the other organs of the State. This process of the publicization of the parties undoubtedly represents, as Kelsen has argued, a form of Weberian 'power rationalization',[66] since it answers to the growing specialization and professionalization of political life in differentiated societies. This in no way negates the view that, as a result of this evolution, parties lose their original character as movements of opinion and political struggle, very often under the guidance of char-ismatic leaders, and tend to abandon even the role traditionally entrusted to them by democratic doctrine: that of *corps intermédiaires* (Montesquieu) intended to act as a political framework for the people and to mediate the requests which arise from below.[67]

The final stage of this evolution is reached with institutionalized public financing of the parties, a course adopted over the last twenty years by the legislatures of almost all the Western democracies. In every case the manner and type of financing are decided by the parties themselves – leading to a reappearance of the familiar figure of absolute power. Public financing, far from removing the perennial shortage of party funds and discouraging secret or illegal forms of private financing,[68] in fact reinforces the party bureaucracies and concentrates power in the hands of central and constituency management, expanding the hierarchy of salaried officers, giving ground still further to expert advisers and marginalizing the simple party workers and grass-roots campaigners.

In the end, even the holders of representative or administrative functions, whether they are elected or appointed, and whether they operate at a central or at a local level, find that they possess no form of autonomous power if they fail to occupy a position of importance within the party's executive hierarchy. The party managements become the all but exclusive holders of the power attributed by Schumpeter to the voters. For it is the managements who 'produce' the governors, and it is the managements whom the governors 'represent'. Meanwhile, the old relation of representation between electors and elected becomes a dead end which leads only to parliamentary assemblies where the power in circulation is no more than a residual one of personalized micro-clientism. The central and local party managements also spawn a 'new class' of political professionals who, especially in Welfare State countries, exercise increasing influence on large sectors of the economy, the financial and information systems, the management of services and the administration of justice. Given the power it has to influence appointments in thousands of concerns which are more or less directly dependent on public administration (from the banking system to public contracts, business credit, foreign trade, town and health planning, the publishing and mass media industries, etc.), this class is finally transformed into a kind of 'proprietary corporation', very little different from the bureaucracies of the socialist countries.[69] Inside these corporations, alongside the many who directly owe their livelihood to politics, exist the multitudes who indirectly benefit from politics. In this situation, it is by no means out of place to resurrect, as Samuel Eisenstadt and Günther Roth have proposed to do, the old category of 'patrimonialistic power'.[70]

Within the parties themselves these developments are followed by the demise of the unpaid political volunteer, especially from among the young, a drastic reduction in the number of door-step campaigners, and the decline, in conjunction with the eclipse of internal democratic debate, of the importance itself of the party organization as a capillary instrument of ideological instruction and recruitment. Once this level of bureaucratic institutionalism has been reached, each party, regardless of its own political stance towards change, tends increasingly to identify the problem of its own preservation with that of the preservation of the party system and, consequently, with the stability of the public bureaucracy as a whole. But by then the single party as an autonomous political-bureaucratic institution and as an 'agent of the constitution' no longer, strictly speaking, exists. Its place has been taken by the entire cluster of parties, the community they form, and the 'unique, structurally complex, organism' which they combine to create.[71] Inter-party competition, insofar as it survives and in the forms in which it survives, is no different in operation from competition between producers in the economic market. Neither parties nor producers will take steps to damage in the slightest degree, indeed they will even attempt to reinforce, the common interest they have in maintaining the general conditions of the market.

The function of general legitimation of the political system fulfilled by the parties is a natural consequence of the fact that there exists for them, as bureaucratic organs of the State, a 'general interest' which is increasingly coincident with the stability of state institutions. Is it really to be imagined that party elites would embark on a fratricidal struggle which could only compromise their collective status as bureaucratic structures of the State, able to supply their own members and clients with an enormous range of advantages and privileges?

The party bureaucracies do not in any sense contribute to the legitimation of the political system through an ability to create channels for the prompt perception and faithful transmission of demands emerging from a pre-existing and autonomous political will. Their legitimation of the democratic system is carried out, above all, through the credit they lend to the institutional fiction of representation. They help to keep alive a public image of the political arena as a *general* and *open* system. The system is general because, thanks to the universality of suffrage, all holders of the right to citizenship are, whether or not they participate in the electoral procedures, 'represented' by the party system. Formally at least, the political sphere can therefore still appear to be the general social system within which, in accordance with the classic schemes of Aristotle and Rousseau, decisions regarding public affairs are taken collectively. It is also an open system because, again on the formal level at least, all citizens can freely associate to create new parties and, above all, they are free to join parties already in existence.

This development leads to an odd contradiction in the composition of the contemporary political party. Despite becoming an arm of the state bureaucracy, the party still preserves the legal structure of a 'free private association' in which any citizen may take part. (Entry into the parties is not in fact subject to conditions imposed, as is the case with all other state organizations, by public examination, direct election or the demonstration of any particular expertise, technical competence or moral attitude.) This structural ambiguity allows the party system to stand for 'representation' in the minds of the citizen body, and to legitimate, on the grounds of prior authorization by large popular masses, what has in fact been decided by the higher echelons of the parties – and so by the higher echelons of the State – on the basis of highly specific, and to some extent 'invisible', systemic logics.

Democratic consensus within the organizational circuits of the parties is envisaged by both the classical and the neo-classical doctrines as flowing from the bottom to the top. In fact the flow of political legitimation follows the opposite direction. From descending lines of bureaucratic power within the parties the process of decision-making receives its justification in retrospect, and legitimation has more to do with the mechanisms of 'political exchange' than with rational persuasion reached 'discursively' through the mutual expression of opinion.

In situations of intense information activity, the higher ranges of the parties possess by and large a remarkable capacity to generate information and to give it prompt distribution through the means of mass communication, which, either directly or indirectly, they normally control.[72] The flow of democratic legitimation which descends from the top of the system thus tends to travel increasingly outside the internal organizational structure of the parties, in order to reach the voting public directly through advertising techniques whose effectiveness has already been demonstrated by commercial firms.[73]

The clearest evidence of the prevalence of this self-referential logic within the party system lies, however, in the progressive weakening of the element which Schumpeter and the neo-classical theorists, Bobbio included, consider to be one of the irremovable conditions of pluralistic democracy – competition between parties. Clearly it is not the case that all forms of competition are at odds with the logic of self-reference. But incompatibility certainly exists when there are forms of competition that run the risk of introducing the antagonistic tension of zero-sum games into inter-party relations and so of jeopardizing the parties' 'general interest' in legitimacy and overall stability. The political market works in just the same way as the economic market in allowing competition to regulate the distribution of market shares, but in proscribing any activity which is not coherent with the logic of exchange and not therefore essentially transactive and co-operative. In other words, as is argued by two otherwise very different authors, Ralf Dahrendorf and Cornelius Castoriadis, within the (self-referential) political system of the post-industrial countries nothing less is proscribed than political opposition itself.[74]

This tendency towards the minimization of 'intrasystemic' conflict leads progressively to the very homologization of political offerings which, as we have seen, Norberto Bobbio considers to violate a central rule of democracy: the need for voters to be confronted with 'genuinely alternative' political proposals. Notwithstanding the attempt each party makes to differentiate its own image for publicity purposes – witness the increasing importance they attach to the visual symbols by which they wish to be recognized (the 'logo') and the names by which, often following professional advice, they choose to be known – the effective differentiation of the 'political offering' tends to be reduced to the point of near monopoly. Attempts to give artificial character to the image of the parties, for example by creating new types of charismatic and presidential leadership or by expending great care on the rhetorical and 'telegenic' aspects of their messages, become all the more necessary, the less the substance of their product is truly differentiated from others.

In addition, this process reinforces the inherent – and by now undisputed – tendency in parliamentary regimes for parties to 'converge towards the centre', where they are able to gather the greatest number of 'volatile' votes.[75] For it is here – and not at the extreme edges – that the parties can expect to find the votes of those who are moderate and ideologically less committed, and who are thus more inclined to alter their electoral behaviour on the basis of marginal evaluations of fluctuating social conditions, without the need for any laborious ideological conversions. Indeed, the 'volatile' electorate even seems to expand in post-industrial societies as a further recursive consequence of the parties' convergence and programmatic homologization.[76] In addition to this tendency, all the parties, even those considerably removed from the centre, have a propensity, on the basis of similar electoral calculations, to enlarge the range of groups to which they offer proposals of political exchange. This tendency leads to another well-recognized phenomenon: the reproduction of the pluralism of prevailing social interests within each party. And this, apart from generating phenomena of decisional stress within the political system as a whole, still further increases the temptation among the 'catch-all' parties[77] to level out their political proposals in the attempt to favour a plurality of mutually inconsonant expectations. Ironically, it is exactly this perverse plurality of the interests 'represented' within each party that seems to produce one of the most specific definitions of the 'pluralistic representation of interests'. In the end, this trend gives 'parliamentary compromise' a meaning entirely opposite to Kelsen's ingenuous supposition which saw in it the essence of democracy.[78]

On this basis I think it is legitimate to conclude that the tendency of differentiated political systems to assume a self-referential structure constitutes one of the most serious 'evolutionary risks' of democracy in post-industrial countries. It violates at least two of the three conditions of democracy defined by the neo-classical model of competitive leadership. Its effect is to paralyse the mechanisms of the political market, making a mockery of its pluralism, marginalizing all non-conforming expectations, and emptying competition between the parties of all its potential for innovation in the face of a growing complexity and mobility in the social environment.

## The inflation of power

The 'self-referential' mechanisms which produce a minimization of conflict and (self-)legitimation are not solely 'intra-systemic' factors in the ability of the party system to reproduce itself. For, at the same time as these mechanisms guarantee the system's stability and self-reproduction, they also lend it credence in the eyes of those agents of 'polyarchy' who operate outside the ritualized political sphere. The self-referentiality of a differentiated and autonomous political system is, in other words, the underlying condition behind the functioning of an 'extra-systemic pluralism'. The bureaucratic assemblage of parties can thus operate with stability as one of the agents of pluralism, making itself a carrier of those interests that arise from its position within a particular social subsystem and putting into the political market its own procedural, financial and communicative resources.

The functional capacity of the parties to produce the specific social element of universally binding power – and to produce it legitimately as a result of the procedural fiction of representation – allows them to occupy a bargaining position of particular importance in the pluralistic political market. Through its offering of protection, backed up in the ultimate instance by the legitimate use of force – in a word, by the power of the State – the party system defends the 'general interest' of all those other groups whose resources are located in subsystems (such as the economic, scientific-technological, religious, etc.) which differ from the political one. In this way, the legitimacy 'produced' by the party system is transferred to the entire range of pluralistic negotiators. This amounts to the firm legitimation of a comprehensive asset of power in its widest sense of normative protection of the social and economic order. In this way too the bureaucratic, hierarchic and even despotic structures which typify a large part of the agents of polyarchy, such as big economic businesses or military and religious organizations, receive a supplement of legitimation which reinforces their links of internal dependence and provides democratic approval of the 'private rule' which they exercise over their own members.[79]

Philippe Schmitter, in common with the theorists of neo-corporativism, has argued that in the experience of numerous Western countries the political system, or more precisely its legal-formal expression, the State, does not operate within bargaining relations as a simple *primus inter pares* or as an impartial arbitrator giving external guarantee to the agreements reached by private groups. Rather, the State possesses a power of 'concertation', i.e. of the attribution of public status to 'interest groups', and it is only the granting of this status that allows them to 'represent' their own members (or, in certain cases, the entire class of related groups) or to apply with authority the agreements reached at the level of corporate negotiation.[80] Without this selective intermediation of the State, the pluralistic system would be unable to function. The figure of the State remains central, therefore, in neo-corporativism, as it was, *mutatis mutandis*, in classic corporativism.

Schmitter is not, in my opinion, mistaken in drawing attention to the specific nature of the contribution the State, i.e. the party system, has to offer to corporative pluralism. It is, however, evident (and has become increasingly so in these years of crisis of the Welfare State) that the logic of negotiation imposes a drastic restriction on the capacity for political government shown by the party system. The production of counterpowers, which the neo-classical school hails as one of the most valuable achievements of the pluralistic system, turns out in reality, far from being a guarantee of individual freedom in a classical sense, to be a constraint on the non-purely repressive functions of political power. The close network of transversal linkings and of visible and 'invisible' exchanges between the bargaining agents – a network multiplied by the technique of role interchange and temporally stabilized by such mechanisms as 'log-rolling' – widens the sphere of the parties' activity, but at the same time inhibits the constructive, and not solely the reactive and adaptive, uses of power.[81] If one then takes account of the great variety, the functional dislocation and the micro-fragmentation of the agents of the polyarchic universe – e.g. individual parties, political currents within those parties, splinters of legislative and executive power, administrative and judicial sectors, single trade-union associations or their whole class, public firms, financial institutions and an infinite variety of private groups – then the context is more clearly seen within which the deficit and 'inflation' of power, to use the monetary metaphor proposed by Talcott Parsons, emerges as one of the central problems afflicting pluralistic societies.[82]

Faced with this political scenario, which overturns the schemes of the representative constitution and requires, as Schmitter himself has argued, a reconstruction of democratic theory',[83] the theoretical contributions of authors such as David Easton and Karl Deutsch, however brilliantly they have taken system theory and cybernetic theory into account, in large part lose their value. An entire series of apparently successful conceptual neologisms based on input–output analysis or the 'communicative' approach of *The Nerves of Government* in practice turn out to be unserviceable because of the causalistic rigidity of their epistemological assumptions and the rudimentary and centralistic nature of their adopted model of decision-making.[84]

'Post-empiricist' writers such as, amongst others, Herbert Simon and Raymond Boudon, have argued that the more the activities of political government expand and increase in complexity, the less secure and controllable are the effects of political decisions. Information assumes the characteristics of a structurally scarce resource, and even short-term social prediction has little credibility, once it is divorced from the inductive support provided by the regularity of recurrent and observable phenomena. Even time becomes scarce, and decisions are taken in situations of chronic emergency. Power fragments itself and is dispersed among a number of relatively independent spheres. 'Limited rationality', 'perverse effects', and polycentrism contradict any idea of the rational programmability of social growth and transformation on the basis of linear causal sequences between input and output, guaranteed by unitary political management.[85]

In view of this development, as Niklas Luhmann has argued in his important study 'Klassische Theorie der Macht. Kritik ihrer Prämissen', a revision of the notion itself of power becomes inevitable.[86] The causal and transitive conception of power needs to be replaced with a relational and reflexive conception, which takes account of the great unpredictability of the effects of each application of power and of the dependence of these effects on the recursive relations which bind the partners of a power relationship in a network structure which has no clearly defined centre. In differentiated and complex societies each agent, under different headings and at different times, exercises alternately roles of inferior and superior power even within the same power relationship. Despite the status accorded to it by the entire liberal-democratic tradition, the theory of the 'constancy of the sum of power' has to be jettisoned.

The idea behind this theory is that power may, in any given social context, be accumulated or distributed, centralized or decentralized, become absolute or balanced, but its total quantity can be neither added to nor diminished. Every loss of power suffered by one agent is matched by an equivalent acquisition by another, and, correspondingly, every acquisition is matched by a loss.[87] But the crucial problems ignored by this theory are those of the actual quantity of power which is socially available in societies with growing levels of differentiation and complexity and of the 'evolutionary risk' involved in the variability of the relative size of power, i.e. of its excess or scarcity in relation to demand.

This phenomenon reveals a dramatic paradox in the relationship between power and social complexity. The more the complexity of the environment grows, the more difficult the control of its variables becomes, since cognition, prediction and programming are then forced to take place in conditions of growing entropy, i.e. of increasing disorder and turbulence. Each political decider is faced with an increased number of essential decisions and within each decision the range of possible alternatives is widened. The broad social burden of the reduction of complexity expands in proportion, and a higher 'quantity of power' has to become socially available in order to bring about the execution and legitimation of the selected courses of action.[88] In other words, complexity is matched by the rapid growth of the functional requirements of decisions (and especially of synchronized, effective and timely decisions) and this leads to a corresponding growth in the social demand for power.

But – and herein lies the paradox – the difficulty of 'producing' and exercising power of a positive (and not purely repressive or adaptive) kind increases simultaneously, as a result of the heterogeneity and fragmentation of the social expectations which emanate from a strongly differentiated society. It becomes increasingly difficult to concentrate power, given the fragmented character of interests and after the expansion, as part of the development of social action, of 'blocking powers': powers, that is, which are unable to achieve anything positive, but which are extremely effective in hampering and dividing, even when they are operated by relatively small groups which occupy strategic or deviant positions. Herein lies the especial vulnerability of complex societies with high functional interdependence which has been lucidly analyzed by Gino Germani.[89] Furthermore, as Ralf Dahrendorf has emphasized in his development of a suggestion by Claus Offe, in societies of segmented stratification, as post-industrial societies most commonly are, the citizens no longer convey a single prevalent political interest. Instead, individual citizens form centres of pluralities of interests and particular preferences which bind them in relationships of solidarity and affiliation to different groups in different 'life spheres'[90] Since each of these groups tends to place itself in either a conflictual or a transactive relationship with competing groups, political expression of individual preferences is totally unable to lead to coherent, well-defined and long-term projects.

A more directly political problem emerges in the democratic 'governability' of post-industrial societies. Here the multiplicity of the subjects of political demand and the competition between antagonistic claims overload the political system and lead to the paralysis of its decisional capacity in a network of pressures and opposing vetoes. The entangled confusion of polyarchic interests is reflected in the 'representative' system both in its entirety and in all of its constituent parts, and it is only the introduction of prompt and efficient mechanisms for the selection and rearrangement of the demands that could make it in any way possible to reduce the system's complexity and to render it at all governable.

Segmented decisional processes, a rigidly selective perception of problems, incrementalist and marginal politics, adaptive, incoherent, and short-term measures are all aspects of what Luhman has called 'decisional opportunism'. It is a technique of 'weak government' which consciously orientates itself in accordance with mutually inconsistent and mutable values, taking the balance of the system as an independent variable and making its strategic objective the easing of the pressures and risks which from time to time become critical.[91]

The conditions which lead post-industrial societies to assume the form of 'weak government' may be summed up in terms of a threefold functional deficit: first, a coherence deficit, arising out of inconsistency or antinomy between the advantages and disadvantages produced by political decision; second, a structural deficit, caused by the absence of a unitary decider and by the presence, instead, of a nexus of uncentred and fragmented political decisions dependent on impulses of horizontal self-co-ordination and resistent to all forms of centralized command (*Politikverflechtung*, in the terminology of Fritz Scharpf); third, a temporal deficit, engendered by the growing unpredictability, even in the short term, of the variables within the political system and of its relations with the external environment, including the international environment. This third deficit exercises an increasing influence on national political systems, restricting the autonomy of governments both in fact and in law.[92]

A fourth element, according to a thesis widely accepted in the theory of law and in administrative science, may also be added: the deficit of regulative capacity possessed by the normative structure of the 'rule of law'.[93] The central legal category of the rule of law, the general law, on which hinges the entire system of the sources of right and of the procedural guarantees of individual freedoms, no longer seems able to express or transmit precise normative contents or to make them work on the level of concrete administrative execution (implementation).[94] The legal system of the 'rule of law', with its formal characteristics of limited flexibility and reduced capacity for adaptation and self-correction, seems ill suited to the exercise of effective and timely control of the growing variety and variability of the cases which emerge from a complex society. And this remains so, despite the flood of legislative production which has arisen from both central and local sources, as well as at an international level, where a growing number of supranational organizations are chaotically superimposing their own norms on the internal ordering of states.[95] The consequence of this is that normative sovereignty, which constitutional texts traditionally – and now, somewhat rhetorically – attribute to the parliamentary legislators, is in fact, as Carl Schmitt would put it, usurped by the interpreters. These are, in the great majority of cases, non-elective bureaucracies who tend to apply to the norms, above all those that show any signs of innovation, their own filters of particularism and preservation, with serious effects for the principle of legality and the certainty of the law.[96] It should not be forgotten, notwithstanding the flood of rhetoric on the 'minimal state' from theorists such as Nozick, that a deficit of power can actually signify the weak protection of individual rights and diffused interests, as is quite unquestionably the case in Italian regions dominated by the power of the Mafia, and as is also shown, again in Italy, by the subordination of transport and communication legislation to private monopolistic interests.[97] Lack of positive power can be no less injurious to the rights of freedom than an excess of negative power.

Directly linked to the syndrome of 'weak government' and a deficit of power is the phenomenon of 'power inflation'. The growing quantity of problems which require a decision, and hence the exercise of 'positive' power, lead to a growing quantity of reformatory projects to which the parties subscribe, yet which they systematically disregard. Power behaves in the same way as a monetary system in which banknotes are multiplied up to the point where money loses its purchasing power. A series of adaptive short-term micro-decisions are made, frequently under the pressure of time, in place of any radically reforming decision which would require the imposition of long-term programmes, a large investment of power and a high degree of legitimation. Micro-decisions, on the other hand, require only a minimum expenditure of positive power and a limited consumption of legitimation, since they restructure social expectations gradually, without provoking frustrations or far-reaching retaliations.

A typical example of power inflation is the weak and incoherent fiscal policies adopted by pluralistic systems, especially by Welfare State regimes. These policies, distorted by the logic of polyarchic negotiation, lie behind what has been termed the 'fiscal crisis' of the State.[98] They lead to chronic cash-shortages being suffered by public agencies and, in the most serious cases, to an irreversible imbalance of the State, which surfaces in a striking and paralysing disproportion between current expenditure and long-term investment. Power inflation is also evident in the helplessness of pluralistic democracies in such matters as environmental care, ecological restoration, sex discrimination, the quality of urban life, youth employment, the rationalizing of transportation, the reform of bureaucratic and military structures, the democratization of the mass media, control of racial conflict and migratory pressures from the countries which have no economic growth. Such decisional inertia comes very close to what Bachrach and Baratz have called 'nondecision-making', and affects the whole range of interests and expectations held by individual agents, not as members of polyarchic organizations, but as simple citizens in all the differentiated variety of the social and functional positions they occupy.[99]

But if the political system fails to succeed in keeping faith with its own 'protective' tasks – i.e. by failing to respond promptly to the demand for assurance against the risks of complexity – and if its functional tardiness continues to form an increasingly stark contrast with the functional speed of the other primary subsystems, especially the scientific-technological and economic ones, then it is in danger of collapsing, in common with the entire range of 'representative' institutions and procedures.[100]

It is at this point, when it develops into a functional need far more than into a conservative political demand, that the syndrome of weak government assumes the alarming features of an 'evolutionary risk'. This is the need for 'governability' to be assured through a drastic selection of social expectations in order to deal with a chronic decisional insufficiency. The relief of the political system from an 'excess of democracy' can thus be presented as the structural condition for the survival of democracy itself.[101]

## The neutralization of consensus

The explanatory hypothesis of the 'political market', both as originally formulated by Schumpeter and in its subsequent neo-classical developments, interprets the political system as a *public market*. Political entrepreneurs formulate their offerings in public, openly display their 'products' in competition with one another, and submit themselves to the final decision of the political consumers whose function it is to pass public judgement on the success or failure of the products and the producers. The political market owes its democratic functionality to the existence of a 'public opinion' which is in a position to evaluate the market's offerings and to control its procedures. This supposes the existence of a collective space – a 'public sphere' – in which a significant and direct interaction takes place between those who produce an offering and those who originate the demand for it. It forms, in addition, the basic condition for the belief that a degree of 'responsiveness' exists between the expectations of citizens and the decisions of politicians, and for the argument that pluralistic democracy, as opposed to the government of non-democratic regimes, is based on the 'consensus' of the citizens.

According to classical theorists of democracy, this condition was satisfied either by the institutions of direct participation or by interaction between public opinion and the elective assemblies, above all parliament. This public opinion was believed to emerge from the 'civil society' and to represent it both at the time of elections and, to an even greater degree, during the course of the legislature. For neo-classical theorists this condition is satisfied if competition between the groups standing for leadership is given free rein in the consultation which takes place at the time of periodic elections. For, given the presence of free competition between a plurality of parties, it can be assumed that the exercise of power 'responds' to the expectations of citizens and is democratically legitimated by the consensus of an autonomous public opinion.

It is evident, however, that the assumptions on which this model rests have already in large measure been overturned by the praxis of polyarchic negotiation between the self-referential party system and the totality of the agents of 'corporate pluralism'. As we have seen, this negotiation is conducted along lines which are transversal or even directly opposed to the formal circuits of representative delegation, creating thereby a sort of hidden substructure of state institutions – Alan Wolfe's 'double state' – which lies beyond the reach of public opinion. Only in certain limited cases and at a macro-structural level does this negotiation occur on the basis of an explicit attribution of negotiative competence to formal organs of the legislative and the executive so as to be in some measure 'visible' and controllable.

Except within this limited sphere, neither parliament nor any other institution constitutes a 'public space' in which citizens are able to examine and give conscious evaluation to the offerings of the political market and the possible alternatives. This is particularly so, given that private bargaining agents behave like pawns on an international chessboard superimposed upon national politics, whose moves are divorced from any control by national parliaments and governments. In practical terms, the agents of polyarchy, whether they belong to parties or not, avoid competing in public between themselves and instead aim for private settlement of the great majority of issues which have any strategic value. This means that there remains only limited scope for political controversy, which would need to be judged by the sovereignty of the political consumers within each state. It is interesting to see that in some European countries it has recently been proposed, *pace* Schumpeter, to grant 'interest groups' official representative status in parliamentary assemblies, and the idea of a ministry for institutional reforms has been actively canvassed in Italy. These notions form revealing attempts to disguise beneath the 'totemic mask' of representation the one element which, as Norberto Bobbio has maintained, is opposed to it in the most radical terms possible, i.e. the corporate representation of interests.

Isolation, secrecy and the fragmentation of the political market have already been identified as elements of a picture of democratic institutions which, to a large extent, sets aside the notion of the consensus of the generality of citizens. For the agents of a polyarchy, under the protection of the institutional fiction of representation, take for granted the consensus of all those who are not directly involved in a specific transaction and are thus in no position to 'see' or to control or to disagree with it. But the thesis which I intend to argue here goes deeper than this. I believe that in complex societies the presumption of 'third-party neutrality' plays a generally legitimating political role, and may in fact be seen as a replacement for the idea of legitimation on the basis of effective consensus.

In complex societies the legitimacy of political decisions is not based on general criteria of a political or juridical nature. Even less is it based, as contractualists aver, on a code of moral rules ideally subscribed to by citizens and used by them in order to evaluate the democratic legitimacy of procedures and political decisions. On the one hand, legitimacy is generated by a situation of diffused social readiness to accept as legitimate the decisions made by the public administration, even if they are eventually held to be 'unjust', incorrect or disadvantageous – i.e. a presumption of legitimacy is accorded to democratic institutions on the basis of purely formal postulates. On the other, it arises from the administration's ability to presuppose this generalized 'readiness to accept' without particular reference to values, rational motives or collective outcomes which may precede or stand in an independent relation to political decisions.

On this point the debate between Jürgen Habermas and Niklas Luhmann in the early 1970s still seems, to my mind, to retain great importance.[102] Habermas criticized the breakdown of legitimacy and rationality in late capitalist institutions and found them to be enmeshed in a growing need circularly to produce their own legitimation. But neither then nor now did he renounce the aim of achieving an inter-subjective communication capable of re-establishing the legitimacy of the State through a rational consensus centred on common values, albeit expressed in the procedural forms inevitably assumed by political legitimation in the modern state.[103] He agreed that in complex societies unthinking acceptance of bureaucratic decisions tends to become an 'uncontested fact of *routine*'. But he rejected as conservative and apologetic all theoretical proposals which established a functional equivalence between political legitimacy and procedural legality. In his view, a position of this type risked condemning to irrelevance a central topic of Western philosophical-political thought which he held to be crucial for democratic theory. This was the topic of the rational, i.e. non-circular, or purely functional, justification of political obligation. To his mind, so serious a renunciation endangered the value itself of personal dignity.[104]

Luhmann, for his part, blamed 'old European' provincialism for formulating the problem of political legitimacy in abstractly normative or axiological terms. In complex societies, he argued, the legitimacy of a political system is an event with sociological, rather than axiological, relevance. It is not, and cannot be, based on any rational or moral consensus of the citizens, but is the a-posteriori acceptance, following no particular motivation and 'without foundation' (*grundlos*), of the results of the decisional process. Legitimacy coincides with whatever involvement of the citizens actually occurs in the political and legal procedures of the State, i.e. of a political system which has radically 'positivized' the sources and relativized the aims of the legal system.[105] Once they have accepted their own role within the procedural mechanism, Luhmann argued, citizens no longer possess any opportunity of repudiating its results and mobilizing for their own ends any third-party political solidarity on the basis of values, interests or general principles. This is why an administration can claim that its decisions correspond to third-party expectations, i.e. that they are considered legitimate in every politically significant sense, without this meaning, so far as the vast majority of the citizens are concerned, any consensus other than that of pure and simple neutrality.[106]

Whilst classical writers of European sociology, such as Durkheim, saw the division of labour as producing political solidarity, for Luhmann social differentiation leads to conflict, lawlessness, turbulence and the increasing danger of the collapse of the system: his main preoccupation is therefore, like that of Parsons, with the stability of the political system in a context of rapid social change, uncertainty, contingency and unpredictability. This is the reason why he views 'legitimation through procedures' (*Legitimation durch Verfahren*) as a valuable evolutionary development and holds it to be not merely compatible with the institutions of modern democracy, but absolutely necessary for their stability.

Although reservations could well be expressed on this last judgement, Luhmann's analysis does seem to me to identify quite clearly the premisses of what I propose to consider the third, and perhaps most serious, 'evolutionary risk' of post-industrial democracy: the *neutralization of consensus*.

If within post-industrial societies expressions of consensus (and of dissent) tend to dissolve into a 'groundless acquiescence' in the results of political decisions, and if, in addition, the political system possesses such a high potential for self-legitimation as to be able to dispense with any input whatever of values or general interests, then it is legitimate to doubt not only the democratic, but even the 'oligarchic-liberal', character of the regimes which govern such societies.

That this danger is actually present today is shown, to my mind, by a number of phenomena which are characteristic of complex societies in their present phase of evolution. These include the relative scarcity of attention which is socially available for the political system, the systemic strategies for the 'absorption of disappointments' and the removal of social conflict and, above all, the mechanisms of political communication and their long-term effects. The increase in functional differentiation in societies of high technological development is matched *pari passu* by an increase in the quantity of attention required of each agent in order to adapt to a more complex and dangerous environment. A relative scarcity of the quantity of socially available attention then ensues. Multifarious topics of information, knowledge and experience surround individual agents with an increasing flow of symbolic stimuli and prescriptive demands which 'consume' a growing share of their potential for conscious attention. There appears to be empirical confirmation that the attention span of *homo sapiens* is a limited resource with little elasticity, either from an individual point of view or from an evolutionary one.[107]

Attention spans vary remarkably little from one individual to another; they do not increase significantly with the growth of knowledge and intellectual ability, nor can they be replaced technologically. Moreover, the underlying biological and neurological conditions of attentiveness do not seem to have undergone any significant modification in the evolution of the species over recent millennia, although there has been an enormous increase, especially in the course of the last century, in the social need for paying attention. We stand therefore at a real evolutionary bottleneck, with the seemingly infinite range of propaganda and publicity techniques through which public communication is transmitted in the information societies presenting a massive positive feedback. Indeed, the more attenuated the attention span of the 'citizen-consumer' becomes, the more insistently are the producers of social communication forced to make demand on it, until the problem comes close to assuming alarming proportions. This circumstance explains why public communication, when faced with the defence mechanism of agents overloaded by information stimuli, which mentally reduces the message to background noise, increasingly resorts to ostensibly harmless persuasion techniques of a repetitive or subliminal kind. These methods attain their objective by converting themselves into psychological routines which place the minimum of strain on the receiver's conscious attention.

It is easily understandable how, within this general context of a deficit of attention, individuals tend to grant the political subsystem a decreasing quota of their conscious attention. They protect themselves from being overloaded with information by relegating to the level of background noise anything which goes beyond the sphere of daily experience, giving preference to information which induces primary emotive impulses. Communication which concerns acquisition and consumerism falls neatly into this category, given its emotionally involving themes such as sex, music, sport, health, travel, dress, etc. Political information, on the other hand, deals with increasingly more specialized problems, and by comparison therefore finds itself penalized, above all in its more 'rational' forms, which evoke no immediate emotive resonances. The consequence, as we shall see in detail in the next chapter, is that such subjects become excluded from political communications in favour of messages which are purely suggestive or spectacular.

The political system is therefore able to operate without, so to speak, being observed, in a sort of penumbra where 'the third parties', i.e. the vast majority made up of those who are not directly involved in a specific political transaction, are chronically distracted spectators, who always have some other object competing for their attention and who consequently 'abstain'. Under such conditions it becomes highly improbable that full, simultaneous and widespread consensus can be established on specific political issues, and the tendency is naturally reinforced for the political system to economize as much as possible in the search for an effective consensus and to find instead institutional and procedural replacements for it.[108]

It appears to be the logic of functional differentiation and of the division of labour, with its appeal to the principle of economy in the use of the resources of power, time and money, that discourages differentiated political systems from expanding their bases of effective consensus beyond restricted circles of professional politicians and specialists. Indeed, such expansion would seem to have become functionally superfluous. Given the high heterogeneity and particularity of the political expectations which. emerge from a differentiated society, the political system can afford to ignore those expectations that have a similar value for all the associates – the so-called 'diffused interests' – and can opportunistically satisfy the particular demands of agents and groups who are positioned in different roles, functions and subsystems. In this way it can carry out a continual 'restructuring of expectations' by excluding from the formalized political process all forms of radical or general conflictuality and any disagreement which militates against a substantial level of 'neutrality'.[109] The absorption of the 'disappointments' which from time to time the political system cannot help imposing on certain groups is achieved through strategies of dilation, differentiation or amalgamation of their particular expectations, while the diffused interests, which possess no negotiating power, can be systematically removed and confined to neutral or politically irrelevant areas.[110]

Furthermore, because they are exposed in complex societies to a minimal amount of conscious attention, pluralistic political systems are able to present their policies in very generic terms (freedom, justice, efficiency, economic development, control of crime, etc.) which, although remaining constant, are nevertheless compatible with frequent alterations in the particular and specialist themes of political communication.[111] The lack of a goal or long-term projection of government action – or of a corresponding form of political communication to reflect it – further contributes to the weakening of the evaluative capacity of 'third parties' and to the disorientation of their motivation. The production of consensus and its 'neutralization' are seen far more in the matter of the choice (and the exclusion) of themes to be submitted to discussion and political decision from time to time than in the matter of specific decisions. More efficacious than strategies intentionally based on 'decision rules' are the mechanisms which modulate political communication and form public opinion according to 'attention rules'. These mechanisms, which may, following Bachrach and Baratz, be called in a broad sense 'nondecisional', have now been given enormous potential by the electronic instruments of mass communication and their long-term cognitive and political effects. This last issue, which I consider crucial to a reconstruction of democratic theory, will form the subject of my final chapter.

## Notes

1   Cf. N. Bobbio, *Il futuro della democrazia*, Eng. trans., p. 40.
2   Ibid., p. 25.
3   Cf. N. Bobbio, 'La crisi della democrazia e la lezione dei classici', in N. Bobbio, G. Pontara and S. Veca, *Crisi della democrazia e neocontrattualismo*, pp. 17–18.
4   Cf. N. Bobbio, *Quale socialismo?*, Engl. trans., pp. 65–6, 89–92; id., 'Democrazia', in N. Bobbio, N. Matteucci and G. Pasquino (eds), *Dizionario di politica*, Turin: Utet, 1983; id., *Il futuro della democrazia*, Eng. trans., pp. 24–6.

5   Ibid., p. 31.
6   Ibid., pp. 43–5; N. Bobbio, *Quale socialismo?*, Eng. trans., pp. 78–82.
7   Cf. N. Bobbio, *Il futuro della democrazia*, Eng. trans., pp. 28–30, 46–9.
8   Ibid., pp. 66–8.
9   Cf. N. Bobbio, *Quale socialismo?*, Eng. trans., pp. 109–10. Bobbio quotes
    K. Kautsky from *Die Agrarfrage* (Berlin, 1899).
10  Cf. N. Bobbio, *Il futuro della democrazia*, Eng. trans., pp. 64–5; see also N.
    Bobbio, 'La regola di maggioranza: limiti ed aporie', in N. Bobbio, C. Offe
    and S. Lombardini, *Democrazia, maggioranza e minoranze*, Bologna: Il
    Mulino, 1981.
11  Cf. N. Bobbio, *Quale socialismo?*, Eng. trans., p. 91.
12  Cf., *contra*, R. D'Alimonte, 'Democrazia e competizione', *Rivista italiana di
    scienza politica*, 19 (1989), 2. 301–19; the starting-point for this article is a
    'minimal definition' of democracy as an 'open electoral political market'
    which, for 'logical reasons', does not include competition and, still less,
    differentiated political offerings. The author does not, however, deny the
    functional utility of competition as a condition of the 'responsiveness' of a
    democratic leadership and of the relevance of political elections themselves.
13  Cf. N. Bobbio, *Quale socialismo?*, Eng. trans., pp. 91–2.
14  Cf. N. Bobbio, *Il futuro della democrazia*, Eng. trans., p. 26.
15  Ibid., p. 70.
16  A term drawn from the titles of two books, politically of opposite persuasion,
    by Vilfredo Pareto and Johannes Agnoli; cf. V. Pareto, *Trasformazione della
    democrazia*, Milan: Corbaccio, 1921, Eng. trans. New Brunswick (NJ):
    Transaction Books, 1984; J. Agnoli and P. Brückner, *Die Transformation
    der Demokratie*, Frankfurt a.M.: Europäische Verlagsanstalt, 1968.
17  The following essays are relevant: 'Quali alternative alla democrazia soci-
    alista?', originally published in *Mondoperaio*, 1975, n. 10, pp. 40–7, repr. in
    *Quale socialismo?*, pp. 42–65; 'La crisi della democrazia e la lezione dei
    classici', a revised version of the paper presented in 1980 to a Symposium
    organized by the Centro Mario Rossi, Siena, repr. in N. Bobbio, G. Pontara
    and S. Veca, *Crisi della democrazia e neocontrattualismo*, pp. 9–33; 'Il futuro
    della democrazia', orginally the text of a lecture given in the Building of the
    Cortes in Madrid in November 1983, repr. in a revised and enlarged version
    in *Il futuro della democrazia*, pp. 3–28. Bobbio's elaboration of this theme
    is not always rigorously systematic. Many modifications are made, not only
    of a merely terminological nature. For instance, in 'La crisi della democrazia
    e la lezione dei classici' Bobbio adds to the previous 'four paradoxes'
    of democracy (the contrast of democracy with the big organizations, the
    bureaucratic structures of the State, the incompetence of citizens, the mass
    society) three 'perverse effects': ungovernability, the privatization of the
    public sphere, invisible power. In the last essay this distinction is dropped
    and in its place Bobbio lists six 'broken promises' of democracy.
18  Cf. N. Bobbio, *Quale socialismo?*, Eng. trans., pp. 69ff; id., 'La crisi della
    democrazia e la lezione dei classici', p. 19.

19  Cf. N. Bobbio, *Quale socialismo?*, Eng. trans., p. 69; id., 'La crisi della democrazia e la lezione dei classici', p. 19; id., *Il futuro della democrazia*, Eng. trans., pp. 27–8.

20  Cf. N. Bobbio, *Quale socialismo?*, Eng. trans., pp. 71–2; id., 'La crisi della democrazia e la lezione dei classici', p. 19.

21  Cf. N. Bobbio, *Quale socialismo?*, Eng. trans., pp. 72–3; id., 'La crisi della democrazia e la lezione dei classici', p. 19; id., *Il futuro della democrazia*, Eng. trans., pp. 35–6.

22  Ibid., pp. 28–31.

23  Ibid., pp. 32–3, 54–7; cf. also N. Bobbio, *Quale socialismo?*, Eng. trans., pp. 82–3. Unlike Dahl, Bobbio does not devote analytical discussion to the theme of 'economic democracy'; he appears, however, to be rather reticent on the possibility of democratic reform of the capitalistic organization of production. On 'industrial democracy' see the recent contribution of M. Kiloh, 'Industrial Democracy', in D. Held and C. Pollitt (eds), *New Forms of Democracy*, pp. 14–50.

24  Bobbio's reference here is to Alan Wolfe's famous analysis in *The Limits of Legitimacy*, New York: The Free Press, 1977.

25  Cf. N. Bobbio, *Il futuro della democrazia,* Eng. trans., pp. 33–5, 79–97; cf. also id., 'La crisi della democrazia e la lezione dei classici', pp. 27–33. On the impressive metaphor of the *Panopticon* see P. Costa, *Il progetto giuridico,* Milan: Giuffrè, 1974; M. Foucault, *Surveiller et punir. Naissance de la prison.*

26  Bobbio's texts are not univocal on this point. Although in the essay 'Il futuro della democrazia', repr. in his *Il futuro della democrazia*, the 'visibility of power' is included among the 'promises' which could not be kept (p. 37), in the Preface to the same collection of essays Bobbio maintains that the visibility of power is the only 'promise' which had to be kept (p. 18).

27  Cf. N. Bobbio, *Il futuro della democrazia*, Eng. trans., p. 18.

28  Ibid., p. 37.

29  Ibid.

30  See R. Rose (ed.), *Challenge to Governance. Studies in the Overloaded Polities,* Beverly Hills (Calif.): Sage Publications, 1975; M. J. Crozier, S. P. Huntington and J. Watanuki, *The Crisis of Democracy: Report on the Governability of Democracy to the Trilateral Commission,* New York: New York University Press, 1975.

31  Cf. N. Bobbio, *Il futuro della democrazia*, Eng. trans., p. 39.

32  Ibid., p. 40.

33  Ibid., pp. 40–1.

34  According to Parry Anderson, an 'unsolved antinomy' exists in Bobbio's political philosophy between the temptations of conservative realism, which he draws from his studies of Italian elitism, and the stimulus of the radical-socialist ideology, which arises from his political experience as an anti-fascist and member of the Italian *Resistenza*, and from his permanent dialogue with Italian communists. This is the reason why Bobbio criticizes liberal democracy from two different and opposite points of view, without realizing

that this antinomy is crucial to his political theory; cf. P. Anderson, 'The Affinities of Norberto Bobbio', *New Left Review*, 170 (1988), 4. 3–36.

35   Cf. N. Bobbio, *Il futuro della democrazia*, Eng. trans., p. 129.

36   In other pages, however, Bobbio's criticism of 'invisible power' is extremely severe: cf. his 'La crisi della democrazia e la lezione dei classici', pp. 30–2.

37   Ibid., pp. 41–2.

38   Cf. N. Bobbio, *L'utopia capovolta*, Turin: La Stampa, 1990, p. xv.

39   Cf. R. Dahl, *Democracy and Its Critics*, p. 223.

40   Cf. D. Held, *Models of Democracy*, pp. 201–5. Held highlights Dahl's new interest in the theme of economic democracy. The term 'neo-pluralism' has already been used in German political culture to designate the theoretical position of Ernst Fraenkel and his followers; cf. W. Steffani, 'Pluralismus – Neopluralismus. Konzeptionen, Positionen und Kritik', in H. Oberreuter (ed.), *Pluralismus. Grundlegung und Diskussion*. Munich: Bayerische Landeszentrale für Politische Bildungsarbeit, 1979, pp. 31–65.

41   R. Dahl, *Democracy and Its Critics*, p. 252.

42   Ibid.: 'A modern, dynamic, pluralist society disperses power, influence, authority, and control away from any single center towards a variety of individuals, groups, associations, and organizations. And fosters attitudes and beliefs favorable to democratic ideas'. For the terms 'corporate pluralism' and 'democratic corporatism' cf. ibid., pp. 296, 297.

43   Ibid.

44   Ibid.: 'Even when the government of the State is restricted to elites, in a modern, dynamic and pluralist society a competitive political system in which compromise is a normal feature is very likely to emerge.'

45   Ibid. ('the dispersion of wealth, income, education, status, and power creates various groups of persons who perceive one another as essentially similar in the rights and opportunities to which they believe themselves entitled, while it simultaneously blurs or frequently changes the boundaries that distinguish the members of one such group from those of another.')

46   Cf. C. E. Lindblom, *The Intelligence of Democracy*, New York: The Free Press, 1965. Other pluralist authors maintain that the informality of the pluralistic representation of interests permits expectations to be satisfied in a way which takes into account not only the number, but also the intensity, of preferences. Furthermore, the defence of personal rights, which is extremely difficult if it is supported only by the resources of individuals and formal legal instruments, becomes a feasible task if individuals are protected by influential groups.

47   R. Dahl, *Democracy and Its Critics*, pp. 295ff.

48   R. Dahl, *Dilemmas of Pluralist Democracy: Autonomy versus Control*, New Haven (Conn.): Yale University Press, 1982, p. 52. Dahl adds: 'As complexity increases in a centrally controlled system, those in charge of steering need more and more information to avoid disaster, let alone arrive close to their chosen destination. Yet in modern democratic countries the complexity of the patterns, processes, and activities of a large number of relatively

autonomous organizations has outstripped theory, existing information, the capacity of the system to transmit such information as exists, and the ability of representatives to comprehend it' (ibid.).

49 Cf. R. Dahl, *Democracy and Its Critics*, p. 336; on the relationship between complexity and the democratic process cf. ibid., pp. 335–341.

50 Ibid., p. 311.

51 Ibid., p. 338; for an optimistic interpretation of the relationship between complexity, technology and democracy see H. D. Forbes, 'Dahl, Democracy and Technology', in B. R. Day, R. Beiner and J. Masciulli (eds), *Democratic Theory and Technological Society*, Armonk (NY): M. E. Sharpe, Inc., 1988, pp. 227–47.

52 Cf. R. Dahl, *Democracy and Its Critics*, pp. 338–41.

53 Ibid., pp. 336ff.

54 See E. E. Schattschneider, *The Semisovereign People*; S. Kariel, *The Decline of American Pluralism*, Stanford (Calif.): Stanford University Press, 1961; H. Marcuse, *One-Dimensional Man*, Boston (Mass.): Beacon, 1964; G. McConnell, *Private Power and American Democracy*, New York: Kopf, 1966; P. Bachrach, *The Theory of Democratic Elitism. A Critique*, Boston (Mass.): Little, Brown and Co., 1967; T. Lowi, *The End of Liberalism*, New York: Norton, 1968; see also S. Halebsky, *Mass Society and Political Conflict*, Cambridge: Cambridge University Press, 1976, pp. 182–233.

55 See J. Agnoli and P. Brückner, *Die Transformation der Demokratie*; F. Naschold, *Organization und Demokratie*, Stuttgart: Kohlhammer, 1969; F. Scharpf, *Demokratietheorie zwischen Utopie und Anpassung*, Kronberg: Scriptor, 1970; W.-D. Narr and F. Naschold, *Theorie der Demokratie*, Stuttgart: Kohlhammer, 1971; C. Offe, *Strukturprobleme des kapitalistischen Staates*, Frankfurt a.M.: Suhrkamp Verlag, 1972; R. Eisfeld, *Pluralismus zwischen Liberalismus und Sozialismus*; see also: F. Nuscheler and W. Steffani (eds), *Pluralismus. Konzeptionen und Kontroversen*, Munich: Piper Verlag, 1972; H.-G. Assel (ed.), *Demokratischer Sozialpluralismus*, Munich and Vienna: Günther Olzog Verlag, 1975.

56 Cf. C. Offe, *Strukturprobleme des kapitalistischen Staates*, pp. 65–105.

57 Cf. R. Dahl, *Democracy and Its Critics*, pp. 97–105.

58 According to Lijphart, the Westminster model is characteristic of pluralist regimes which respect the principle of majority decision, while the 'consociative model' virtually denies this principle; see A. Lijphart, *Democracies. Patterns of Majoritarian and Consensus Government in Twenty-One Countries*, London: Yale University Press, 1984.

59 See N. Luhmann, 'Klassische Theorie der Macht. Kritik ihrer Prämissen', *Zeitschrift für Politik*, 16 (1969), 2; N. Luhmann, *Macht*, Eng. trans. in N. Luhmann, *Trust and Power*; J. Habermas and N. Luhmann, *Theorie der Gesellschaft oder Sozialtechnologie*; J. Habermas, *Legitimationsprobleme im Spätkapitalismus*, Frankfurt a.M.: Suhrkamp Verlag, 1973, Eng. trans. London: Heinemann, 1976.

60 Cf. H. Kelsen, *Vom Wesen und Wert der Demokratie*, pp. 75ff.

61    All of this far exceeds the functional need of each political majority to delegate the implementation of its programmes to dependable and competent political personnel. This brings us to the problems which continental literature has termed 'institutional colonization' and *lottizzazione*. On the (in many ways emblematical) Italian situation, see, e.g., G. Pasquino, *Restituire lo scettro al principe*, Rome-Bari: Laterza, 1985.

62    Cf. N. Luhmann, *Soziologische Aufklärung*, I. 9–53, 154–77.

63    Cf. N. Luhmann, *Grundrechte als Institution*, Berlin: Dunker und Humblot, 1965, pp. 16ff, 186ff.

64    Cf. N. Luhmann. *Legitimation durch Verfahren*, pp. 32ff; id., *Politische Planung*, pp. 9–34.

65    Cf. G. Leibholz, *Das Wesen der Repräsentation unter besonderer Berücksichtigung des Repräsentativsystems*, Berlin–Leipzig: De Gruyter, 1929.

66    Cf. H. Kelsen, *Vom Wesen und Wert der Demokratie*, p. 20.

67    On the development, transformation and crisis of party systems see S. Neumann (ed.), *Modern Political Parties*, Chicago: Chicago University Press, 1956; L. D. Epstein, *Political Parties in Western Democracies*, London: Pall Mall, 1967; M. Duverger, *Les parties politiques*, Paris: Colin, 1951; K. Von Beyme, *Parteien in westlichen Demokratien*, Munich: Piper Verlag, 1984, Engl. trans. Aldershot: Gover, 1985; L. Maisel and P. M. Sacks (eds), *The Future of Political Parties*, London: Sage Publiations, 1975; L. Maisel and J. Cooper (eds), *Political Parties: Development and Decay*, London: Sage Publications, 1978; W. J. Crotty and G. C. Jacobson, *American Parties in Decline*, Boston: Little, Brown and Co., 1984.

68    In fact public financial support does not in itself rule out the use of numerous other economic sources, from donations to financial speculations, to secret or illegal economic activities; cf. A. J. Heidenheimer and F. C. Langdon, *Business Associations and the Financing of Political Parties: A Comparative Study*, The Hague: Martinus Nijhoff, 1968; R. Kraehe, *Financement des partis politiques*, Paris: Presses Universitaires de France. 1972; H. E. Alexander, *Financing Politics: Money, Elections, and Political Reform*, Washington (DC): Congressional Quarterly Press, 1980; K. Z. Paltiel, 'Campaign Finance: Contrasting Practices and Reforms', in D. Butler, H. R. Penniman and A. Ranney (eds), *Democracy and the Polls*, Washington (DC) and London: AEI Studies, 1981. On the Italian situation see G. Pasquino, *Restituire lo scettro al principe, passim*; and my 'Una legge per i partiti politici', *Micromega*, 1 (1986), 2. 34–49.

69    Cf. A. Manzella, 'La casa comune partitocratica', *Micromega*, 5 (1990), 4. 48.

70    See S. N. Eisenstadt, *Traditional Patrimonialism and Modern Neopatrimonialism*, Beverly Hills (Calif.): Sage Publications, 1973; G. Roth, *Politische Herrschaft und persönliche Freiheit. Heidelberger Max Weber-Vorlesungen 1983*, Part I, *Charisma und Patrimonialismus heute*, Frankfurt a.M.: Suhrkamp Verlag, 1987.

71    Cf. A. Manzella, 'La casa comune partitocratica', pp. 44–55.

72 The Italian situation provides a good example of this: political control over the three public TV channels is distributed among the majority parties and the opposition, while free-market TV is also under the patronage of some political parties. More precisely, however, free-market TV is dominated by the quasi-monopoly of Fininvest (Silvio Berlusconi). Fininvest has close links with the Italian Socialist Party (Bettino Craxi), which is already entitled to control of the second channel of public TV. Silvio Berlusconi and Bettino Craxi are known to be close personal friends.

73 See L. D. Epstein, 'Political Parties: Organization', in D. Butler, H. R. Penniman and A. Ranney (eds), *Democracy and the Polls*, pp. 52–74; G. Benjamin (ed.), *The Communication Revolution in Politics*, New York: Academy of Political Science, 1982; J. B. Abramson, F. C. Arterton and G. R. Orren, *The Electronic Commonwealth: The Impact of New Media Technologies on Democratic Politics*, New York: Basic Books, 1988.

74 Cf. R. Dahrendorf, 'Declino delle opposizioni e minoranze morali', *Micromega*, 3 (1988), 2. 77–100; M. Gauchet and C. Castoriadis, 'L'idea di rivoluzione ha ancora senso?' *Micromega*, 5 (1990), 1. 197–202. Dahrendorf maintains that within major European countries such as England, France, Germany, Italy, Switzerland and Belgium, opposition is marginalized or confused and has no ideas or programmes. Dissenters steer clear of public engagements and give their support at most to forms of 'moral opposition'. According to Castoriadis, the unlimited expansion of production and consumerism is the universal paradigm of the collective imagination and of political decision-making by the 'conservative oligarchies' which dominate industrial countries. A deep-seated, generalized conformity kills individual autonomy and deprives the 'right–left' opposition of any real content.

75 See H. Daalder and P. Mair (eds), *Western European Party Systems. Continuity and Change*, London: Sage Publications, 1983; I. Crewe and D. Denver, *Electoral Change in Western Democracies: Patterns and Sources of Electoral Volatility*, London: Croom Helm, 1985.

76 See S. Bartolini and P. Mair, *Identity, Competition, and Electoral Availability*, Cambridge: Cambridge University Press, 1990.

77 See Otto Kirchheimer, 'The Transformation of the Western European Party System', in J. La Palombara and M. Weiner (eds), *Political Parties and Political Development*, Princeton (NJ): Princeton University Press, 1966.

78 Cf. H. Kelsen, *Vom Wesen und Wert der Demokratie*, p. 57; H. Kelsen, *Das Problem des Parlamentarismus*, Vienna–Leipzig: W. Braumüller, 1924.

79 Cf. R. J. Harrison, *Pluralism and Corporatism. The Political Evolution of Modern Democracies*, London: George Allen and Unwin, 1980, pp. 64–73.

80 See P. C. Schmitter and G. Lehmbruch (eds), *Trends Toward Corporatist Intermediation*, Beverly Hills (Calif.): Sage Publications, 1979; P. C. Schmitter, 'Democratic Theory and Neocorporatist Practice', *Social Research*, 50 (1983), 4. 885–928; id., 'Neo-corporatism and the State', in W. Grant (ed.), *The Political Economy of Corporativism*, London: Macmillan,

1985, pp. 32–62; R. Benjamin, *The Limits of Politics. Collective Goods and Political Change in Postindustrial Societies*, Chicago: The University of Chicago Press, 1980; C. Offe, 'The Attribution of Public Status to Interest Groups', in S. D. Berger (ed.), *Organizing Interests in Western Europe: Pluralism, Corporatism and the Transformation of Politics*, Cambridge: Cambridge University Press, 1981, pp. 123–58; W. Grant, 'Introduction' to W. Grant (ed.), *The Political Economy of Corporativism*, pp. 1–31.

81    Cf. F. W. Scharpf, *Politischer Immobilismus und ökonomische Krise*, Kronberg/Ts: Athenäum, 1977, N. Bobbio, *Il futuro della democrazia*, Eng. trans., p. 127.

82    Cf. T. Parsons, 'On the Concept of Political Power', in *Proceedings of the American Philosophical Society*, 1963, vol. 107, no. 3; N. Luhmann, 'Soziologie des politischen Systems', in N. Luhmann, *Soziologische Aufklärung*, I. 154–77; N. Luhmann, *Macht*, pp. 81–9, Eng. trans., pp. 161–6.

83    Cf. P. C. Schmitter, 'Democratic Theory and Neocorporatist Practice', p. 886.

84    See D. Easton, *The Political System;* id., *A Framework for Political Analysis*; K. Deutsch, *The Nerves of Government*. For a comparative evaluation of Easton's and Luhmann's political thought see my 'Teoria dei sistemi e analisi politica' in my collection of essays *Complessità e democrazia*, Turin: Giappichelli, 1987, pp. 51–67.

85    See H. Simon, 'Bounded Rationality', in C. B. McGuire and R. Radner (eds), *Decision and Organization*, Amsterdam: North Holland, 1971; R. Boudon, *Effets perverses et ordre social*, Paris: Presses Universitaires de France, 1977, Eng. trans. New York: St Martin's Press, 1982.

86    Cf. N. Luhmann, 'Klassische Theorie der Macht. Kritik ihrer Prämissen', *passim*.

87    There is also a similar theory of 'zero-sum' power; cf. H. D. Lasswell and A. Kaplan, *Power and Society*, New Haven (Conn.): Yale University Press, 1950.

88    Cf. N. Luhmann, 'Klassische Theorie der Macht. Kritik ihrer Prämissen', p. 168; id., *Macht*, pp. 83–4, Eng. trans., pp. 163–4.

89    Cf. G. Germani, 'Democrazia e autoritarismo nella società moderna', *Storia contemporanea*, 11 (1980), 2. 212–7.

90    Cf. R. Dahrendorf, 'Declino delle opposizioni e minoranze morali', pp. 85–6; C. Offe, 'Politische Herrschaft und Klassenstrukturen', in G. Kress and D. Senghaas (eds), *Politikwissenschaft*, Frankfurt a.M.: Europäische Verlagsanstalt, 1969.

91    Cf. N. Luhmann, 'Opportunismus und Programmatik in der öffentlichen Verwaltung', in N. Luhmann, *Politische Planung*, pp. 165–80. On the notion of incremental and marginal policy-making seen as a process which develops through a sequence of short steps towards the margin, see D. Braybrooke and C. E. Lindblom, *A Strategy of Decision: Policy Evaluation as a Social Process*, New York: The Free Press, 1963.

92    See F. W. Scharpf, 'Politische Planung zwischen Anspruch und Realität', in

M. Lendi and W. Linder (eds), *Politische Planung in Theorie und Praxis*, Bern and Stuttgart: Haupt, 1980; F. W. Scharpf, *Politikverflechtung*, II, Kronberg/Ts.: Scriptor, 1977.

93  See, e.g., G. Teubner (ed.), *Dilemmas of Law in the Welfare State*, Berlin and New York: De Gruyter, 1984; G. Teubner and H. Willke, 'Kontext und Autonomie: Gesellschaftliche Selbststeuerung durch reflexives Recht', *Zeitschrift für Soziologie*, 6 (1964), 1. 4–35.

94  See R. Maintz (ed.), *Implementation politischer Programme. Empirische Forschungsberichte*, Königstein/Ts: Athenäum, 1980; E. Bardach, *The Implementation Game: What Happens After a Bill Becomes a Law*, Cambridge (Mass.): Harvard University Press, 1977.

95  See A. Cassese, *International Law in a Divided World*, Oxford: Oxford University Press, 1986. On the relationship between the 'process of globalization' and the limitations of the sovereignty of national states cf. D. Held, *Political Theory and the Modern State*, Stanford (Calif.): Stanford University Press, 1989, pp. 214–42.

96  See L. Ferrajoli, *Diritto e ragione*, Rome–Bari: Laterza, 1989, *passim*. However, violation by the interpreter of the explicit statements of the law is very frequently the condition for the implementation of the law. In other instances, a more or less deliberate *ignorantia legis*, as is proved a *contrario* by the 'white strikes', is the condition for the functioning of whole administrative structures. In such a situation as this, the 'decisionist' option may well be very tempting.

97  I refer to the virtually unlimited power exerted by Fiat on Italian transport policy and, in the area of telecommunications, by Fininvest and its director, Silvio Berlusconi. Fininvest occupies a large portion of the Italian TV market (with important offshoots in France and Spain). It is strongly supported by moderate parties, particularly by the PSI and its leader Bettino Craxi, and makes valuable contributions to these parties in terms of discounts on the tariffs for political advertisements. When in 1990 the Italian parliament finally passed a law regulating the private telecommunications sector it was decided to postpone for two years the enforcement of rules limiting the interruption of films by commercial advertisements in order to safeguard the interests of Fininvest, which still had large stocks of film to be sold.

98  Cf. J. O'Connor, *The Fiscal Crisis of the State*, New York: St Martin Press, 1973.

99  Schmitter grants that the corporatist limitation of power frustrates the expectations of simple citizens such as 'consumers, taxpayers, youths, feminists, irregular workers, foreigners, cultural minorities, nature lovers, pedestrians', etc.; cf. P. Schmitter, 'Democratic Theory and Neocorporatist Practice', pp. 915–9.

100  On the *décalage* in terms of the functional velocity between the political subsystem and the other primary social subsystems see my 'Il tempo della politica', *Iride*, 1 (1989), 2. 141–8.

101  See M. J. Crozier, S. P. Huntington and J. Watanuki, *The Crisis of Demo-*

*cracy: Reports on the Governability of Democracy to the Trilateral Commission*, New York: New York University Press, 1975; W. Hennis et al., *Regierbarkeit*, Stuttgart: Klett-Cotta, 1977; on the same subject see also C. Offe, 'Unregierbarkeit. Zur Renaissance konservativer Krisentheorien', in J. Habermas (ed.), *Stichworte zur geistigen Situation der Zeit*, Frankfurt a.M.: Suhrkamp Verlag, 1973.

102   Cf. J. Habermas and N. Luhmann, *Theorie der Gesellschaft oder Sozialtechnologie*, pp. 260–9; J. Habermas, *Legitimationsprobleme in Spätkapitalismus*, pp. 178–93; J. Habermas, *Zur Rekonstruktion des Historischen Materialismus*, pp. 276–81. In this work Habermas criticizes Schumpeter's model of democracy which denies the relevance of procedures and premises of a 'free agreement and discursive formation of the will' (ibid., p. 279).

103   Ibid.

104   Cf. J. Habermas, *Legitimationsprobleme im Spätkapitalismus*, pp. 194–6.

105   Cf. N. Luhmann, 'Positivität des Rechts als Voraussetzung einer modernen Gesellschaft', *Jahrbuch für Rechtssoziologie und Rechtstheorie*, 1 (1970). 175–202; N. Luhmann, *Soziologische Aufklärung*, I. 178–202.

106   Cf. N. Luhmann, *Legitimation durch Verfahren*, p. 32; N. Luhmann, *Rechtssoziologie*, pp. 72, 259–66.

107   On voluntary attention (or 'durable concentration') see A. Bale, *L'attention*, Paris: Presses Universitaires de France, 1970.

108   Cf. N. Luhmann, *Rechtssoziologie*, p. 72: 'It is impossible to know which school reform will be preferred by peasants, which trial system will be preferred by housewives, which trade conditions will be preferred by middle-school teachers. It is necessary therefore realistically to admit that these kinds of opinion do not exist and cannot be produced, and that nowadays only the institutional fiction of opinions can be produced'; N. Luhmann, *Politische Planung*, pp. 15–7.

109   Cf. N. Luhmann, *Legitimation durch Verfahren*, pp. 171–3.

110   Cf. C. Offe, 'Politische Herrschaft und Klassenstrukturen', in G. Kress and D. Senghaas (eds), *Politikwissenschaft*, Frankfurt a.M.: Europäische Verlagsanstalt, 1971, pp. 155–89; C. Offe, 'Krisen des Krisenmanagement: Elemente einer politischen Krisentheorie', in M. Jänicke (ed.), *Herrschaft und Krise*, Opladen: Westdeutscher Verlag, 1973, pp. 197–223.

111   Cf. N. Luhmann, *Politische Planung*, pp. 12–17, 24–7.

# 5 The Principality of Communication

A prince should appear, upon seeing and hearing him, to be all mercy, all faithfulness, all integrity, all kindness, all religion. And men in general judge more by their eyes than their hands; for everyone can see but few can feel. Everyone sees what you seem to be, few touch upon what you are, and those few do not dare to contradict the opinion of the many who have the majesty of the state to defend them.

Machiavelli, *Il Principe*

## The sovereignty of the political consumer

As we have seen in chapter 3, one of the constitutive axioms of the neo-classical doctrine of democracy – alongside pluralism and the competition between elites for political leadership – is the sovereignty of the political consumer. Political competition, according to Schumpeter and Plamenatz, can call itself democratic only when it is a 'free competition for a free vote'.[1] Dahl, for his part, maintains that pluralist democracy differs from 'guardianship' in that it starts from the postulate of personal autonomy and therefore takes for granted that each individual is, by virtue of his capacity for psychological and moral self-determination, the best judge of his own interests.[2]

In accordance with this postulate, he argues, democratic institutions work towards the realization of the maximum possible freedom by guaranteeing equal opportunity to all to have their own expectations entered onto the agenda of the decisional process.[3] In a democracy, all citizens should be free to participate in the political competition, either as candidates or as voters, and should be able to give public expression to their opinions, including their dissent, without this laying them open to any serious personal risk.[4] Freedom of public opinion, Sartori then adds, should be considered 'the substantive and effective foundation' of democracy because it constitutes 'the element which gives substance and effect to popular sovereignty'.[5] These conditions quite clearly exclude the possibility of violence being used in a democracy as an instrument of political competition. But they entail, above all else, as Schumpeter argues, 'a considerable amount of freedom of speech *for all*' and in particular 'a considerable amount of freedom of the press'.[6]

The neo-classical doctrine therefore cannot avoid positing freedom of public opinion and the autonomy of the political agent (in a sense other than the purely formal or negative) as 'procedural' conditions of democracy. However, as we have seen, the sovereignty of the political consumer, especially in Schumpeter's analysis, is in the end found to be compromised by the ability of political and economic groups to use methods borrowed from commercial propaganda to influence the process by which our political will is formed. In seriously contradictory terms, as we shall shortly see, Schumpeter comes to argue that consumers, whether they are buyers of economic or of political products,

> are so amenable to the influence of advertising and other methods of persuasion that producers often seem to dictate to them instead of being directed by them. The technique of successful advertising is particularly instructive. There is indeed nearly always some appeal to the reason. But mere assertion, often repeated, counts for more than rational argument and so does the direct attack upon the subconscious which takes the form of attempts to evoke and crystallize pleasant associations of an entirely extra-rational, and very frequently of a sexual, nature.[7]

Political propaganda is successful, therefore, precisely to the extent to which, through its recourse to persuasive techniques of a suggestive and repetitive kind, it avoids committing itself to rational arguments which could arouse the critical capacities of the recipient of the message and stimulate his awareness.[8] In this respect, the consumer of 'political products', according to both Schumpeter and, subsequently, Sartori, is distinctly less advantaged than the consumer of economic goods, in that the quality of products in everyday use, from food to clothing or cigarettes, can to some extent be controlled.[9] Political products, in contrast, are so indeterminate and unrelated to everyday experience that no 'sense of reality', and hence no 'sense of responsibility', operates to give rational direction to the political consumer's choices.[10] If Jefferson's dictum that 'in the end the people are wiser than any single individual can be' is to have any sense at all, it can only be true, according to Schumpeter, retrospectively and over considerably extended periods of time.[11]

In any event, he goes on to argue, it is pointless to expect that political preferences have effects analogous to those exercised by economic preferences for consumer goods. While it is true that the public's economic preferences can clearly reward or punish producers on the basis of the quality or price of their goods, political reaction and behaviour is much less obviously expressed or interpreted. It is practically impossible for political information not to be in some way 'adulterated or selective'. This is a result not only of the prejudice and inevitable slant of those who aim to further certain ideals or interests, but also of the biased position of the actual recipients of any political message.[12] It is precisely this bias that, as he most acutely observes, acts as a positive selector of the contents of the message, with the result that an increase in political information is normally also accompanied by an increase in political bias.[13]

At this point, then, it seems entirely proper for us to ask wherein, for Schumpeter, lies the free competition for a free vote, the freedom of speech for all and freedom of the press, if political and economic oligarchies are, as he shows, in a position to 'create the will of the people' by using propagandist techniques. It is amazing that, for all the strength of his realism, it never occurred to him to counter this with the suggestion that there might be a political or legal reaction or at least some critical resistance to the new techniques of persuasion operated by both economic and political entrepreneurs. Nor, equally surprisingly, did he entertain any doubts on the democratic nature of this kind of political market. On the contrary, he maintained that the manipulation of citizens' political opinions was 'an essential part of the democratic process' and that the psychological techniques employed in the administration and propaganda of the political parties were no mere accessories, but in fact 'the essence of politics'.[14] The essence of democracy would then, according to this argument, lie in the use of civil and political liberties to suppress the autonomy of individuals. It is worth recalling, in this context, his principle that voters should abide strictly by their procedural function, which is that of contributing to the production of a government through the acceptance of a political leadership, without in any way interfering with the activity of parliament or the executive organs.[15]

A similar level of ambiguity is equally apparent in the work of those theorists of democratic pluralism who have followed in Schumpeter's footsteps – in particular Dahl, Plamenatz, Sartori and Aron, as well as Downs and the other 'economists' of democracy[16] – and have maintained that in a democratic regime public opinion, despite the influence of political and economic groups, still has an essential part to play.

John Plamenatz grants the illusoriness of the notion of 'popular will' and acknowledges limitations to the political competence and psychological autonomy of the average citizen. But he rejects the idea that these limitations have anything to do with the freedom of electoral procedures and their democratic nature. What counts for him is that the voter should be able 'freely' to express his political preferences in the context of a 'free competition between a plurality of parties. Whether or not the political preferences of an individual voter are acquired with freedom is not a relevant consideration. 'Whether his vote is free or not does not depend on how he acquired his preferences: it depends on how elections are conducted and on his being aware of what he is doing when he votes.'[17]

Freedom of political elections is thus, in his view, fully compatible with an absence of autonomy in the participating agents. Sartori has expressed this thesis even more pointedly: the autonomy of individual voters extends as far as their volition, but not as far as their behaviour in elections. For these writers, autonomy is a concept which may have some relevance in ethics, but is misleading, and even dangerous, in politics.[18] Given that the means of communication and political propaganda are at the disposal of all groups who present themselves as candidates for the acquisition of power, and given that there is no limit to the freedom each group has to promote its own candidacy, it is then supposed by the democratic pluralists that in a democratic regime public opinion is substantially free.

The 'necessary and sufficient condition' of our ability to speak of the freedom of public opinion is, as Giovanni Sartori affirms in characteristically forthright terms, the polycentric structure of the means of mass communication. Thus, in the United States, where polycentrism is at its greatest, the greatest liberty of public opinion is also to be found. In totalitarian or despotic regimes, on the other hand, public opinion is unable to find free expression because competition between elites, even when it takes place in the presence of the people or takes the form of actual election, is not submitted to the decision of the people except in a wholly formal sense. In such regimes there is no freedom of the press, information, discussion or political propaganda – the citizens are not in fact in a position to choose between alternative sources of political information.[19] It is the existence of this choice that marks out a democratic regime from a totalitarian one.[20] And, according to Raymond Aron, following Hannah Arendt, the 'fundamental feature' of a democratic regime is, alongside the plurality of its 'governing categories', the pluralism of its means of mass communication, such as radio, the press and television, and the independence of these from the political system. Conversely, the chief characteristic of a totalitarian regime is an ideological monopoly governing both political and cultural communication.[21]

According to the theorists of democratic pluralism, therefore, citizens are 'sovereign' in the sense that they freely exercise their function as 'political consumers'. Although they do not participate – except entirely marginally and then only occasionally – in the processes of political decision, and although as voters they are in no plausible sense mandators of members of parliament and the other elective assemblies, still they are not merely passive consumers of the political spectacle.[22] They are not comparable to supporters in a sports stadium whose influence on the outcome of the game can only be indirect or contrary to the rules. Rather, they are like buyers of goods in a supermarket who possess the ability, over the long term, to contribute to the success or failure of a producer or of a product.

In a pluralistic democracy the citizens are effective in fulfilling the role of judges of the electoral contest between political elites because it is 'electoral consensus', i.e. an acceptance which is explicit and formalized (not tacit or plebiscitarian), which gives legitimacy to the governing elite. The procedure which requires a political elite to subordinate its 'will to power' to the outcome of an electoral competition is democratic because it is through this free competition that the electorate succeeds, albeit within the bounds of the reduction of choices already effected by the competitors, in expressing a wish of its own and in having it taken up as one of the elements of the democratic game. Out of this procedure, as we have seen, there arises the especial characteristic of pluralist regimes, the responsiveness of governments to the political demands of the electors.[23]

The judgement of the average voter may not extend to precise points of view on individual problems, nor is it reasonable to expect the electorate to give competent, responsible guidance on the general direction a government should take, particularly concerning questions which do not touch on the experience of everyday life. All the same, the voters' political judgement is substantially autonomous and endowed with rationality. Citizens, Plamenatz argues, even if they cannot be expected to show the political competence of an expert or a leader, are still able autonomously to evaluate the qualifications of the elites as legitimate aspirants to leadership and to grant victory to what they see as the politically most meritorious candidacy. This is, indeed, the only competence which is required of them.[24] In an 'electoral democracy', as Giovanni Sartori unequivocally explains, the citizens' incompetence and lack of political knowledge can be absorbed by the system without serious dysfunctions, because the job entrusted to them is not the delicate matter of deciding upon individual questions, but simply that of deciding who should decide. That public opinion should be well or badly informed matters much less than its 'liberty' and therefore its suitability, institutionally guaranteed, to appoint, via free electoral procedures, the leadership of government.[25]

But it is clear from all this that the theorists of democratic pluralism cannot, for all the deep scepticism they express about the classical assumption of the autonomy, rationality and moral responsibility of the citizen, entirely rid themselves of this premiss without irreparably compromising their desire to present themselves as 'democratic' theorists.[26] If it were not so, democracy, which they intend as a simple side effect of a *modus procedendi* which involves freedom of information, speech and the press, would be in danger of appearing as an entirely casual and irrational product of liberty.[27] Without some sort of autonomy or rationality of public opinion, even the 'procedural' requirements of pluralism and electoral competition would be empty of content. They would lead to results which would be not simply casual and irrational, but also, in the long term, counter-productive. For they would end by debasing all standards of efficiency in political choice, and by threatening retroactively the free character of the democratic procedures themselves.

These, then, are the reasons behind my belief that the theory of public opinion advanced by the upholders of democratic pluralism can be seen today to be just as ambiguous, rudimentary and unrealistic as, fifty years ago, the classical liberal-democratic doctrine appeared to Schumpeter.

For the classic writers on liberal-democratic thought – from Locke to Kant, Burke, Bentham and Constant – the institution of an elective parliament was closely associated with the idea of a public opinion which could control the activity of the legislative assembly and legitimize its authority. The members of the parliament, free from the restraint of any imperative mandate, were to answer morally and politically only to public opinion, because this was the authentic, rational expression of the general interest.

But, as we should be careful to note, public opinion was not held to coincide exactly either with the opinion of the electorate or with any majority of it. Public opinion expressed the general interest of the citizens because it emerged from the centres of civil society – newspapers, magazines, professional associations, clubs, salons, universities, the stock exchange, markets, etc. – which ensured that the character of such opinion would be both public and rational.[28] Public opinion occupied, in sum, a kind of uncertain intermediate position between the electorate and the legislative power. It, rather than parliament, was held to be autonomous and incorruptible, and therefore formed the supreme embodiment of political legitimization. It had the particular function of expressing consensus, in the people's name, to the government between one election and the next. Naturally, in order that this could happen, it was necessary for publicity and transparency – as opposed to censorship and state secrecy – to be leading characteristics of the actions of parliament and government, and for full freedom of speech and of the press to be guaranteed.

It is highly significant that, in the course of the nineteenth century, at a time when the liberal State was emerging in the forms of liberal democracy and then of so-called 'mass democracy', the liberal-democratic theory of public opinion underwent a far-reaching revision. It is equally significant that this revision represents the state of theoretical affairs which immediately preceded the formulations arrived at by Schumpeter and the neo-classical theorists.[29]

With the decline of the narrow oligarchies of the liberal State and the extension of electoral suffrage, along with the appearance of new powerful agents in European politics such as trade unions, liberal-democratic theory abandoned the idea that public opinion emanated from the culture, rationality and morality of civil society. Instead it was presented, following the lines laid out by de Tocqueville and Mill, as the expression of social majorities influenced by new ideologies, whether conformist or subversive, which spelt danger for the intellectual and moral autonomy of individuals.[30] That these ideologies were rudimentary, acritical, inconsistent, confused, changeable, and the product of sentimental or purely emotional collective impulses, was shown by the work of Scipione Sighele[31] and Gustave Le Bon[32] on the 'irrationality of the masses' and was further argued for by Graham Wallas in his *Human Nature in Politics*.[33] The last two of these writers, as we have seen, provided direct inspiration for Schumpeter.

On the basis of such premisses, public opinion finally comes to be identified with the ideas prevailing at any given time among the undifferentiated public of ordinary citizens. It drops the feature of 'rationality', because it no longer aims, through public dialogue, at universality of opinions, but instead is guided by acquisitive and opportunistic criteria. The elements of autonomy and competence disappear also, confronted by the influence of a cultural force which extends the logic of the marketplace to information, knowledge and moral values.[34]

From these developments there arose the widespread philosophico-political literature of the early years of this century which emphasized the decline, or the outright demise, of public opinion.[35] But this literature also fell foul of a deep contradiction. For it held too firmly that the principle of freedom of information and of an open and critical debate between political agents was an unalterable foundation of democracy. The reason for this affirmation was again that the possibility of a free, conscious choice on the part of the voters was said to depend on the freedom of the press and on public competition between the parties. But it was also acknowledged at the same time that the assumption of the sovereignty, rationality and moral autonomy of the ordinary citizen was an ideal postulate which industrial society and 'mass democracy' had by then proved false.

The consequence of this, as is seen in the work of liberal-democratic theorists such as Lippmann, Kornhauser and Key,[36] was the need for a 'realistic' conception of democracy which no longer claimed to link the legitimacy of political decision with consensus or the control of an unreliable (treacherous or, alternatively, amorphous) public opinion. In other words, it was necessary to recognize openly that even democracy was a regime in which majority opinion played, and could not but play, a marginal role.

Clearly Schumpeter and the theorists of democratic pluralism have worsened, and even increased, the ambiguity of this 'revisionist' doctrine. This ambiguity surfaces, as we have seen, in the principle that freedom of information, of the press and propaganda is a condition of the autonomy of public opinion (and of the democratic character of political competition) and in the simultaneous acknowledgment – at times explicit, but more often concealed – of the deleterious effects this freedom has on the ability of voters autonomously to orient themselves and reach decisions. There can be no doubt, however, that Schumpeter's realistic analysis does take clear note of the eclipse of citizenship in modern 'large and highly differentiated'[37] industrial societies and lays bare, with equal clarity, the limitations to political rationality in voting behaviour. He is not of course wrong in maintaining that, *rebus sic stantibus,* the individual agent can no longer be considered the pivot of political action and judgement. But the suspicion arises that the taking of this position, in Schumpeter just as in Dahl, Plamenatz and Sartori, is motivated solely by the intention to re-establish, in the name of the principle of leadership, the sovereignty of the elites and the acknowledgement of their irreplaceable 'democratic' function.

The vital factor in this argument seems to be the recognition that the effective actors in the democratic game are those political, economic, professional and ideologico-religious groups who are able to make their own expectations prosper and to present them as corresponding to the common good or 'general interest'. The freedom of these groups is therefore of prime importance, along with a good measure of 'negative freedom' guaranteed to consumers (of both the economic and political kinds), because this condition governs the functioning of both the economic and the political markets. Negative freedom – e.g. free access to information and political communication – does not, however, mean the autonomy of political agents but, to some degree, the direct opposite. Everything else, including electoral procedures, is seen as only a ritual for the procedural legitimization of power – a ritual of 'protection' and social integration – which has no bearing, except wholly marginally, on the effective contents of political decisions. The electorates passively accept the normative framework and applaud the general results of a political game whose only actors are, as it is well that they should be, the narrow oligarchies that peacefully take turns between themselves at exercising power. Recourse to the ballot box has, if anything, the aim of regulating the relative strengths of the elites, not of affecting the choice between them. In short, the principle of leadership is seen as requiring democracy to be understood as something which has much more regard for the relations between the elites than for the relations of the elites with the majority of the citizens. Democracy is, then, little more than a name for good relations between the ruling groups.

In my opinion, these positions do not stop at mere ambiguity and an incompatibility with what, following Norberto Bobbio's criteria, would be even a minimal definition of democracy. Above all they are turning out today to possess little, if any, realism when applied to the situation which has come into being since the end of the last war as a result of the massive increase of the means of mass communication. They take no account at all of the theme – which is, to my mind, crucial – of the cognitive, emotional and behavioural effects brought about by mass communication over a long period in advanced industrial societies subjected to the 'information revolution'. Nor do they take account of the impact these effects have on the functioning of modern political systems, both in general terms and with respect to the specific interference they have on the circuits of political communication and the processes by which public opinion is formed. These are themes to which neither Dahl nor Sartori, for example, dedicates a single line of their recent large treatises, distancing themselves at least in this respect from Schumpeter's position.[38] My own view, however, is that it remains critically important for a rebuilding of democratic theory that political philosophy should turn its most central attention to the political effects of mass-media communication. Consideration should, in particular, be given to the problems raised by communication research, which is now reaching an especially active stage of its development. These are the aims I shall have in mind in the succeeding sections of this chapter.

## Long-term political effects

The contents of this section should be introduced by a few preparatory remarks of a general character. Research into the social effects of mass-media communication is naturally subject, in the same way as any other sociological investigation, to a number of differing, and to a large extent mutually incompatible, epistemological orientations.[39] These orientations have some considerable relevance to the results of the research. If the standpoint I have outlined in chapter 1 – i.e. a reflexive epistemology centred on the notion of complexity – is accepted, then certain consequences inevitably follow for the methods and outcome of communication research. Most of all, a 'reflexive epistemology' denies any relevance to the neo-empiricist approach, which was in fact precisely the approach which dominated initial research into the political effects of the mass media and still continues today to condition a large part of the studies on political communication.[40] Karl Deutsch, for instance, tried to construct a general theory of the political system as a 'communicative network' by relying on a particularly rigid version of empiricism, combined with elements drawn from system theory and cybernetic theory.[41]

The first systematic research into the effects of journalism and of the radio and cinema of the day was carried out, as is well known, by Lazarsfeld, Berelson and Gaudet as part of their studies on electoral behaviour conducted under the auspices of Columbia University. Their work owed much to the explanatory models of empirical sociology and 'political science' and was directed towards practical and cognitive ends within the media system. Their findings challenged the basis of the 'omnipotence' of the instruments of mass communication. Instead, it was argued, the effect of electoral propaganda was for the most part actually to reinforce voters' original inclinations, and very rarely to bring about any political 'conversion' in the form of a change from one political leaning to another.[42] The conclusion they drew from this was that the way media messages are received is by its nature 'selective'. Audiences tend to decode a transmitted message in differentiated forms, giving preference to the information which matches their own beliefs and blocking out what does not. A further selective function was located, even more precisely, in the 'mediation' carried out by 'leaders of opinion' within the particular subcultures in which audiences come together.

On the basis of such empirical results, a kind of academic orthodoxy very rapidly gained currency in the United States, from where it spread to Europe, and was later abridged by Joseph Klapper in the early 1960s to form the thesis of the 'limited effects' of media communication.[43] The receivers of mass communication, this concluded, instead of being manipulated by it, were in fact themselves in a position to manipulate its effects. On this basis, and in harmony with the methodological assumptions of 'political science' and the general theses of democratic pluralism, the theory was advanced that the recipients of mass communication essentially adjust their use of the media in order to fit their own criteria of personal gratification.

In democratic regimes, it was argued, citizens are not exposed to the influence of the media within such a situation of passive isolation as is found in totalitarian countries. Rather they experience it within a rich framework of social relations which media communication itself serves to make still more complex. Citizens in a democracy were to be thought of therefore as active, aware, socialized and critical agents with regard to the contents of the messages they received through media communication. 'Media behaviour' was, in short, intentional, utilitarian, guided by stable interests, and therefore impervious to persuasion.[44] It was the behaviour of people endowed with high levels of critical ability and of autonomy.

It is hard, however, to accept that the interpretation of empirical data in the work of Lazarsfeld and Berelson was not appreciably conditioned both by the methodological bias of the former and by the apologetic intentions of the latter. Lazarsfeld applied to media research the most rigid criteria of neo-positivist sociology, while Berelson exalted the American democratic system for its (alleged) ability to function democratically without the need for the presence of 'democratic citizens'. It was from this position that he derived his famous justification of apathy and political non-participation as functional elements in democracy, if not indeed proof of a democratic regime's good state of health.[45]

But these lines of research, for all their empirical basis, proved in practice to be as unreliable as the generalization later attempted by Joseph Klapper. Not unsurprisingly, the 'limited-effects' model has, since the early 1960s, come under increasing critical pressure within the general crisis of empiricist epistemology.[46] The problem with this type of research was that it had failed in any sense to address the question of the long-term general relationship between the media system and the social system as a whole. In following the prescriptions laid down by empirical experimentalism, Lazarsfeld and Berelson had rigidly circumscribed the range both of experience and of time covered by their analyses. The 'limited-effects' model and the idea of the active nature of media reception were therefore established on the basis of research restricted to single communication events and with attention given almost exclusively to finding the direct consequences of this communication upon the politico-ideological attitudes of the recipients.[47] However faithful they may have been to the canons of empirical research, Lazarsfeld and Berelson simply found what they set out to find, i.e. that political communication exercises no more than a negligible *direct ideological influence* on its recipients.

As for the neo-positivist epistemology which continues to motivate many of the political communication studies carried out today – predictably by American political scientists for the most part[48] – here I believe that a different theoretical position is called for. I suggest that the central questions in political-communication studies should in fact be the classical questions of the sociology of knowledge and the hermeneutics of culture.[49] For it is necessary, as I see it, to begin by realizing that the means of mass communication are under present circumstances the agencies not simply of political socialization, but also, more generally, of the production and social distribution of knowledge.

Nowadays it is essentially the press and electronic media that mould our perceptual attitudes and establish the collective criteria which enable us to understand our surroundings, acting as a constant context of reference even for our personal experiences. Cognitive sociological research, although it should not reject empirical investigation and the techniques of 'content analysis', should nevertheless vigorously assert the need for a holistic and multi-disciplinary approach capable of coping not only with the increasing complexity of the communication phenomenon, but also with the rapid integration it is undergoing both in functional terms (i.e. the expanding multiplicity of media) and in territorial (i.e. globalized) terms. The approach should also be capable of dealing with the ability of the communication phenomenon to use the instruments of propaganda and commercial publicity to fashion and homologize both public and private forms of social experience.[50]

A fresh, holistic investigation of the relationship between the media subsystem and the social system as a whole is, to my mind, the necessary premiss for the development of a socio-cognitive approach to the question of the long-term political effects of media communication. Above all, it should aim to supersede the optimism and reductionism which vitiated the early research carried out in American universities. But it is also necessary to remove the simplistic assumptions and dogmatic pessimism which lie behind the conspiracy theories. By these I have in mind not just the Frankfurt theorists, such as Adorno, Marcuse and Horkheimer, but also Western Marxism, especially Althusser's doctrine of the mass media as 'ideological state apparatuses'.[51]

A crucial area of study for a socio-cognitive approach is the processes through which the different forms of mass communication selectively construct and transmit to the public an image of social reality and then, using this as a basis, mould that same social reality politically over the long terms.[52] We need to clarify by what ways – and up to what limit, if it is accepted that there is a limit – the mass media succeed in self-referentially imposing their own 'reality' as the only one open to the recipients of their messages and therefore in making a selective and distorted image of 'reality' into the only true social reality, unchallengeable by any alternatives other than silence, inertia or madness.

## Asymmetry, selectivity and non-interaction

From the epistemological point of view which I have outlined in this book, the credit for having first opened the way to the new 'post-empiricist' tendencies – which may be defined as holistic, long-term and multi-disciplinary – belongs to the functionalist theories of mass communication. The basic question which functionalism set itself, from the time of the first media studies of C. R. Wright, had no regard for the (to varying degrees) intentional effects of individual communication acts.[53] Instead, it was concerned with the general functions fulfilled by mass communication within a social group. For this reason, short-term results which followed (or could follow) from specific information acts designed to advance either the aims of the communicator or the interests of the recipient were not an object of interest. Interest did focus, however, on the situation of normal routine communication composed of the production, diffusion and every-day consumption of media messages.[54]

From a holistic and long-term point of view, functionalist analysis of the multi-media system can be seen to have concentrated, regardless of the diverse institutional arrangements and technical elements specific to each medium, on a wide range of 'general functions' (and also, implicitly, of general hypotheses concerning the long-term effects of exposure to the media). These 'general functions' comprise cognitive-information functions, integration functions of self-identification and absorption of dis-appointments, ethico-rhetorical functions of the reinforcement of social norms, meritocratic functions of the distribution of authority and prestige and, above all, functions which stand as surrogates for direct experience. According to functionalist analysis, contact with the social milieu which is *mediated* and indirect, in conjunction with the increasing flow of information available, brings about the tendency to economize on *immediate, direct* experience. The reception of media communication becomes, there-fore, a substitute for action itself.

But the element on which the holistic approach throws most light is the deep dissymmetry which exists between the communicative roles of those agents who put out information and those who receive it. From the point of view both of communicative ability and of social structuring there are extremely wide differences between these two classes. The first consists of highly cohesive professional groups formally organized as capitalist business concerns or as bureaucratic structures. They are geared to seeing their professional activity as a contribution to an objectively true rep-resentation of reality although at the same time they are systematically engaged in procedures of information selection. The second class consists of agents who have no specific form of social cohesion, possess no collective perception of themselves as a group with a role to play, and make use of – to varying degrees selectively, but still without their possessing any overall capacity for communicative interaction – a symbolic universe already severely reduced in scale through the selections of the information-producing class.

The emphasis laid by functionalism on the asymmetric, selective and non-interactive nature of media communication (which is explicitly denied or simply left unmentioned by the 'limited-effects' and 'use-and-gratifications' theories) has received powerful support from certain recent developments in communication research which also appear to have significant importance for political research. Two lines of enquiry seem to me to be especially worthy of attention: the sociology of the communication-producing class and, still more, on account of its close connection with the theory of public opinion, the 'agenda-setting' hypothesis.

The sociology of the communication-producing class involves analysis of the procedures which govern the production of communication, and especially the production of information. These procedures tend to be kept apart from the contents of the communication itself: under normal circumstances media procedures do not divulge to the public the means by which they have obtained their product or what 'ingredients' have gone into it. The law has not yet gone so far as to require declarations of the kind which are obligatory for many other types of technological product. News-products, in particular, are presented as direct images of objective events or states of affairs, and are not accompanied by any 'reflexive' communication either on the intricate net of procedures through which the item has been sifted or on the selective decisions which led to the final form of the communication, as if such elements had no importance or did not even exist.

By contrast, the aim of systematic research into the organizational structures, forms of recruitment, shared values, career standards, and professional deontologies of the communities of information producers – newsmaking producers in particular – would be to show the crucial importance of the part played by selective procedures in determining the final form of the news-item. It would attempt to identify the 'filter zones' in which the agents work who have the power to open or close doors for the passage of information and who control the type and quality of the 'ingredients' which go into it. There is every reason to believe that in deciding whether to accept or reject items of news these selectors do not principally turn for guidance to the expectations of the public to whom the information is addressed. The public is a generally unclear entity whose views can only be hazarded in unfocused and purely intuitive ways. Instead, therefore, the context of reference tends to be the 'professional-organizational-bureaucratic' one, which comprises both the network of sources (e.g. the large national and international information agencies) and the professional community of colleagues and their superiors, and is subject only to the general limits set by sponsors and audience or reader ratings.

The kind of 'communication distortion' which results from this – and which could also in itself serve as a further refutation of the 'conspiracy' theories – is predominantly an 'unwitting bias' which has very little to do with any subjective intention to transmit specific ideological messages or with any necessity to implement instrumental pressures imposed by external agents. Thus there can be no support in this for the Orwellian 'Big Brother' idea. The distorting effect is owed not to the imposition of a totalitarian ideology, but to the actual structure of the medium of electronic communication – to its 'functional code' – which itself very obviously shows the effects of its positioning within broad technological, economic and political contexts. If a totalitarian element does exist, it can be ascribed more to the omnipresence and pervasiveness of the electronic instruments of multimedia communication than to any plan for universal political homologization.

From this functional standpoint the most effective criteria are those of the prominence of a news item and, above all, the 'newsworthiness' (i.e. suitability to become a news item) of an event or a situation. Naturally not all happenings, no more than all people or ideas, are equally 'telegenic'. From this it comes about, at least in the case of television-based information, that newsworthiness demands a systematic decontextualization and fragmentation of events. Background situations simply cannot be established in the very short time-spans allowed by newsmaking, and news items can only be such if they are in fact new, that is, in some measure sudden, unexpected and spectacular. They have therefore to be offered up to the consumer in the most immediate and concise form possible. Each item has to be constructed in the form of a narrative flash which is self-standing and conclusive in itself. Thus the focus of a narration inevitably tends to be upon what has happened, and very rarely touches upon any of the deeper reasons why it has happened.[55]

The hypothesis of the 'agenda-setting effect' is closely bound up with this idea of the selective functions and distorting effects of the process by which media communication is produced.[56] Its main argument is that the selective and distortive procedures which produce information not only convey to the recipients the contents of a selected and distorted piece of information, but also transmit to them the mental framework through which the selection and distortion takes place. In the course of a long period this framework establishes itself in the psychology of the public until it is transformed into objective criteria for the prominence of news items and into structures for the selective organization of the recipients' attention, awareness and motivation.

Analysis of prominence listings made by audiences has shown, when compared (in terms both of range and/or frequency of information) with the prominence values attributed to the same topics by the media themselves, the cognitive dependence of the first upon the second, both in deciding a 'daily order' for items, in which topics which are thought to be relevant oust others which are not, and in establishing hierarchies of individual topics.

These analyses corroborate a hypothesis which seems to me to be highly significant from the point of view of political theory: mass communication has the effect, over the long term, of defining the range of public attention and the extent therefore of the areas which are held to be socially relevant and even, at the extreme, to exist. Or, to look at it from the other end of the spectrum, the effect consists in determining which matters, through their failure to cross the threshold of multimedia communication, will be relegated to neglect and non-existence. The mass media issue no ideologically binding prescriptions on specific topics – in this respect, paradoxically, the findings of Lazarsfeld and Berelson do receive support – but instead they concentrate public attention on some topics, while diminishing the importance of others or even wholly excluding them from the cognitive horizon. The media play a decisive part in selecting what the public perceives as relevant because, by virtue of being the most effective modulators of public attention, they have the function of establishing and distributing what may well be called 'attention values'.

The electronic media in particular succeed in fulfilling this selective function because they, unlike any form of direct experience, possess such basic properties as 'cumulativity' and 'consonance'.[57] Their ability to impose a topic on public attention is the result of an infinite number of repetitions, whose total effect is to consolidate communicative similarities and to iron out dissonances. Their power of persuasion is derived from their being widely perceived as the repository of 'public wisdom' in that they exist as the single, effective and legitimized 'public sphere' within industrial societies of the information era. The final outcome, to quote one acute observation, is that the effective distribution of public opinion becomes a reproduction of the distribution which the media, following a 'self-fulfilling prophecy', themselves reflect.[58] The 'agenda-setting hypothesis' is in sum, therefore, recursive and self-referential.

# Teledemocracy

Such is the framework of problems and related research upon which a modern theory of political communication now needs to be constructed. It is also the background against which the whole question of public opinion and its autonomy within contemporary democratic regimes should now be rethought in realistic terms, by which I mean ones which are neither superficially optimistic nor the product of 'conspiracy' theories.

Above all, this aim is least well served by continued consideration of Karl Deutsch's over-ambitious attempt – of which the influence is still to be seen behind the work of those who favour a 'cybernetic theory of politics'[59] – to construct a general theory of the political system as an information-communication network. In *The Nerves of Government* Deutsch set out to elaborate a 'communication theory of politics' by borrowing such concepts as information, message, recall, communication net, retroaction, learning, self-correction, etc., from communication science and cybernetics.[60] On the assumption that information phenomena would be susceptible to measurement and calculation, he endeavoured to create a kind of physics of the communication of politics which would admit of rigorous explanation and prediction.

But this attempt, rooted as it was in a rigidly physicalist epistemological conception and elaborated within the empiricist-behaviourist paradigm of political science, has turned out to be of little heuristic value, and has consequently remained isolated and devoid of any significant consequences.[61] The implicit assumption which it contains – that the essential nature of political experience is representable as a system of communication processes – cannot, to my mind, be sustained. It fails to take account either of the power effects which social structures exercise on citizens without their being mediated through any form of communication or of the directly coercive and violent types of political power which require no specific linguistic transmission. Moreover, it ignores the phenomenology of 'invisible' power, i.e. the large area of power whose effective exercise is secured precisely because it is successful in avoiding any form of explicit political communication.

From the standpoint which most concerns me here – a reconstruction of the democratic theory of public opinion – the elaboration of a 'theory of political communication' would be far more relevant. Such a theory would need to take account of the new morphology which communication processes are currently acquiring within political systems subject to the information revolution. By political communication I mean in this instance the cascade of information with an explicitly political content which descends on the ordinary citizen from the elective or bureaucratic organizations at the top of the political system.[62]

Even more important, however, would be the development of a 'political theory of communication'. For the problem is one of studying the interaction between modern forms of mass communication and the functioning of the political system. Attention should be given both to the impact mass communication has on the techniques by which political power is exercised and on the general political effects which in the long term the flow of electronic information, even in its not explicitly political forms, has on the public. The assumption I make here is that 'non-political' communication – probably more than communication of an explicitly political kind – has a central role to play in social integration and the formation of public opinion in terms of influence, authority, control, negotiation and symbolized interaction.[63]

The first aim of such research should be to concentrate on the problems which arise in modern political systems as a result of the use political parties make of information instruments to communicate between themselves and with the public. It is already a well-recognized fact that parties are increasingly turning, for the creation and diffusion of their image, to advertising agencies who are skilled in applying the criteria of commercial propaganda to political communication. This is leading, hand in hand with the more widespread invasion of advertising standards into the whole communicative system, to the penetration of advertising techniques deep into the political system. Their effect extends now not merely to the production mechanisms of party images, but even to the actual content of political communication and decisions. The functional logic of commercial advertising, neatly encapsulated in the television 'spot', exerts its influence on criteria for the competition between candidates, the recruitment of personnel and the selection of topics for political debate according to their level of 'telegenicity'.[64]

In the United States in particular, electoral competition has now widely assumed the features of a 'teledemocracy' functioning almost entirely outside the party bureaucracies and resting in the hands of the demoscopic (i.e. public-opinion assessment) agencies, the political-consultancy firms and the 'Political Action Committees' (PACs), which exist for the specific purpose of financing, via extra-party means, the personal advertising campaigns of the various candidates.[65] The result of this phenomenon is a growing 'spectacularization' of politics, dominated by the attention-gathering abilities of candidates – or rather the *ad hoc* images constructed for them by their publicity agents – to the detriment of any rational presentation or discussion of the problems needing political decision or the available alternative solutions to them.[66] This process leads to unprecedented procedures of 'televisual legitimization' of the political system and its leaders, procedures which not only dispense with party participation, but also prejudge the selection and decision functions traditionally exercised by the democratic electorates. Central to these is the charisma of 'teledemocratic' leadership – itself a product of media manipulation – which exists in the short circuit between consumer/spectator expectations implanted by the media themselves in the mind of the public and the realization of these expectations in the form of personalized and idealized televisual images.[67] Judgement on the political aptitude of candidates is pronounced, long before they reach the electorate and even before they reach the television audiences, by the publicity specialists who assess and enhance their 'telecharismatic' gifts in order to make credible, and therefore financeable, their electoral campaigns.

As has now been acknowledged even by Giovanni Sartori, the election of representatives in the United States nowadays depends, more than upon any other factor, on the provision of financial resources which candidates can use to employ their own strategists, speech-writers, pollsters and advertisers, and to buy television space. This leads to what we are surprised to find the same writer, otherwise taken to be one of the most intransigent upholders of democratic elitism, describing as the 'paradox of American public opinion' by which the United States is 'the country that bows most to public opinion, and yet the country that has probably less public opinion worthy of the name than any other Western democracy'.[68]

A prime example of this degeneration of public opinion may be seen in the subliminal effects achieved by the political communication of Ronald Reagan. His ability to play up the protective father-figure image, and to paint himself as guardian of certain idealized American values, meant that any attack by his adversaries could only be seen as an attack on the American nation itself. The same goes, though in more general terms, for the personalization of political communication in the political campaigns of other Western countries, which show an increasing tendency to publicize the biographical details of charismatic leaders (or aspirants to such) – from the medical operations they have undergone to their domestic, sporting and sexual life – at the expense of any deeper investigation of their actual political programmes.

Another prominent aspect of televisual democracy is the growing transformation of political campaigns into 'meta-campaigns' and of electorates into 'meta-electorates'. The ability of demoscopic agencies to conduct (electronic) research into the political orientations of the public, to communicate their findings instantaneously and, often enough, to provide accurate projections of results long in advance of elections, creates a surrogate electorate alongside the real one. The real electors see themselves

replaced by their own demoscopic and televisual projection, which anticipates them and leaves them the passive observers of themselves. Individual
citizens, despite being the true holders of the right to vote, find themselves
subjected to the pressure of public predictions which tend circularly to be
self-fulfilling by edging them out of the electoral event. For when victory
of the opposite party is taken for granted, citizens' participation is discouraged just as much as when victory is predicted for their own parties.
In both cases personal initiative on the voter's part appears to become
superfluous. Thus the opinion poll replaces democracy, 'image' anticipates
and drains the content from reality and reinforcement is given to existing
tendencies towards abstentionism and political apathy.[69]

## Narcotizing dysfunction and political silence

Research into mass communication achieves its most significant results
when, according to the epistemological view which I have attempted to
advance in this work, it stresses the hidden, indirect and long-term effects
of the media. A connection needs to be made, I shall now argue, between
these results and not simply the democratic doctrine of public opinion,
but the theory of democracy *tout court*.[70]

Political debate on the democratic control of the means of mass communication tends, especially on the continent of Europe, to be concentrated
on the influence the political parties and large economic and financial
groupings exercise on the communication content which they consider to
have direct political or economic relevance. Thus the debate focuses on
problems such as the relationship between state television and the free
market, appropriation of state television by the political parties, the vulnerability of the market to 'cornering' by individual concerns, distortions
introduced by the advertising market into the running both of commercial
and state television or the interweaving (in most instances untraceable) of
'invisible' political power with the television industry. Such legal, political
and constitutional problems must of course be regarded as crucial for the
outcome of 'democratic' political institutions. But, from a wider standpoint
of political theory, there must also be added to them the problems which
arise from the long-term political influence of the cognitive effects of mass
communication.

From this broader perspective we seem now to be faced with problems
which call into question the very nature of the democratic system in
information societies and make its ultimate fate wholly uncertain. The
situation is one which offers a further – and probably decisive – argument
against the neo-classical doctrine of democracy and adds increased urgency
to the need for an entire reconstruction of democratic theory.

From this last point of view there are two principal aspects which should now be taken into account. The first of these is the asymmetric, non-interactive nature of mass-political communication. It will perhaps be objected that political communication has always been – and, even in democratic societies, can only be – unidirectional and in all significant respects closed to dialogue. But this does not remove the fact that electronic and telematic forms of mass communication are now producing cumulative and consonant effects wholly unparalleled in terms of the pre-information-revolution media.

The communication world is nowadays made up of a series of self-standing, but interconnected, professional groups, for the most part directed towards profit, who are intent on establishing their own strong positions within the international business community. For, like the large multinational corporations (on whom they are often dependent), they operate outside the limits of any democratic control. Internally their power relations reproduce the hierarchical structure of capitalist firms and public bureaucracies. Following their aim of ensuring the good functioning of the market, these national and international information agencies consistently play down (or 'consume' through the continual repetition of stereotyped representations) the most controversial social issues, e.g. the effects of the international market on the standard of living for Third World populations, racial discrimination in the United States, Israel and Europe, apartheid in South Africa, the problem of the South in Italy. In accordance with their standard functional logic – a logic which, even within state television agencies, inclines more towards the market – the tendency of the sources of multimedia communication is naturally to favour those organizations that represent governing interests, to take the side of producers' rather than of consumers' expectations, to marginalize the 'diffused interests' of weaker social agents and to discourage political innovation.

Insurmountable political obstacles, quite apart from the technical and economic difficulties connected with satellite and cable transmission, have rapidly shown up the utopian nature of the idea of the 'electronic democracy' envisaged some decades ago by sociologists such as Charles Cooley and R. E. Park[71] or statisticians and political scientists such as George Gallup and Harold Lasswell.[72] The availability of new techniques for interactive communication (teleconferencing, opinion-polling systems, automated feedback programmes, two-way cable television, etc.) would, it was claimed, lead to unprecedented forms of participative democracy, i.e. to a full-scale electronic *agora*. Electoral procedures would be replaced by devices for permanent popular consultation brought into being by the opinion-sounding and referendum possibilities created by two-way television. Today we can see that the democracy of instant referenda is, and will in all likelihood always remain, a scientistic mirage. Those who continue to espouse the idea close their eyes to the growing specialization of political functions and the profound scarcity of resources of time and attention available in societies of heightened complexity and functional differentiation.[73]

The second crucial theme from the point of view of a reconstruction of democratic theory is the further contribution to the dispersion of the 'public sphere' offered by the 'narcotizing dysfunction' to which functionalist research in particular has alerted us. Mediated contact with the social world, once acclimatized, results in a tendency to economize on direct political experience, given that an equal level of gratification appears to be obtainable from symbolized experience and that such experience also carries greatly reduced exposure to any risks of being disappointed. In addition, the 'dependency effect', which is caused by the fact that a large part of transmitted information refers to areas of experience which are unreachable by the recipients, has the habit of also spilling over into the range of experience which would normally be within their grasp. 'Narcotizing dysfunction' therefore surfaces in torpor and operational inertia, particularly in connection with the traditional forms of collective participation in social and political life. The increase in transmitted information is accompanied by a tendency to take refuge in the inner sphere of private experience and personal relationships, where control of one's environment and assertion of some residual personal identity still seems possible. Similarly, the large quantity of political information transmitted by the media – distorted as it is by the needs for 'newsworthiness' and 'spectacularization' – does not lead to a better spread or to better quality of political knowledge, or to increased motivation, or to a higher level of popular participation. In the long term it seems to produce exactly the opposite effect.

The 'public sphere' may be said, therefore, to transform itself into a reflexive area, a timeless meta-dimension in which the 'real' public passively assists, as if in a sort of permanent television broadcast carried out in real time, in the exploits of an 'electronic' public. Meanwhile, the overload of information disorientates all those – who are of course the large majority – who are not employed on the side of information input and have no access to privileged resources. The 'cognitive differential' between transmitting agents and receiving subjects, far from diminishing as a result of the information they 'share', tends instead to multiply. Those agents who possess greater cultural, economic and political résources find that they can put the information they receive to good profit, while those who are less gifted simply find themselves unable to decode it or to extract any benefit at all. This only serves to strengthen the asymmetric nature of political communication and the 'narcotizing dysfunction' which substitutes the non-interactive reception of communication for personal responsibility and participation.

One of the odd phenomena we have found to exist in complex societies is that individuals show an increasing tendency to obey commands from political authority 'for no particular reason'. I suspect that a cause of this unquestioning obedience can be seen in the 'narcotizing' transmission of political consensus which has begun to render obsolete one of the classic aspects of Western political philosophy and democratic theory – the requirement for power to be legitimized and for political obligation to be justified in a non-circular manner.[74]

Furthermore, if, as seems reasonable, there is some force in the theory of nondecision-making, which sees the exercise of power as involving 'nondecisions' more than it involves decisions (i.e. problems which endanger the stability of the political system are tacitly removed from the channels of political decision), then another important key is provided for understanding the political systems of post-industrial societies. Analysis should therefore be made of the 'nondecisional' consequences of the long-term effects of exposure to the media, and especially of exposure to the 'agenda-setting effect'.[75]

The political influence of the means of mass communication, as must now be beyond doubt, does not depend upon any supposed aptitude they have for inculcating the elements of a particular ideology or upon the capability they might be taken to possess of exercising a capillary influence on individuals' opinions and behaviour. This belief was the weak point in the 'conspiracy' interpretations advanced by Orwell, Marcuse, Althusser and others. The experience – and now the failure – of the ideological and authoritarian management of political communication in the countries of 'actually existing socialism' provides definite proof of this criticism. It has shown how, in complex societies, forms of political despotism can only maintain themselves by becoming more refined and complex in that they are forced to rely increasingly on persuasion rather than on intellectual repression and indoctrination.[76] Ideological propaganda finds itself at its greatest disadvantage precisely when it attempts, in its ingenuously catechistic way, to focus individuals' attention on, and obtain their agreement to, the explicit contents of its political communication. The capacity, however, for conscious attention is greatly reduced in a public which is surrounded by a constant, growing flow of symbolized stimuli. Also, as Schumpeter rightly observed, conscious attention represents more of a hindrance than a help to the transmission of ideologically loaded messages. For this reason, paradoxically, the media achieve their greatest potential for influence in democratic countries, where the explicit ideological content of their messages is relatively small and their capacity for indirect persuasion is consequently increased.[77]

In practice, the political effects of mass communication are closely linked with the tendencies towards conformity, apathy and political 'silence' which stem not so much from what is said as from what is unsaid, from what the communication filters tacitly exclude from the daily order of public attention. Silence is beyond doubt the most effective agent for subliminal persuasion in mass communication,[78] and the most suitable instrument for a kind of negative homologization of an information-based public. The political integration of information-based societies comes about far more through tacit reduction in the complexity of the topics of political communication than through any positive selection or discussion of them.

Silence is not restricted solely to themes already formulated for inclusion on the political agenda. It also extends to the ability to conceive and express these themes in the first place. For, once they go beyond the bounds of the political code standardized by the media, political agents seem unable to form any proper outline of problems, to establish a clear conception of their own interests or to articulate them in a communicable and socially effective manner.[79] When they run out of stereotyped expressions, political consumers fall silent and become effectively dumb, the range of their possibilities of expression and experience having run up against the restriction already placed there by a previous 'reduction of complexity'. Like the slaves and foreigners in the *polis* democracy, they become *aneu logou,* losing the ability to speak or to communicate.[80] They then find themselves, as Elizabeth Noelle-Neumann has argued, subject to the intellectually intimidating pressure caused by their anxiety about disregarding the laws of social conformity.[81] Being swallowed up by the 'spiral of silence' thus becomes a comforting alternative for those who dare not incur the risk of isolation posed by contravening mass-media 'public opinion'. If they remain silent, they know that they can count on the complicity guaranteed by a political group to those who show that they share the prejudices and particularisms on which that group is founded.

It is possible that, in accord with Schattschneider, Bachrach and Luhmann, power in information-based societies should be envisaged as a means of communication through which certain agents 'reduce complexity for others' by pre-emptively limiting the choices open for their decision and thus by restricting the horizon of their possibilities.[82] If this is true, then it is clear where, in such societies, the hidden and uncontrollable core of inner power is concentrated. It is also evident that 'democracy', in an information-based context, coincides largely with the margin of visibility in the communication processes and, symmetrically, with the extent to which the *arcana communicationis* are reduced.

The realism of both Schumpeter and the neo-classical doctrine now clearly emerges as both rudimentary and obsolete. It is equally clear that the line of demarcation between democracy and totalitarianism which is drawn by the theorists of pluralism is highly vulnerable. As we have seen, the notions of the 'autonomy' of public opinion and of the polycentrism of the means of mass communication which they take to be decisive turn out, on the contrary, to be weak and ambivalent. In total contradiction to the classical theses of democratic pluralism, scientific research and historical experience have both shown that the persuasive capacity of the mass media has far more effectiveness in the countries of pluralistic democracy (and of the market economy) than in totalitarian ones.

Nor is it possible to accept that the paucity of information, scant competence and weak sense of responsibility which are almost universally taken by neoclassical theorists to epitomize democratic electors are, quite simply, the characteristics of the average citizen. As we have seen, Schumpeter even came to formulate a sort of 'law of intellectually diminishing efficiency'. For him the average citizen became the less efficient the further he or she moved away from the restricted area of direct experience and reached a peak of inefficiency when dealing with general political topics where their judgements received no support from any 'sense of reality'.

It is easy to add to this analysis and observe, with Gehlen, that in societies of high technological development it is now extremely difficult to identify any sphere even of direct experience in which individuals operate with a secure sense of reality, confident that they are using autonomous criteria of judgement and staying at the height of their intellectual efficiency. The overload of communication and symbolized stimulation appears to have reserved its most powerful effect for the domain of private life, including the sexual emotions. The explosive increase in North America of recourse to psychoanalysis and other, very disparate, forms of private counselling may be taken as an index of the general decline of the 'sense of reality' and of the growing insecurity in information-based societies which have reached a high level of complexity. The phenomenon of teenage suicide, now constantly increasing in the United States and in many European countries, may well also deserve to be seen in the same light.

There are also good reasons for believing that exposure to the media exercises its deforming influence not only on ordinary citizens, but also (and even principally) on those who belong to the higher strata of active society – the very individuals who, classically, were taken to be the authentic source of public opinion. Lack of political information is now to be found even at the highest levels of specialist culture, while abstentionism and political apathy, once the almost exclusive preserve of the poorer rural and uneducated social classes, are now also found, in the United States and Europe, among an increasingly large number of young individuals of good educational attainment.[83]

Nevertheless, the political effects of mass communication cannot be simplistically understood as the intentional result of a manipulatory capacity exercised by particular political, economic or intellectual elites within each state, the result effectively being counteracted by 'polycentrism' and competition. It cannot in practice be maintained that the pluralism of information-producing agencies, either local or national, provides anything of an antidote to the dependency and distortion effects of the mass media, given that in this area pluralism creates no significant forms of competition between producers or of differentiation between their products.[84]

The problem is more one of a 'systemic' phenomenon which has taken on world-wide proportions and is bringing about a second 'structural transformation of the public sphere' even more radical than the one classically analysed by Jürgen Habermas. No aspect of public or of private life, and no individual, whether ordinary citizen or member of the governing elites, can be separated, at least in the present phase, from something that is taking on more and more of the characteristics of an 'anthropological mutation'.

Under such circumstances the improbability of the thesis advanced implicitly by Schumpeter, and explicitly by Plamenatz and Sartori, can only become more apparent: that there is perfect compatibility between the level of competence required of the average citizen in the role of political consumer and their weak rationality and submission to political propaganda. On the contrary, it seems to me that the sovereignty of the political consumer – i.e. the autonomy, rationality and moral responsibility of the citizen called upon to pass sovereign judgement on the competition between parties – can now hardly amount to more than empty verbiage in the context of the massive spectacularization of teledemocracy to which pluralistic competition between the parties, by no means merely in the United States, is being reduced. Such sovereignty seems to me to have even less substance when put in the perspective established by communication research of the narcosis, cognitive dependence, dissociation and 'political silence' induced by long-term exposure to the media.

# Notes

1   Cf. J. Schumpeter, *Capitalism, Socialism and Democracy*, p. 271; J. Plamenatz, *Democracy and Illusion*, pp. 117ff.
2   Cf. R. Dahl, *Democracy and Its Critics*, pp. 97–105.
3   Ibid., pp. 83–96, 106–18.
4   Ibid., pp. 220–4.
5   Cf. G. Sartori, *Elementi di teoria politica*, p. 166; id., *The Theory of Democracy Revisited*, pp. 96–110.
6   Cf. J. Schumpeter, *Capitalism, Socialism and Democracy*, pp. 271–2.
7   Ibid., pp. 257–8.
8   Ibid., p. 263.
9   Cf. G. Sartori, *Elementi di teoria politica*, p. 188.
10  On this point Arnold Gehlen is in warm agreement with Schumpeter: cf. *Die Seele im technischen Zeitalter*, Eng. trans., p. 65.
11  Cf. J. Schumpeter, *Capitalism, Socialism and Democracy*, p. 264.
12  Ibid., pp. 263–4.
13  Ibid., p. 263.
14  Ibid., pp. 282–3.
15  Ibid., p. 295. F. Bealey sees the most explicit limitation of Schumpeter's theory of democracy as lying in his underestimation of the dangerousness of power and the need for permanent vigilance against it: F. Bealey, *Democracy in the Contemporary State*, Oxford: Oxford University Press, 1988, pp. 53–7.
16  Downs, as is well known, maintains that it is irrational to be well informed on political topics because of the low yield political information gives in terms of economic return. Clearly, therefore, a large number of citizens vote without either adequate information or clear motivation (see A. Downs, *An Economic Theory of Democracy*, pp. 207–19, 298–9).
17  Cf. J. Plamenatz, *Democracy and Illusion*, p. 126.
18  Cf. G. Sartori, *The Theory of Democracy Revisited*, pp. 318ff.
19  Cf. R. Dahl, *Democracy and Its Critics*, p. 221–2; see also N. Bobbio's definition of the minimal requisites of democracy in *Quale socialismo?*, Eng. trans., p. 66.
20  Cf. J. Plamenatz, *Democracy and Illusion*, pp. 122–9.
21  Cf. G. Sartori, *Elementi di teoria politica*, Bologna: Il Mulino, 1987, p. 176–82; id., *The Theory of Democracy Revisited*, pp. 96–102; R. Aron, *Démocratie et totalitarisme*, Paris: Gallimard, 1965, Eng. trans. London: Weidenfeld and Nicolson, 1968, pp. 52–64, 192–204; R. Aron, 'Catégories dirigeantes ou classe dirigeante?', *Revue française de science politique*, 15 (1965), 1. 7–27.
22  Dahl seems to share Berelson's opinion that wide popular concern with political problems is not an essential feature of a democratic regime: cf. R. Dahl, *A Preface to Democratic Theory*, p. 81; R. Dahl, *Who Governs?*, New Haven (Conn.): Yale University Press, pp. 71, 279–80.
23  Given, however, the obvious condition that those demands are expressed by politically organized groups; cf. R. Dahl, *A Preface to Democratic Theory*,

p. 131; id., *Who Governs?*, p. 164; cf. also C. B. Macpherson, *The Life and Times of Liberal Democracy*, pp. 81–2.

24   On the kind of political knowledge which should be expected from ordinary citizens in a pluralistic democracy see J. Plamenatz, *Democracy and Illusion*, pp. 194–5; also D. Miller, 'The Competitive Model of Democracy', pp. 139–40; G. Parry, 'Citizenship and Knowledge', in P. Birnbaum, J. Lively and G. Parry (eds), *Democracy, Consensus and Social Contract*, Beverly Hills (Calif.): Sage Publications, 1978, pp. 37–57; G. Parry, 'Democracy and Amateurism – the Informed Citizen', *Government and Opposition*, 24 (1989), 4. 490–2.

25   Cf. G. Sartori, *Elementi di teoria politica*, pp. 195–6.

26   Cf. D. Held, *Models of Democracy*, pp. 179–80.

27   Cf. D. F. Thompson, *The Democratic Citizen*, Cambridge: Cambridge University Press, 1970, pp. 22–6.

28   See J. Habermas, *Strukturwandel der Öffentlichkeit*, Neuwied: Luchterhand, 1971, pp. 112–43.

29   Cf. T. H. Qualter, *Opinion Control in the Democracies*, London: Macmillan, 1985, pp. 1–29.

30   Cf. J. Habermas, *Strukturwandel der Öffentlichkeit*, pp. 158–71.

31   See S. Sighele, *La folla delinquente*, Turin: Bocca, 1891.

32   See G. Le Bon, *La psychologie des foules*, Paris: Alcan, 1895.

33   See G. Wallas, *Human Nature in Politics*, London: Constable, 1908; cf. M. Margolis, *Viable Democracy*, London: Macmillan, 1979, pp. 103ff.

34   See J. Ortega y Gasset, *La rebelión de las masas*, Madrid: Revista de Occidente, 1930.

35   See F. A. Allport, 'Toward a Science of Public Opinion', *Public Opinion Quarterly*, 1 (1937), 1. 7–23.

36   See W. Lippmann, *Public Opinion*, London: Allen and Unwin, 1922; id., *The Phantom Public*, New York: Macmillan, 1925; W. Kornhauser, *The Politics of Mass Society*, London: Routledge and Kegan Paul, 1960; V. O. Key, *Public Opinion and American Democracy*, New York: Knopf, 1961.

37   Cf. J. Schumpeter, *Capitalism, Socialism and Democracy*, p. 286.

38   In *Democracy and Its Critics*, a kind of general *summa* of his thought, Robert Dahl devotes no attention to the theme of the relationship between democracy, public opinion and mass-media communication. The same may also be said of Sartori's comprehensive book, *The Theory of Democracy Revisited*, where there are only some very generic hints in the direction of the problem (pp. 92–6). Sartori appears only very recently to have become aware of the relevance of the effects of mass-media communication to democratic theory.

39   See D. D. Nimmo and K. R. Sanders (eds), *Handbook of Political Communication*, Beverly Hills (Calif.): Sage Publications, 1981; J. B. Thompson, *Ideology and Modern Culture*, Cambridge: Polity Press, 1990, pp. 20–7, 272–327.

40   See D. J. O'Keefe, 'Logical Empiricism and the Study of Human Communication', *Speech Monographs*, 42 (1975), 2. 169–83.

41   See K. Deutsch, *The Nerves of Government*.

42   See P. F. Lazarsfeld, B. Berelson and H. Gaudet, *The People's Choice*, New York: Columbia University Press, 1940. Of the sample who were exposed to electoral propaganda over several months, 53 per cent turned out to have been confirmed in their original political attitude. Only 5 per cent reacted to the political communication by 'converting' to a new political stance. On the basis of further research Lazarsfeld, Berelson and their collaborators reached the conclusion that the perception and memorizing of mass-media messages is basically selective and indirect (see B. Berelson, P. Lazarsfeld and W. McPhee, *Voting*, Chicago: University of Chicago Press, 1954).

43   See J. T. Klapper, *The Effects of Mass Communication*, New York: Free Press, 1960.

44   On 'uses-and-gratifications' theory see J. G. Blumler and D. McQuail, *Television in Politics*, Chicago: University of Chicago Press, 1969; J. G. Blumler and E. Katz (eds), *The Uses of Mass Communications: Current Perspectives on Gratifications Research*, Beverly Hills (Calif.): Sage Publications, 1974.

45   Cf. B. Berelson, P. Lazarsfeld and W. McPhee, *Voting*, pp. 306–23.

46   Cf. M. Wolf, *Teorie delle comunicazioni di massa*, Milan: Bompiani, 1985, pp. 12–14.

47   See K. Lang and G. E. Lang, 'The Mass Media and Voting', in W. Schramm and D. Roberts (eds), *The Process and Effects of Mass Communication*, Chicago: University of Illinois Press, 1972.

48   See the Introduction in D. D. Nimmo and K. R. Sanders (eds), *Handbook of Political Communication*, Beverly Hills (Calif.): Sage Publications, 1981, pp. 11–36.

49   A recent, interesting attempt to interpret the influence of mass media on everyday life according to the principles of hermeneutics may be seen in J. B. Thompson, *Ideology and Modern Culture*, pp. 274–303.

50   See P. Elliot, *The Making of a Television Series. A Case Study in the Production of Culture*, London: Constable, 1972; id., 'Uses and Gratifications Research: A Critique and a Sociological Alternative', in J. G. Blumler and E. Katz (eds), *The Uses of Mass Communications: Current Perspectives on Gratifications Research*; id., 'Intellectuals, the Information Society and the Disappearance of the Public Sphere', in R. Collins et al. (eds), *Media, Culture and Society. A Critical Reader*, London: Sage Publications, 1986; J. B. Thompson, *Ideology and Modern Culture*, pp. 19, 182–215.

51   See R. L. Lanigan, 'A Critical Theory Approach', in D. D. Nimmo and K. R. Sanders (eds), *Handbook of Political Communication*, pp. 141–67; J. Curran, M. Gurevitch and J. Woollacott, 'The Study of the Media: Theoretical Approaches', in O. Boyd-Barret and P. Braham (eds), *Media, Knowledge and Power*, London: Croom Helm, 1987, pp. 60–3; cf. also the analysis of the relationship between ideological transmission and the mass media in J. B. Thompson, *Ideology and Modern Culture*, pp. 12–20, 216–71.

52   See D. L. Swanson, 'A Constructivist Approach', in D. D. Nimmo and K. R. Sanders (eds), *Handbook of Political Communication*, pp. 169–91.

53   Cf. C. R. Wright, 'Functional Analysis and Mass Communication', *Public Opinion Quarterly*, 24 (1960), 4. 605–28.

54   Cf. M. Wolf, *Teorie delle comunicazioni di massa,* pp. 58–79.

55   Ibid., pp. 177–254.

56   See K. Lang and G. E. Lang, 'The Mass Media and Voting', in W. Schramm and D. Roberts (eds), *The Process and Effects of Mass Communication*; M. E. McCombs, 'The Agenda Setting Approach', in D. D. Nimmo and K. R. Sanders (eds), *Handbook of Political Communication*; M. E. McCombs and D. L. Shaw, 'The Agenda-Setting Function of the Mass Media', *Public Opinion Quarterly,* 36 (1972), 2. 176–87.

57   See E. Noelle-Neumann, 'Return to the Concept of Powerful Mass Media', *Studies of Broadcasting,* 9 (1973), 1. 67–112.

58   Cf. M. Wolf, *Teorie delle comunicazioni di massa,* p. 142.

59   See J. D. Steinbruner, *The Cybernetic Theory of Decision. New Dimensions of Political Analysis,* Princeton (NJ): Princeton University Press, 1974.

60   See K. Deutsch, *The Nerves of Government*; id., 'Toward a Cybernetic Model of Man and Society', in W. Buckley (ed.), *Modern Systems Research for the Behavioral Scientist,* Chicago: Aldine, 1968; id., 'On Political Theory and Political Action', *American Political Science Review,* 65 (1971), 1. 11–27.

61   The only attempt to apply Deutsch's cybernetic model to an actual political system seems to be that of I. Galnoor, *The Israeli Political System,* Beverly Hills (Calif.): Sage Publications, 1981.

62   See R. R. Fagen, *Politics and Communication,* Boston (Mass.): Little, Brown, 1966; S. H. Chaffee (ed.), *Political Communication,* Beverly Hills (Calif.): Sage Publications, 1975.

63   See D. V. J. Bell, *Power, Influence and Authority,* New York: Oxford University Press, 1975; C. Mueller, *The Politics of Communication,* New York: Oxford University Press, 1973.
versity Press, 1975; C. Mueller, *The Politics of Communication,* New York: Oxford University Press, 1973.

64   See L. L. Kaid, 'Political Advertising', in D. D. Nimmo and K. R. Sanders (eds), *Handbook of Political Communication,* pp. 249–71.

65   See T. Luke, 'Televisual Democracy and the Politics of Charisma', *Telos,* 19 (1986), 4. 59–79; F. C. Arterton, *Teledemocracy. Can Technology Protect Democracy?,* Newbury Park (Calif.): Sage Publications, 1987.

66   See, e.g., M. Edelman, *Constructing the Political Spectacle,* Chicago: The University of Chicago Press, 1988; on the general theme of political manipulation see E. Etzioni-Halevy, *Political Manipulation and Administrative Power,* London: Routledge and Kegan Paul, 1979; R. E. Goodin, *Manipulatory Politics,* New Haven (Conn.): Yale University Press, 1980.

67   J. B. Thompson recognizes that modern mass media endow political leaders with unprecedented opportunities for reaching and influencing a large number of individuals, but he also maintains that this situation increases the vulnerability of their power because it renders them much more visible to audiences which are more extensive and endowed with more information and power than ever before (*Ideology and Modern Culture,* p. 115).

68   Cf. G. Sartori, 'Video-Power', *Government and Opposition,* 24 (1989), 1. 52.

69   See L. J. Martin (ed.), *Polling and the Democratic Consensus,* Beverly Hills

(Calif.): Sage Publications, 1984; D. Kavanagh, 'Public Opinion Polls', in D. Butler, H. R. Penniman and A. Ranney (eds), *Democracy and the Polls*, pp. 196–215.

70  See C. Zukin, 'Mass Communication and Public Opinion', in D. D. Nimmo and R. K. Sanders (eds), *Handbook of Political Communication*, pp. 359–90.

71  See C. H. Cooley, *Social Organization*, Glencoe (Ill.): The Free Press, 1956; R. E. Park, *Society: Collective Behavior, News and Opinion. Sociology and Modern Society*, Glencoe (Ill.): The Free Press, 1955.

72  See G. Gallup and S. F. Rae, *The Pulse of Democracy: The Public-Opinion Poll and How it Works*, New York: Simon and Schuster, 1940; cf. H. D. Lasswell, *Democracy Through Public Opinion*, Menasha (Wis.): Banta, 1941, p. 15.

73  Cf. K. C. Laudon, *Communication, Technology and Democratic Participation*, New York: Praeger Publishers, 1977, pp. 1–48; M. Traber, *The Myth of the Informatic Revolution*, London: Sage Publications, 1986, pp. 1–6.

74  Cf. N. Luhmann, 'Öffentliche Meinung', *Politische Vierteljahresschrift*, 11 (1970), 1. 2–28.

75  See P. Bachrach and M. S. Baratz, *Power and Poverty*.

76  Confirmation of this may be seen in recent political events in the German Democratic Republic. Here the old methods of Marxist-Leninist despotism have been defeated by West German mass media which have for many years exerted a tacit persuasive influence on East Germany. The influence of the 'consumeristic model' was also responsible, according to many analysts, for the remarkable success of conservative parties in the first pluralist elections held in East Germany (March 1990).

77  Although admitting the asymmetric and scarcely interactive character of mass-media communication, J. B. Thompson criticizes the 'myth of the passive recipient'. In my view there can be no doubt about the difficulty of transmitting direct ideological contents via the mass media caused by the selective attitude of receivers, but it must be added that one of the most efficient communication techniques consists in bypassing the selective ability of the receiver by means of subliminal messages (cf. *Ideology and Modern Culture*, pp. 24–5, 114–15, 319).

78  See D. D. Nimmo and J. E. Combs, *Subliminal Politics*, Englewood Cliffs (NJ): Prentice-Hall, 1980.

79  Cf. E. Noelle-Neumann, *Die Schweigespirale: Öffentliche Meinung, unsere soziale Haut*, Munich: Piper Verlag, 1980, Eng. trans. Chicago: University of Chicago Press, 1984, pp. 170–3.

80  It should perhaps be mentioned that, contrary to this, Gianni Vattimo maintains that 'the world of generalized communication' leads to 'a liberation of differences'. The erosion of the reality principle caused by the mass media permits the explosion of 'a variety of "local" rationalities – ethnic, sexual, religious, cultural or aesthetic – which finally take the floor, since they are no longer repressed by the idea of a unique, true form of humanity' (see *La società trasparente*, pp. 16–17). The 'bewilderment effect', which many analysts consider to be a dysfunction associated with the excessive acts of selection

required by the overload of non-interactive communication, is interpreted by Vattimo as an opportunity for human emancipation. These views seem to me suggestive, but hardly convincing.

81   Cf. E. Noelle-Neumann, *Die Schweigespirale: Öffentliche Meinung, unsere soziale Haut*, Eng. trans., pp. 37–57.

82   Cf. E. E. Schattschneider, *The Semisovereign People*, p. 68: 'the definition of the alternatives is the supreme instrument of power'; P. Bachrach and M. S. Baratz, *Power and Poverty*, pp. 38–51; N. Luhmann, *Macht*, Eng. trans. in N. Luhmann, *Trust and Power*.

83   On political apathy within complex societies see, amongst others, G. Di Palma, *Apathy and Participation: Mass Politics in Western Societies*, New York: The Free Press, 1970. A quite opposite, although in my opinion unconvincing, hypothesis has been formulated by R. Inglehart in *Culture Shift in Advanced Industrial Societies*, Princeton (NJ): Princeton University Press, 1990. He sees increasing levels of public instruction, the declining political relevance of sexual differences and the diffusion of 'postmaterialistic values' as tending to promote an increasing cognitive political involvement of the new generations in post-industrial societies.

84   G. Sartori also now seems to agree with this opinion: cf. 'Video-Power', p. 51.

# Conclusion

## A new model of democracy?

One of the essential tasks of modern political philosophy, according to the famous 'map' drawn by Norberto Bobbio, is to ask radical questions on subjects such as the justification of power, the basis of political obligation, the nature of good government and the very meaning of the word 'politics'. In my own view, the concern of political philosophy could usefully be extended so as to include problems arising from the more deeply entrenched categories of political theory, including those belonging to the Western humanistic and democratic tradition and to its programme of emancipation. This would then, it seems to me, allow some basis for political philosophy to claim, in the 'post-modern' cultural climate of today, a measure of public utility, in that it could cease to take refuge in redundant defence of the conditions of existing power.

But, when extended in this manner, the study of political theory becomes a risky intellectual exercise which can provoke, even in times of widespread ideological disenchantment, reactions of distrust and irritation, not only within the intellectual establishment. Such reactions are by no means unreasonable, however, when the radicality of the questions is not – and has no hope of being – matched by answers of corresponding depth. And this is of course all the more the case under present circumstances when the classical problems of political philosophy are becoming increasingly complicated as a result of the growing globalization and world-wide interlocking of political resources, social risks and causes of conflict. It would seem that in political philosophy, beginning at least in Rousseau and Kant, there is an inevitable element of intellectual and moral velleity, and that this is all the more so, the more rigour is applied.

These remarks will, I hope, serve to explain my reluctance to present anything that might amount to a true conclusion to this book or, more particularly, to an actual proposal for a new model of democracy. I doubt very much whether such a model could in fact be constructed in such a way as to have any interest or importance outside purely academic circles. My aim here will not be to build a model, therefore, but to deal with a number of general points which in my opinion establish beyond doubt the need for a reconstruction of democratic theory. Their purpose is principally to distinguish my realist position, albeit in perhaps too rigid a form, from other philosophico-political paradigms. But they will also, I hope, provide some constructive indications, however incomplete, which may conceivably serve to outline some first steps towards a deeper study.

I should perhaps also mention at this point the disquiet it gives me that my views on the future of democracy and the probable fate of information-based societies will in all likelihood seem unduly pessimistic to some. There is of course an already over-abundant literature on the crisis of modernity and the enlightened philosophy in which it is rooted, so that some apology may be in order for adding to it. In some ways I should not be sorry if my views were found to be mistaken and if I were proved wrong by different interpretations of the 'facts' and by different forecasts. The possibility is by no means to be ruled out that other observers, more sociologically imaginative and sanguine than I, will find the means to develop more consoling, and perhaps even edifying, theoretical standpoints.

To my eyes, however, the prospects not merely of the development, but even of the simple preservation, of democratic institutions in post-industrial countries seem decidedly uncertain. Nor is this solely because of the 'evolutionary risks' – i.e. the tendencies inherent in the political systems which govern increasingly complex societies – which I have attempted to outline in this book. There are also 'external risks' threatening the future of democracy which have necessarily had to lie outside the scope of this book, but which seem to me to cry out for a broad interdisciplinary study.

By 'external risks', I have in mind phenomena which now affect the whole world: the current demographic explosion, coupled with the growing disparity between the small number of democratic (and rich) countries and the large number of non-democratic countries which, far from experiencing economic growth, are actually seeing the living standards of millions of their people progressively worsen; the mass movements of population which these conditions are likely to cause, and the racist reactions and violent conflicts over the apportionment of citizenship which the objective pressure for equality behind these movements seems certain to provoke; the ever-present military threat, now further increased by the widescale diffusion of nuclear, chemical and biological weapons in the countries experiencing growth and, in the poorer countries, by an uncontainable spread of terrorism, which has now been taken to international levels – indeed terrorism may even be said to be the 'poor' alternative today to the economic and military leadership of the great powers and their increasing attempts to form themselves into a world government under the aegis of the United Nations; the escalation of the trend towards ecological disequilibrium with incalculable consequences not only for the quality of life on the planet, but also for the political structures themselves of industralized countries.

The most alarming aspect of this possibility of disorder, over-crowding and pollution is the 'insufficiency of the polis' referred to by David Bell. By this phrase he meant the absence of a political thought or the ability to govern which matches the same level of broadness, complexity and interdependence evident in the problems which have to be faced. To my mind, however, the outlook does not justify the taking of any catastrophic or apocalyptic position, if for no other reason than the extreme uncertainty of all wide-ranging predictions regarding the future of the planet. But it does not seem to justify either the conservative optimism of such thinkers as Friedrick Hayek, Karl Popper or their followers now widely dispersed, even in the formerly socialist countries. Nor does it justify the different kind of optimism shown by those, such as Ralf Dahrendorf, who see in 'post-communism' a situation particularly favourable to the progress of freedom, prosperity and democracy. Nor, finally, does it lend any support to Jürgen Habermas's persistent attempt to sew together the shreds of modern discourse and to offer the resulting Penelope's web as a kind of 'philosophical first-aid' to soften the frustrations of both democrats and socialists. Rather, in my view, the fear should now be that the demise of socialism, together with the failure of its epochal expectation of the defeat of capitalism and representative formalism, will, rather than restore vigour to liberal-democratic and social-democratic ideals, instead drag them into the sort of 'democratic melancholy' – the interweaving of apathy, greed and consumeristic frustration – which Pascal Bruckner and Cornelius Castoriadis have recently called to mind.

## Some starting-points

Here I intend to set out some of the firm ground which I hope has been established by my study. On the epistemological level, it is designed to form a realistic alternative both to political science and to neo-Kantian moralism. On the level of political theory, it is intended to provide reasons for a rejection of the classical and neo-classical doctrines of democracy and for acceptance of a 'post-classical' attempt at a reconstruction of democratic theory[1].

1    *Beyond the idea of representation.*   A large part of the European political encyclopedia, and in particular the idea of 'representative democracy', must now, I maintain, be considered obsolete. This is a view for which I hope to have provided a number of sound reasons. Recent attempts to re-establish the idea of 'representative democracy' on the universalistic basis of a 'public ethic' of Kantian type are, in my opinion, little more than academic exercises, which are in practice daily disproved by the particularistic violence of political conflicts.

A realistic conception of democracy should in fact abjure any definition of 'public ethics' used, as in Rawls, to design a 'public' anthropological model, to select needs, establish common values and found universal rights. It should, on the contrary, recognize its own limitations and its own radical contingency and leave to other social spheres – culture, art, music, friendship, love, scientific study, and even religious belief – the enquiry into ultimate ends and the promotion of values. Politics should therefore be restored, even in the more demanding and radical democratic schemes, to its laical functions of the organization of particular interests, the mediation of conflicts, the guarantee of security and the protection of civil rights.

Obviously I do not propose that, in order to realize these objectives, it should be necessary to start from zero. Neither in political philosophy nor in any other discipline is there any possibility of research from a Cartesian *tabula rasa*. My point is more simply that the theoretical vocabulary and syntax which we currently use for the description of Western political systems are gravely misleading, and should therefore be translated, insofar as that is still possible, into a different, more realistic and more complex, theoretical language.

Even the theory of democratic pluralism, including also the more open-minded forms in which it is found, still remains within the representative paradigm and the language connected with it. This is particularly true of the notion of 'responsiveness', which constitutes the extreme attenuation of the political paradigm derived from Aristotle and Rousseau as the search for the common good and the execution of a general will. In this sense, even the model of democracy as a political market belongs to a classical conception of politics, however watered-down.

What I do propose is that this archaic theoretical model should now be set aside, and that in its place the heuristic fecundity of a liberalized systemic standpoint should be given the chance to be tried. Within this fresh perspective the political system is seen as a social structure which fulfils the essential function of reducing fear through the selective regulation of social risks. The central issue of modern political philosophy thus becomes the relation between the provision of security, guaranteed by the power institutions, and the threat posed to the protective function of the political system by the growing differentiation of contemporary societies. This process tends to challenge all the State's claims to universality and demands individual rights of liberty itself. This development will lead to the dissolution of Aristotelian political philosophy, which lay behind the medieval idea of the political city and has inspired an odd collection of utopian projects even in modern times. It will, in addition, mean the end of the organicistic and consensualistic model of the political community which has been dramatically, but vainly, proposed in Europe first by romanticism and subsequently by communism, and which today is reduced to being the object of the futile academic nostalgia of the North American 'communitarians'.

2 *Differentiated and limited autocracies.* From this new theoretical standpoint, the regimes which today we call democratic are seen to be the regimes in which increasing functional differentiation has demanded explicit limitation of the political system – by its very nature monocratic and unlimited – and recognition of the functional autonomy of other social subsystems, especially the economic and scientific ones and those made up by private and religious life. The regimes which are known as democratic are more properly *differentiated and limited autocratic systems*, that is, in traditional terminology, liberal oligarchies. In these regimes, there has emerged a wholly new, i.e. 'modern', balance between the opposed demands of security and complexity/freedom. The oligarchic (not monocratic) structure of power is guaranteed in them by the pluralism of the 'private governors', and this pluralism is functionally interconnected with the multiplicity of the differentiated and autonomized social domains.

Both the internal articulation of power functions (i.e. the division of powers) and the constitutional recognition of 'negative' freedoms (i.e. the rule of law) answer to the need to preserve the level of differentiation and complexity reached by modern industrial societies. Individual rights of freedom – private property, freedom of exchange, *habeas corpus*, protection of physical integrity and privacy, religious tolerance – form the institutions and procedures through which reciprocal autonomization of the political subsystem and the other social subsystems comes into being and receives formal sanction. In particular, the market economy demands the freedom of the economic agent as an inalienable functional condition, so that it would be possible to say, paraphrasing Schumpeter, that liberal democracy is a by-product not of inter-party competition, but of differentiation between the political and the economic systems.

In this sense the protection of social complexity against the functional predominance of any particular subsystem – e.g. the productive, the scientific-technological, the religious, the trade-union, or, above all, the political subsystem itself – is the crucial 'promise' which democracy must keep if it intends to distinguish itself in any other than wholly formal terms from despotic or totalitarian regimes.

In the effective functioning of those systems that we call democratic, however, there is practically nothing that seems to correspond to what political theorists – and the language of politicians, journalists and the media in general – intend by terms such as 'popular sovereignty', 'participation', 'representation', 'public opinion', 'consensus', 'equality'. The last in particular – the idea of equality understood in any sense other than a purely formal one – seems to possess no significant link with modern political institutions, be they called liberal-democratic, social-democratic or socialist. This is one of democracy's 'broken promises' which no modern political system appears to be in a position to keep.

3   *Negative liberties versus autonomy: The 'Singapore model'.*   Such is the theoretical context behind the central hypothesis of this work, that the process of increasing differentiation and complexity which is under way in post-industrial societies is, in political terms, ambiguous and 'risk-filled'. The ambiguity and the risks which follow from it arise from the 'modern' balance, realized in the West in the oligarchic-liberal forms of the rule of law, between political protection and social complexity, between security and freedom, between administration and individual rights. This balance, in which lies what Bobbio calls the 'minimum content' of democracy, seems today to be on the point of disintegration, and the liberal oligarchies are in danger of turning into illiberal oligarchies through a series of those imperceptible functional shifts that occur within political structures devoid of alteration or alternatives.

On the one hand, the increase in differentiation and the great expansion of mobility, knowledge and the possibilities of experience promoted by technological innovation foster acute needs in post-industrial societies for functional independence and individual freedom. The centrifugal tendency of the differentiated subsystems runs counter to the centralism of the public bureaucracies, whilst individuals, emancipated from the bonds of organicism and political consensualism, take on increasingly detached attitudes in their dealings with the traditional forms of socialization and political integration. Even the actual increase in levels of information and quality of consumer goods seems to create the premises of a 'post-materialistic' claiming of positive freedom – the intellectual and moral autonomy which classical doctrine dogmatically took for granted – on the part of agents, both men and women, who are oriented towards forms of expressive and existential self-assertion in their pursuit of a well-defined individual identity.

But on the other hand, as we have seen, the autonomy of individuals is threatened by the exercise of negative freedoms, in particular the exercise of civil and political rights such as the freedom of political, economic and trade-union activity or freedom of thought, the press and propaganda. Under the hegemony of the collective agents of democratic polyarchy – i.e. political parties, trade unions, and the other 'private governors' – the exercise of negative freedoms tends in fact to erode both the public dimension of social life and the domain of individual autonomy. In one respect, in fact, the process of differentiation serves to render improbable the democratic management of complex societies, because the variety and changeability of differentiated interests makes it very difficult to arrive at a consensus which does not depend on single particularistic decisions. Hence the appeal of 'decisionism', inasmuch as it is a strategy of opportunistic political decision-making, divorced from any general consideration of interests. In another respect, it is the growing vulnerability of informatic societies that seems to demand increasingly drastic and underhand forms of the reduction of social complexity, including even subliminal persuasion.

The 'open society' propounded by theorists such as Hayek and Popper, tends therefore to become closed and rigid within the 'nondecisional' process of consumeristic and multimedia homologization of the citizen-consumers. This process threatens individual autonomy at its deepest level, since it impinges on the cognitive and emotive formation of preferences and political will. These societies seem to realize a maximum of social integration not by recourse to the imposition of totalitarian ideologies or to direct repression, but through the de-structuring of the public sphere and the isolation and dispersion of political agents. This new, sophisticated form of 'guardianship', which seems to dispel the very idea of the political city, finds daily confirmation in many democratic countries. These now appear to be governed by outright 'electoral oligarchies' with increasingly restricted social bases. They are restricted both with regard to the irremovability of the political personnel of the parties – the new proprietary corporation which establishes neo-patrimonialistic relations with the State – and with regard to the growing rates of political abstentionism not only in countries such as the United States, France and Switzerland, but, more surprisingly, in post-communist countries such as Poland and Hungary.

At this point reference to the 'Singapore model' will not be out of place. Second only to Japan, Singapore has risen to be the richest and most technologically advanced country in South-East Asia. For more than thirty years, this modern city-state has been governed by its own kind of philosopher-king, Lee Kuan Yew. Without adhering to any precise political ideology, Lee has minutely prescribed for his 3,000,000 fellow-citizens such details of life as the environment, living patterns, individual and collective interests and aims, going right down to the prohibition of such behaviour as spitting in public and smoking. In today's world, no more perfect example could be found of the modern *antipolis*, characterized as it is by the highest technological efficiency, extensive use of information instruments, widespread prosperity, excellent public services (especially schools and hospitals), high levels of employment, efficient and enlightened bureaucracy, social relations aseptically mediated by exclusive functional requirements and a total lack of political ideologies or public discussion.

# Notes

1   In very tentative and hypothetical terms it is possible to envisage some institutional solutions that might in some measure offset the 'evolutionary risks' which democracy faces. First, the constitutionalization of the political parties. This formal recognition should, however, be accompanied by a rigorous definition of the juridical and economic status of the party, to be realized in the form of a full constitutional statute governing parties and political operatives. Secondly, the need should be recognised for a new division of powers to take into account the functional decline of the legislative assemblies. The function of promulgating ordinary laws could be given to the executive power while elected organs could receive wider powers of inspection and control over the activities of the administration. Direct election of the highest echelons of the administration would further contribute to limiting the power of intermediation by the parties and to assuring greater stability to the government. A third, extremely difficult but probably crucial, requirement is the promotion of a communicative democracy. Institutional solutions would be necessary which have the strength to free multimedia communication from its subordination both to the political system and to the productive system and to liberate it from the advertising paradigm which increasingly joins these two sub-systems together.

# Select Bibliography

## Theories of complexity and social complexity

Anderson, C. W., 'Public Policy and the Complex Organization', in L. N. Lindberg (ed.), *Politics and the Future of Industrial Society*, New York: David McKay, 1976.

Ashby, W. R., 'Principles of the Self-Organizing System', in W. Buckley (ed.), *Modern System Research for the Behavioral Scientist*, Chicago: Aldine, 1968.

Atlan, H., *Entre le cristal et la fumée. Essai sur l'organisation du vivant*, Paris: Seuil, 1979.

Bertalanffy, L. von, *General System Theory*, New York: Braziller, 1968.

Bocchi, G., and Ceruti, M. (eds), *La sfida della complessità*, Milan: Feltrinelli, 1985.

Boudon, R., *Effets perverses et ordre social*, Paris: Presses Universitaires de France, 1977, Eng. trans. New York: St Martin's Press, 1982.

Buckley, W., *Sociology and Modern System Theory*, Englewood Cliffs (NJ): Prentice-Hall, 1967.

—— (ed.), *Modern System Research for the Behavioral Scientist*, Chicago: Aldine, 1968.

Casti, J., *Connectivity, Complexity and Catastrophe in Large-scale Systems*, New York: John Wiley and Sons, 1979.

Delattre, P., *Théorie des systèmes et épistémologie*, in J. Lesourne, *La notion de système dans les sciences contemporaines*, II, Aix-en-Provence: Librairie de l'Univesité, 1982.

Emery, F. E. (ed.), *Systems Thinking*, Harmondsworth: Penguin Books, 1969.

Gottinger, H. W., *Coping with Complexity*, Dordrecht and Boston (Mass.): D. Reidel, 1983.

Hayek, F. A., 'The Theory of Complex Phenomena', in M. Bunge (ed.), *The Critical Approach to Science and Philosophy*, New York: The Free Press, 1964.

Hofstadter, D. R., *Gödel, Escher, Bach*, Harmondsworth: Penguin Books, 1979.

Klages, G., and Nowak, J., 'The Mastering of Complexity as a Problem of the Social Sciences', *Theory and Decision*, 2 (1971), 2.

La Porte, T. R. (ed.), *Organized Social Complexity. Challenge to Politics and Policy*, Princeton (NJ): Princeton University Press, 1975.

Loasby, B. J., *Choice, Complexity and Ignorance*, New York: Cambridge University Press, 1976.

Luhmann, N., *Soziologische Aufklärung*, I, Opladen: Westdeutscher Verlag, 1970.

—— *The Differentiation of Society*, New York: Columbia University Press, 1981.

—— (ed.), *Soziale Differenzierung*, Opladen: Westdeutscher Verlag, 1985.

Morin, E., *La Méthode*, I. *La Nature de la Nature*, Paris: Éditions du Seuil, 1977.

Neurath, O., *Foundations of the Social Sciences*, Chicago: University of Chicago Press, 1944.

Parsons, T., *The Evolution of Societies*, Englewood Cliffs (NJ): Prentice-Hall, 1977.

Prigogine, I., and Stengers, I., *La Nouvelle Alliance: Métamorphose de la science*, Paris: Gallimard, 1979, Eng. trans. Boulder (Colo.) and London: Shambhala, 1984.

Scharpf, F., 'Komplexität als Schranke der politischen Planung', *Politische Vierteljahresschrift*, Special Issue 4, 1972.

—— 'Komplexe Demokratietheorie', in F. Nuscheler and W. Steffani (eds), *Pluralismus. Konzeptionen und Kontroversen*, Munich: Piper Verlag, 1972.

Scott, R. W., *Organizations. Rational, Natural and Open Systems*, Englewood Cliffs (NJ): Prentice-Hall, 1981.

Simmel, G., *Über soziale Differenzierung. Soziologische und psychologische Untersuchungen*, Leipzig: Duncker and Humblot, 1890.

Simon, H. A., 'The Architecture of Complexity', *Proceedings of the American Philosophical Society*, 106 (1962), pp. 467–82, now also in H. A. Simon, *The Sciences of the Artificial*, Cambridge (Mass.): The MIT Press, 1981.

—— 'Bounded Rationality', in C. B. McGuire and R. Radner (eds), *Decision and Organization*, Amsterdam: North Holland, 1971.

Thom, R., *Stabilité structurelle et morphogénèse*, Paris: Interéditions, 1972, Eng. trans. Reading (Mass.): W. A. Benjamin, 1975.

Tyrell, H., 'Anfragen an die Theorie der gesellschaftlichen Differenzierung', *Zeitschrift für Soziologie*, 7 (1978), 2.

Zeeman, C., *Catastrophe Theory*, Reading (Mass.): Benjamin, 1977.

Zolo, D., 'Reflexive Selbstbegründung der Soziologie und Autopoiesis', *Soziale Welt*, 36 (1985), 4.

—— 'Function, Meaning, Complexity', *Philosophy of the Social Sciences*, 16 (1986), 1.

—— *Reflexive Epistemology*, Boston Studies in the Philosophy of Science, Dordrecht, Boston (Mass.) and London: Kluwer Publications, 1989.

—— 'The Epistemological Status of the Theory of Autopoiesis and Its Applications to the Social Sciences', in A. Febbrajo and G. Teubner (eds), *State, Law, Economy as Autopoietic Systems: Regulation and Autonomy in a New Perspective*, Milan, Munich and London: European Book Pool, 1990.

—— 'Reflexive Epistemology and Social Complexity: The Philosophical Legacy of Otto Neurath', *Philosophy of the Social Sciences*, 20 (1990), 2.

Political knowledge

Almond, G. A., and Genco, S. J., 'Clouds, Clocks, and the Study of Politics', *World Politics*, 29 (1977), 4.

Berlin, I., 'Does Political Theory Still Exist?', in P. Laslett and W. G. Runciman (eds), *Philosophy, Politics and Society*, Oxford: Blackwell, 1962.

Bobbio, N., 'Scienza politica', in N. Bobbio, N. Matteucci and G. Pasquino, *Dizionario di politica*, Turin: Utet, 1983.

Breton, A., *The Economic Theory of Representative Government*, Chicago: Aldine, 1974.

Buchanan J., and Tullock, G., *The Calculus of Consent. Logical Foundations of Constitutional Democracy*, Ann Arbor (Mich.): University of Michigan Press, 1962.

Dahl, R. A., 'The Behavioural Approach in Political Science: Epitaph for a Monument to a Successful Protest', *American Political Science Review*, 55 (1961), 4.

Deutsch, K., 'Recent Trends in Research Methods', in J. Charlesworth (ed.), *A Design for Political Science: Scope, Objectives, and Methods*, Philadelphia: The American Academy of Political and Social Science, 1966.

Downs, A., *An Economic Theory of Democracy*, New York: Harper and Row, 1957.

Easton, D., 'The Current Meaning of "Behavioralism"', in G. C. Charlesworth (ed.), *The Limits of Behavioralism in Political Science*, Philadelphia: The American Academy of Political and Social Science, 1962.

—— 'Political Science in the United States. Past and Present', *International Political Science Review*, 6 (1985), 1.

Euben, P. J., 'Political Science and Political Silence', in P. Green and S. Levinson (eds), *Power and Community. Dissenting Essays in Political Science*, New York: Random House, 1970.

Eulau, H., *The Behavioral Persuasion in Politics*, New York: Random House, 1963.

Falter, J. F., *Der 'Positivismusstreit' in der amerikanischen Politikwissenschaft*, Opladen: Westdeutscher Verlag, 1962.

Hayward, J., 'The Political Science of Muddling Through: The *de facto* Paradigm?', in J. Hayward and P. Norton (eds), *The Political Science of British Politics*, Brighton (Sussex): Wheatsheaf Books, 1986.

Laslett, P. 'Introduction', in P. Laslett (ed.), *Philosophy, Politics and Society*, Oxford: Basil Blackwell, 1956.

Lerner, D., and Lasswell, H. D. (eds), *The Policy Sciences: Recent Developments in Scope and Method*, Stanford (Calif.): Stanford University Press, 1951.

Lindblom, C. E., 'Still Muddling, not yet Through', *Public Administration Review*, 39 (1979), 6.

MacIntyre, A., 'Is a Science of Comparative Politics Possible?', in P. Laslett, W. G. Runciman and Q. Skinner (eds). *Philosophy, Politics and Society*, Oxford: Basil Blackwell, 1972.

—— 'The Indispensability of Political Theory', in D. Miller and L. Siedentop (eds), *The Nature of Political Theory*, Oxford: Clarendon Press, 1983.

Partridge, P. H., 'Politics, Philosophy, Ideology', *Political Studies*, 9 (1961), 3.

Pasquino, G., 'Natura ed evoluzione della disciplina', in G. Pasquino (ed.), *Manuale di scienza della politica*, Bologna: Il Mulino, 1986.

Plamenatz, J., 'The Use of Political Theory', in A. Quinton (ed.), *Political Philosophy*, Oxford: Oxford University Press, 1967.

Ricci, D. M., *The Tragedy of Political Science*, New Haven (Conn.): Yale University Press, 1984.

Ryan, A., ' "Normal" Science or Ideology?', in P. Laslett, W. G. Runciman and Q. Skinner (eds), *Philosophy, Politics and Society*, Oxford: Basil Blackwell, 1972.

Sartori, G., 'The Tower of Babel', in G. Sartori, F. W. Riggs and H. Teune, *Tower of Babel*, Pittsburgh (Pa.): International Study Association, 1975.

Strauss, L., 'What is Political Philosophy?', in L. Strauss, *What is Political Philosophy and Other Studies*, Glencoe (Ill.): The Free Press, 1959.

Taylor, C., 'Neutrality in Political Science', in P. Laslett and W. G. Runciman (eds), *Philosophy, Politics and Society*, New York: Barnes and Noble, 1967.

—— 'Political Theory and Practice', in C. Lloyd (ed.), *Social Theory and Political Practice*, Oxford: Clarendon Press, 1983.

Voegelin, E., *The New Science of Politics*, Chicago: The University of Chicago Press, 1952.

Wolin, S. S., 'Political Theory as a Vocation', *American Political Science Review*, 63 (1969), 4.

Zolo, D., 'Theoretical Language, Evaluations and Prescriptions: A Post-Empiricist Approach', in *Reason in Law*, ed. E. Pattaro, Milan: Giuffré, 1988.


## The contemporary debate on democracy

Arblaster, A., *Democracy*, Milton Keynes (Bucks): Open University Press, 1987.

Aron, R., *Démocratie et totalitarisme*, Paris: Gallimard, 1965, Eng. trans. London: Weidenfeld and Nicolson, 1970.

Assel, H.-G., *Demokratischer Sozialpluralismus*, Munich and Vienna: Günther Olzog Verlag, 1975.

Bachrach, P., *The Theory of Democratic Elitism. A Critique*, Boston (Mass.): Little Brown and Co., 1967.

—— (ed.), *Political Elites in a Democracy*, New York: Atherton Press, 1971.

Bachrach, P., and Baratz, M. S., *Power and Poverty*, New York: Oxford University Press, 1970.

Barber, B. R., *Strong Democracy*, Berkeley (Calif.): University of California Press, 1984.

Barry, B., *Sociologists, Economists and Democracy*, Chicago: The University of Chicago Press, 1978.

Bealey, F., *Democracy in the Contemporary State*, Oxford: Oxford University Press, 1988.

Benjamin, R., *The Limits of Politics. Collective Goods and Political Change in Postindustrial Societies*, Chicago: The University of Chicago Press, 1980.

Benn, T., *Arguments for Democracy*, London: Cape, 1981.

Birnbaum, P., Lively, J., and Parry, G. (eds), *Democracy, Consensus and Social Contract*, London: Sage Publications, 1978.

Bobbio, N., 'Democrazia', in N. Bobbio, N. Matteucci and G. Pasquino (eds), *Dizionario de politica*, Turin: Utet, 1983.

—— *Il futuro della democrazia*, Turin: Einaudi, 1984, Eng. trans. Cambridge: Polity Press, 1987.

—— *Stato, governo, società*, Turin: Einaudi, 1985, Eng. trans. *Democracy and Dictatorship*, Cambridge: Polity Press, 1989.

Bruckner, P., *La mélancolie démocratique*, Paris: Éditions du Seuil, 1990.

Burnheim, J., *Is Democracy Possible?*, Cambridge: Polity Press, 1985.

Butler, D., Penniman, H. R., and Ranney, A. (eds), *Democracy and the Polls*, Washington (DC) and London: AEI Studies, 1981.

Cnudde, C. F., and Neubauer, D. E. (eds), *Empirical Democratic Theory*, Chicago: Markham, 1969.

Coe, R. C., and Wilber C. K. (eds), *Capitalism and Democracy: Schumpeter Revisited*, Notre Dame (Ind.): University of Notre Dame Press, 1985.

Cohen, C., *Democracy*, Athens (Ga.): University of Georgia Press, 1971.

Connolly, W. (ed.), *The Bias of Pluralism*, New York: Atherton Press, 1969.

Coombes, D., *Representative Government and Economic Power*, London: Heinemann Educational Books, 1982.

Crozier, M. J., Huntington, S. P., and Watanuki, J., *The Crisis of Democracy: Report on the Governability of Democracy to the Trilateral Commission*, New York: New York University Press, 1975.

Dahl, R. A., *A Preface to Democratic Theory*, Chicago: The University of Chicago Press, 1956.

—— *Who Governs?*, New Haven (Conn.): Yale University Press, 1961.

—— *Democracy, Liberty and Equality*, London: Norwegian University Press, 1966.

—— *Polyarchy*, London: Yale University Press, 1970.

—— 'Procedural Democracy', in P. Laslett and J. Fishkin (eds), *Philosophy, Politics and Society*, Oxford: Basil Blackwell, 1979.

—— *Dilemmas of Pluralist Democracy: Autonomy versus Control*, New Haven (Conn.): Yale University Press, 1982.

—— *A Preface to Economic Democracy*, Cambridge: Polity Press, 1985.

—— *Controlling Nuclear Weapons. Democracy versus Guardianship*, Syracuse (NY): Syracuse University Press, 1985.

—— *Democracy and Its Critics*, New Haven (Conn.) and London: Yale University Press, 1989.

Day, B. R., Beiner, R., and Masciulli, J. (eds), *Democratic Theory and Technological Society*, Armonk (NY): M. E. Sharpe, 1988.

Duncan, G. (ed.), *Democratic Theory and Practice*, Cambridge: Cambridge University Press, 1983.

—— and Lukes, S., 'The New Democracy', *Political Studies*, 11 (1963), 2.

Dunn, J., *Western Political Theory in the Face of the Future*, Cambridge: Cambridge University Press, 1979.

Edelman, M., *Constructing the Political Spectacle*, Chicago and London: The University of Chicago Press, 1988.

Erlich, S., *Pluralism on and off Course*, Oxford: Pergamon Press, 1982.

Etzioni-Halevy, E., *Bureaucracy and Democracy*, London: Routledge and Kegan Paul, 1983.

Frei, D. (ed.), *Überforderte Demokratie?*, Zurich: Schulthess Polygraphischer Verlag, 1978.

Gould, C. G., *Rethinking Democracy. Freedom and Social Cooperation in Politics, Economy and Society*, Cambridge: Cambridge University Press, 1988.

Grube, F., and Richter, G. (eds), *Demokratietheorien. Konzeptionen und Kontroversen*, Hamburg: Hoffmann and Campe 1975.

Guggenberger, B., and Kempf, U. (eds), *Bürgerinitiativen und repräsentatives System*, Opladen: Westdeutscher Verlag, 1978.

Habermas, J., *Legitimationsprobleme im Spätkapitalismus*, Frankfurt a.M.: Suhrkamp Verlag, 1973, Eng. trans. London: Heinemann, 1976.

—— and Luhmann, N., *Theorie der Gesellschaft oder Sozialtechnologie*, Frankfurt a.M.: Suhrkamp Verlag, 1971.

Harrison, R. J., *Pluralism and Corporatism. The Political Evolution of Modern Democracies*, London: George Allen and Unwin, 1980.

Hättich, M., *Gefährdete Demokratie*, Munich: Olzog Verlag, 1988.

Held, D., *Models of Democracy*, Cambridge: Polity Press, 1987.

—— *Political Theory and the Modern State*, Stanford (Calif.): Stanford University Press, 1989.

—— and C. Pollitt (eds), *New Forms of Democracy*, Beverly Hills (Calif.): Sage Publications, 1986.

Holden, B., *The Nature of Democracy*, London: Nelson, 1974.

—— 'New Directions in Democratic Theory', *Political Studies*, 36 (1988), 2.

Kainz, H. P., *Democracy East and West. A Philosophical Overview*, London: Macmillan, 1984.

Kariel, H. (ed.), *Frontiers of Democratic Theory*, New York: Random House, 1970.

Keane, J., *Democracy and Civil Society*, London: Verso, 1988.

Kelsen, H., *Vom Wesen und Wert der Demokratie*, Tübingen: J. C. B. Mohr, 1929.

—— 'Foundations of Democracy', *Ethics*, 66 (1955–6), 1.

Key, W. O., *Public Opinion and American Democracy*, New York: Knopf, 1961.

Kornhauser, W., *The Politics of Mass Society*, London: Routledge and Kegan Paul, 1960.

Kremendahl, H., *Pluralismustheorie in Deutschland*, Leverkusen: Heggen Verlag, 1977.

Leca, J., and Papini, R. (eds), *Les démocraties sont-elle gouvernables?*, Paris: Economica, 1985.

Lefort, C., *L'invention démocratique*, Paris: Fayard, 1981.

Lindblom, C., *The Intelligence of Democracy*, New York: The Free Press, 1965.

Lively, J., *Democracy*, Oxford: Basil Blackwell, 1975.

Luhmann, N., 'Klassische Theorie der Macht. Kritik ihrer Prämissen', *Zeitschrift für Politik*, 16 (1969), 2.

—— *Legitimation durch Verfahren*, Neuwied–Berlin: Luchterhand, 1969.

—— *Politische Planung*, Opladen: Westdeutscher Verlag, 1971.

—— *Vertrauen*, Stuttgart: Enke Verlag, 1973, Eng. trans. in N. Luhmann, *Trust and Power*, Chichester (Sussex): John Wiley and Sons, 1979.

—— *Macht*, Stuttgart: Enke Verlag, 1975, Eng. trans. in N. Luhmann, *Trust and Power*, Chichester (Sussex): John Wiley and Sons, 1979.

—— *Politische Theorie im Wohlfahrtsstaat*, Munich–Vienna: Olzog, 1981.

—— *Rechtssoziologie*, 2 vols, Reinbek bei Hamburg: Rowohlt, 1972, Eng. trans. London: Routledge and Kegan Paul, 1985.

Macpherson, C. B., *The Real World of Democracy*, Oxford: Clarendon Press, 1966.

—— *Democratic Theory*, Oxford: Clarendon Press, 1973.

—— *The Life and Times of Liberal Democracy*, Oxford: Oxford University Press, 1977.

Margolis, M., *Viable Democracy*, London: Macmillan, 1979.

Massing, P., *Interesse und Konsensus*, Opladen: Leske Verlag, 1979.

Matz, U. (ed.), *Grundprobleme der Demokratie*, Darmstadt: Wissenchsaftliche Buchgesellschaft, 1973.

Mura, V., 'Democrazia ideale e democrazia reale', *Teoria politica*, 6 (1990), 1.

Naschold, F., 'Demokratie und Komplexität', *Politische Vierteljahresschrift*, 9 (1968), 4.

—— 'Die systemtheoretische Analyse demokratischer politischer Systeme', *Politische Vierteljahresschrift*, Special Issue 2, 1970.

Nelson, W. N., *On Justifying Democracy*, London: Routledge and Kegan Paul, 1980.

Nicholls, D., *The Pluralist State*, London: Macmillan, 1971.

Nordlinger, E. A., *On the Autonomy of the Democratic State*, Cambridge (Mass.): Harvard University Press, 1981.

Oberreuter, H. (ed.), *Pluralismus. Grundlegung und Diskussion*, Munich: Bayerische Landeszentrale für Politische Bildungsarbeit, 1979.

Offe, C., *Strukturprobleme des kapitalistischen Staates*, Frankfurt a.M.: Suhrkamp Verlag, 1972.

—— 'Democracy against the welfare State? Structural Foundations of Neoconservative Political Opportunities', *Political Theory*, 15 (1987), 4.

—— and Preuss, U. K., 'Democratic Institutions and Moral Resources', Zentrum für Sozialpolitik, Universität Bremen, Working paper no. 5, 1990, now in D. Held (ed.), *Political Theory Today*, Cambridge: Polity Press, 1991.

Parry, G., *Political Elites*, London: George Allen and Unwin, 1969.

Pateman, C., *Participation and Democratic Theory*, Cambridge: Cambridge University Press, 1970.

—— *The Problem of Political Obligation*, Chichester (Sussex): John Wiley and Sons, 1979.

Pennock, J. R., *Democratic Political Theory*, Princeton (NJ): Princeton University Press, 1979.

Plamenatz, J., *Democracy and Illusion*, London: Longman, 1973.

Rödel, U., Frankenberg, G., and Dubiel, H., *Die demokratische Frage*, Frankfurt a.M.: Suhrkamp Verlag, 1989.

Sartori, G., *The Theory of Democracy Revisited*, Chatham (NJ): Chatham House Publishers, 1987, voll. 2.

Schmitter, P., and Lehmbruch, G. (eds), *Trends Toward Corporatist Intermediation*, Beverly Hills (Calif.): Sage publications, 1979.

Seurin, J.-L. (ed.), *La démocratie pluraliste*, Paris: Economica, 1980. Stankiewicz, W. J., *Approaches to Democracy*, London: Edward Arnold, 1980.

Steffani, W. (ed.), *Parlamentarismus ohne Transparenz*, Opladen: Westdeutscher Verlag, 1977.

Thompson, D. F., *The Democratic Citizen*, Cambridge: Cambridge University Press, 1970.

Williams, R., *Towards 2000*, London: Chatto and Windus, 1983.

—— *Democracy and Parliament*, London: The Socialist Society, 1982.

Wolfe, A., *The Limits of Legitimacy*, New York: Free Press, 1977.

Zolo, D., 'The Evolutionary Risks of Democracy', *Praxis International*, 9 (1989), 3.

## Communication research and political communication

Abramson, J. B., Arterton, F. C., and Orren, G. R., *The Electronic Commonwealth: The Impact of New Media Technologies on Democratic Politics*, New York: Basic Books, 1988

Altheide, D. L., *Media Power*, Beverly Hills (Calif.): Sage Publications, 1985.

Arterton, F. C., *Teledemocracy. Can Technology Protect Democracy?*, Newbury Park (Calif.): Sage Publications, 1987.

Atkin, C., 'Effects of Campaign Advertising and Newscasts on Children', *Journalism Quarterly*, 54 (1977) 3.

Benjamin, G. (ed.), *The Communication Revolution in Politics*, New York: Academy of Political Science, 1982.

Berelson, B., 'Democratic Theory and Public Opinion', In B. Berelson and M. Janowitz (eds), *Reader in Public Opinion and Communication*, New York: The Free Press, 1966.

—— Lazarsfeld, P., and McPhee, W., *Voting*, Chicago: University of Chicago Press, 1954.

Blumler, J. G., and McQuail, D., *Television in Politics*, London: Faber, 1968.

Carey, J. W. (ed.), *Media, Myths and Narratives. Television and the Press*, Newbury Park: Sage Publications, 1988.

Chaffee, S. H. (ed.), *Political Communication*, Beverly Hills (Calif.): Sage Publications, 1975.

Collins, R., et al. (eds), *Media, Culture and Society. A Critical Reader*, London: Sage Publications, 1986.

Curran, J., Gurevitch, M., and Woollacott, J. (eds), *Mass Communications and Society*, London: The Open University Press, 1977.

Curran, J., Smith, A., and Wingate, P. (eds), *Impact and Influences. Essays on Media Power in the Twentieth Century*, London: Methuen, 1987.

Deutsch, K. W., *The Nerves of Government*, New York: The Free Press, 1966.

Diamond, E., and Bates, S., *The Spot: The Rise of Political Advertising on Television*, Cambridge (Mass.): The MIT Press, 1984.

Door, A., *Television and Children*, Beverly Hills (Calif.): Sage Publications, 1986.

Elliot, P., *The Making of a Television Series. A Case Study in the Production of Culture*, London: Constable, 1972.

Ellul, J., *Histoire de la propagande*, Paris: Presses Universitaires de France, 1967, Eng. trans. New York: Vintage Books, 1973.

Entman, R. M., *Democracy without Citizens*, New York and Oxford: Oxford University Press, 1989.

Gerber, C.-P., and Stosberg, M., *Die Massenmedien und die Organisation politischer Interessen*, Bielefeld: Bertelsmann Universitätsverlag, 1969.

Golding, P., Murdock, G., and Schlesinger, P. (eds), *Communicating Politics: Mass Communications and the Political Process*, Leicester (Leics): Leicester University Press, 1986.

Goodin, R. E., *Manipulatory Politics*, New Haven (Conn.): Yale University Press, 1980.

Graber, D. A., *Verbal Behavior and Politics*, Urbana (Ill.): University of Illinois Press, 1976.

—— *Mass Media and American Politics*, Washington (DC): Congressional Quarterly Press, 1980.

Habermas, J., *Strukturwandel der Öffentlichkeit*, Neuwied: Luchterhand, 1962, Eng. trans. Cambridge (Mass.): MIT Press, 1989.

Himmelweit, H., et al., *How Voters Decide*, London: Academic Press, 1983.

Klapper, J. T., *The Effects of Mass Communication*, New York: The Free Press, 1960.

Kraus, S., and Davis, D., *The Effects of Mass Communication on Political Behavior*, University Park (Pa.): Pennsylvania State University Press, 1976.

Laudon, K. C., *Communication, Technology and Democratic Participation*, New York: Praeger, 1977.

Lazarsfeld, P. F., Berelson B., and Gaudet, H., *The People's Choice*, New York: Columbia University Press, 1940.

Leigh, D., *The Frontiers of Secrecy*, London: Junction Books, 1980.

Lippmann, W., *Public Opinion*, London: Allen and Unwin, 1922.

—— *The Phantom Public*, New York: Macmillan, 1925.

Luhmann, N., 'Öffentliche Meinung', *Politische Vierteljahresschrift*, 11 (1970), 1.

Luke, T., 'Televisual Democracy and the Politics of Charisma', *Telos*, 19 (1986), 4.

Lyon, D., *The Information Society: Issues and Illusions*, Cambridge: Polity Press, 1988.

McCombs, M. E., and Shaw, D. L., 'The Agenda-Setting Function of the Mass Media', *Public Opinion Quarterly*, 36 (1972), 2.

McLeod, J. M., and Becker, M. D., 'Testing the Validity of Gratification Measures through Political Effects Analysis', in J. G. Blumler and E. Katz (eds), *The Uses of Mass Communication: Current Perspectives on Gratification Research*, Beverly Hills (Calif.): Sage Publications, 1974.

McLuhan, M., *Understanding Media*, New York: New American Library, 1964.

McQuail, D., *Mass Communication Theory. An Introduction*, London: Sage Publications, 1983.

Meadow, R. B., *Politics as Communication*, Norwood (NJ): Ablex Publishing, 1980.

Mendelsohn, H., and Crespi, I., *Polls, Television and the New Politics*, Scranton (Pa.): Chandler, 1970.

Mueller, C., *The Politics of Communication: A Study in the Political Sociology of Language, Socialization and Legitimation*, London: Oxford University Press, 1973.

Nimmo, D. D., *Political Communication and Public Opinion in America*, Santa Monica (Calif.): Goodyear, 1978.

—— and Sanders, K. R. (eds), *Handbook of Political Communication*, Beverly Hills (Calif.): Sage Publications, 1981.

Noelle-Neumann, E., 'Return to the Concept of Powerful Mass Media', *Studies of Broadcasting*, 9 (1973).

—— *Die Schweigespirale: Öffentliche Meinung, unsere soziale Haut*, Munich: Piper Verlag, 1980, Eng. trans. Chicago: University of Chicago Press, 1984.

Paletz, D., and Entman, R. M., *Media, Power, Politics*, New York: The Free Press, 1981.

Patterson, T. E., and McClure, R. D., *The Unseeing Eye*, New York: Putnam, 1976.

Plasser, F., Ulram, P. A., and Welan, M. (eds), *Demokratierituale. Zur politischen Kultur der Informationsgesellschaft*, Vienna: Hermann Böhlaus, 1985.

Qualter, T. H., *Opinion Control in the Democracies*, London: Macmillan, 1985.

Ranney, A., *Channel of Power: The Impact of Television on American Politics*, New York: Basic/American Enterprise Institute, 1983.

Schatz, H., and Lange, K. (eds), *Massenkommunikation und Politik*, Frankfurt a.M.: Haag–Herchen, 1982.

Thompson, J. B., *Ideology and Modern Culture*, Cambridge: Polity Press, 1990.

Traber, M., *The Myth of the Informatic Revolution*, London: Sage Publications, 1986.

Wright, C. R. (1960), 'Functional Analysis and Mass Communication', *Public Opinion Quarterly*, 24.

## Social and political theory

Anderson, P., 'The Affinities of Norberto Bobbio', *New Left Review*, 170 (1988), 4.

Aron, R., *Dix-huit leçons sur la société industrielle*, Paris: Gallimard, 1962.

—— 'Machiavelli et Marx', in *Machiavelli nel quinto Centenario della nascita*, ed. M. Boni, Bologna: Boni Editore, 1973.

Arrow, K. J., *Social Choice and Individual Values*, New Haven (Conn.): Yale University Press, 1963.

Bell, D., *The Coming Post-Industrial Society*, New York: Basic Books, 1973.

Bellamy, R., *Modern Italian Social and Political Theory*, Cambridge: Polity Press, 1987.

——'Defining Liberalism: Neutralist, Ethical or Political?' in R. Bellamy (ed.), *Liberalism and Recent Legal and Social Philosophy*, Stuttgart: Franz Steiner, 1989.

Berger, S. D. (ed.), *Organizing Interests in Western Europe: Pluralism, Corporatism and the Transformation of Politics*, Cambridge: Cambridge University Press, 1981.

Bobbio, N., *Quale socialismo?*, Turin: Einaudi, 1976, Eng. trans. Cambridge: Polity Press, 1987.

Crespi, F., *Le vie della sociologia*, Bologna: Il Mulino, 1985.

Dahrendorf, R., *Pfade aus Utopia. Arbeiten zur Theorie und Methode der Soziologie*, Munich: Piper Verlag, 1967.

—— *Reflections on the Revolution in Europe. In a Letter Intended to Have Been Sent to a Gentleman in Warsaw, 1990*, London: Chatto and Windus, 1990.

Dallmayr, F. R., *Polis and Praxis. Exercises in Contemporary Political Theory*, Cambridge (Mass.): The MIT Press, 1984.

Dearlove, J., and Saunders, P., *Introduction to British Politics*, Cambridge: Polity Press, 1984.

Dunn, J., *Rethinking Modern Political Theory*, Cambridge: Cambridge University Press, 1985.

Easton, D., 'The Relevance of Biopolitics to Political Theory', in A. Somit (ed.), *Biology and Politics*, Mouton: International Social Science Council, 1976.

Ferrajoli, L., *Diritto e ragione*. Rome and Bari: Laterza, 1989.

Field, G. L., and Higley, J., *Elitism*, London: Routledge and Kegan Paul, 1980.

Foucault, M., *Surveiller et punir*, Paris: Gallimard, 1975, Eng. trans. New York: Vintage Books, 1979.

Gehlen, A., *Die Seele im technischen Zeitalter*, Reinbek: Rowohlt 1957, Eng. trans. New York: Columbia University Press, 1981.

—— *Der Mensch. Seine Natur und seine Stellung in der Welt*. Wiesbaden: Akademische Verlagsgesellschaft Athenaion, 1978, Eng. trans. New York: Columbia University Press, 1988.

Grant, W. (ed.), *The Political Economy of Corporativism*, London: Macmillan, 1985.

Habermas, J., *Zur Rekonstruktion des Historischen Materialismus*, Frankfurt a.M., Suhrkamp Verlag, 1976.

Hamilton, A., Madison, J., and Jay, J., *The Federalist Papers*, New York: Anchor, 1961.

Hirschman, A. O., *Exit, Voice and Loyalty*, Cambridge (Mass.): Harvard University Press, 1970.

Kan Ori, R. B., *Tradition and Change in Postindustrial Japan*, New York: Praeger Publishers, 1981.

Leibholz, G., *Das Wesen der Repräsentation unter besonderer Berücksichtigung des Repräsentativsystems*, Berlin–Leipzig: De Gruyter, 1929.

Lindberg, L. N., *Politics and the Future of Industrial Society*, New York: David McKay, 1976.

Lukes, S., *Power: A Radical View*, London: MacMillan, 1975.

Machiavelli, N., *Il Principe*, in *Opera Omnia*, Verona: Valdonega, 1968–80, Eng. trans., ed. P. Bondanella, Oxford: Oxford University Press, 1984.

Marx, K., *Kritik des Hegelschen Staatsrechts*, in K. Marx and F. Engels, *Werke*, Berlin: Deitz Verlag, 1956–69, vol. 1, Eng. trans. in K. Marx and F. Engels, *Collected Works*, London: Lawrence and Wishart, 1975.

—— *Zur Judenfrage*, in K. Marx and F. Engels, *Werke*, Berlin: Dietz Verlag, 1956–69, vol. 1, Eng. trans. New York: Philosophical Library, 1959.

—— *The Civil War in France*, in *Archiv Marxa i Engelsa*, III (VIII), Moscow, 1934.

Masters, R. D., 'The Impact of Ethology on Political Science', in A. Somit (ed.), *Biology and Politics*, Mouton: Maison des Sciences de l'Homme, 1976.

Michels, R., *Zur Soziologie des Parteiwesens in der modernen Demokratie: Untersuchungen über die oligarchischen Tendenzen des Gruppenlebens*, Leipzig: Werner Klinkhardt, 1911, Eng. trans. Gloucester (Mass.): P. Smith, 1978.

Mosca, G., *Elementi di scienza politica*, Turin: Bocca, 1896, Eng. trans. Westport (Conn.): Greenwood Press, 1980.

Mueller, D. C., *Public Choice*, London: Cambridge University Press, 1979.

Neurath, O., *Gesammelte philosophische und methodologische Schriften*, Vienna: Hölder-Pichler-Tempsky Verlag, 1981.

Nozick, R., *Anarchy, State, and Utopia*, New York: Basic Books, 1974.

Offe, Claus, *Contradictions of the Welfare State*, London: Hutchinson, 1984.

—— *Disorganized Capitalism*, Cambridge: Polity Press, 1985.

Olson, M., *The Logic of Collective Action*, Cambridge (Mass.): Harvard University Press, 1965.

Pareto, V., *Trasformazione della democrazia*, Milan: Corbaccio, 1921, Eng. trans. New Brunswick (NJ): Transaction Books, 1984.

Parry, G., 'The Machiavellianism of the Machiavellians', in B. Parekh and R. N. Berki (eds). *The Morality of Politics*, London: George Allen and Unwin, 1972.

Parsons, T., 'On the Concept of Political Power', in T. Parsons, *Politics and Social Structure*, New York: The Free Press, 1969.

Pitkin, H. F., *The Concept of Representation*, Berkeley (Calif.): University of California Press, 1972.

Pocock, J. G. A., *The Machiavellian Moment: Florentine Political Thought and the Atlantic Republican Tradition*, Princeton (NJ): Princeton University Press, 1975.

Poggi, G., *The Development of the Modern State*, London: Hutchinson, 1978.

Rawls, J., *A Theory of Justice*, Cambridge (Mass.): Harvard University Press, 1971.

Schattschneider, E. E., *The Semisovereign People*, New York: Holt, Rinehart and Winston, 1960.

Schmitt, C., *Der Begriff des Politischen*, Berlin: Verlag Walther Rothschild, 1928, Eng. trans. New Brunswick (NJ): Rutgers University Press, 1976.

——*Geistesgeschichtliche Lage des heutigen Parlamentarismus*, Berlin: Dunkler and Humbolt, 1979, Eng. trans. Cambridge (Mass.): MIT Press, 1985.

Schumpeter, J., *Capitalism, Socialism and Democracy*, London: Allen and Unwin, 1987.

Skinner, Q., *The Foundations of Modern Political Thought*, Cambridge: Cambridge University Press, 1978.
—— *Machiavelli*, Oxford: Oxford University Press, 1981.
Whynes, D., and Bowles, R., *The Economic Theory of the State*, London: Oxford University Press, 1981.

# Index